THE LIMITS
OF INFLUENCE

THE LIMITS OF INFLUENCE

America's Role in Kashmir

HOWARD B. SCHAFFER

An ADST-DACOR Diplomats and Diplomacy Book

BROOKINGS INSTITUTION PRESS
Washington, D.C.

Copyright © 2009
HOWARD B. SCHAFFER

Library of Congress Cataloging-in-Publication data

Schaffer, Howard B.
  The limits of influence : America's role in Kashmir / Howard B. Schaffer.
    p.   cm. — (ADST-DACOR diplomats and diplomacy ; 36)
  Includes bibliographical references and index.
  Summary: "Draws on interviews, historical research, and decades of experience in South Asia to explain and evaluate three generations of U.S. activities and policies toward Kashmir. Brings the discussion up to the current day, concluding with recommendations on the role Washington might usefully play in resolving the long-simmering dispute"— Provided by publisher.
  ISBN 978-0-8157-0290-0 (hardcover : alk. paper)
    1. United States—Foreign relations—India—Jammu and Kashmir. 2. Jammu and Kashmir (India)—Foreign relations—United States. 3. Jammu and Kashmir (India)—International status. I. Title. II. Series.
  E183.8.I4S33 2009
  327.73054'6—dc22   2009009060

9 8 7 6 5 4 3 2 1

The paper used in this publication meets minimum requirements of the American National Standard for Information Sciences—Permanence of Paper for Printed Library Materials: ANSI Z39.48-1992.

Typeset in Minion

Composition by Cynthia Stock
Silver Spring, Maryland

Maps by Meridian Mapping
Minneapolis, Minnesota

Printed by R. R. Donnelley
Harrisonburg, Virginia

To my granddaughter
Eleanor Rose Hawkins Schaffer

and my grandson
Nicholas Christopher Schaffer

Contents

Maps

Preface

The Kashmir problem has been with us for six decades, ranking it among the world's longest-running, most intractable international disputes. A by-product of the bloody 1947 partition of the British India Empire into two immediately hostile successor states, predominantly Hindu India and Muslim Pakistan, it has led to three wars and repeatedly sparked crises that have threatened to ignite further violent conflict. Indian and Pakistani acquisition of nuclear weapons has made the problem even more dangerous.

From the time the Kashmir issue came to world attention in January 1948 to the mid-1960s, successive American administrations played a leading part in trying to help India and Pakistan resolve the problem. Their efforts uniformly failed despite the personal involvement of Presidents Harry S. Truman, Dwight D. Eisenhower, and John F. Kennedy. Later administrations preferred a more limited U.S. role. They welcomed bilateral negotiations between India and Pakistan but did not become involved in them. Washington also made high-level interventions to defuse crises when dangerous confrontations between the two claimants sparked by the Kashmir problem brought them to the brink of war. The administrations of Bill Clinton and George W. Bush repeatedly asserted that they would be willing to play a "facilitating" role in trying to help India and Pakistan reach a settlement but only if both governments wanted Washington's help.

A number of recent developments suggest that the United States should again look for opportunities to play a more active role, this time with a better chance of success. The United States and India have dramatically strengthened their relations and crafted a serious strategic partnership. As the stronger, status quo power in the Kashmir dispute, India has long opposed any outside intervention. Its enhanced ties with Washington may lead it to recognize that American involvement could actually prove beneficial. New Delhi's heightened, increasingly attainable ambition to play a major role on the international stage could prompt it to regard Kashmir as a troubling obstacle to the recognition it seeks and make it willing to look more seriously for ways, including American help, to rid itself of this albatross. The Indian and Pakistani positions on the terms of a settlement have grown closer over the past few years. A quiet shove by Washington may be more likely than before to help push the two governments over the elusive finish line they have never been able to cross on their own. The critical part Pakistan plays in the fight against terrorism in Afghanistan and in its own territory also has added to the importance of the Kashmir issue and strengthened the case for a more active U.S. role in helping resolve it.

During his campaign for the presidency, Barack Obama suggested that if he won the election his administration might take a more forthcoming approach. During its last year in office, the lame-duck administration of George W. Bush was too weak and its foreign policy agenda too over-stretched to encourage it to undertake an intervention in Kashmir. Any interest it might have had in doing so was further inhibited by the political weaknesses of the governments in Islamabad and New Delhi. These problems are unlikely to go away soon. In Pakistan, the relatively new and still shaky coalition headed by President Asif Ali Zardari faces a host of daunting political, economic, and security challenges. Until it feels more secure and confident, it is unlikely to follow its predecessor Pervez Musharraf's bold lead in offering to India the broad concessions needed to bring about a settlement. In India, Prime Minister Manmohan Singh's Congress Party–led coalition government is fighting for its political life as it prepares for elections against an aggressive opposition spearheaded by Hindu nationalist forces that call for a tough line on Kashmir. It has been in no position to adopt a forthcoming position on the issue. Whether the next Indian government will be prepared to do so will depend on both its composition and its self-confidence. Neither can be realistically forecast at this time.

As South Asia moves upward on America's agenda and as Washington considers which policies toward the Kashmir issue will best advance its increasingly significant interests in the region, it is important to understand the evolution of the U.S. role in the state since the Truman administration came to grips with the problem at the United Nations sixty-one years ago. Many historians have written about the American experience in Kashmir in broader studies of U.S. South Asia policy. It has also figured in conflict resolution literature. But America's role in efforts to resolve or manage the problem has not been systematically studied at any length.

My account is designed to fill this surprising gap. It focuses on the activities, recommendations, and policy decisions of three generations of often frustrated U.S. officials as they dealt with the problem in Washington, the United Nations, and the subcontinent. The book also refers more briefly to the efforts of private American citizens and organizations to develop formulas that they hoped could contribute to progress toward a settlement. I have written it from an American perspective. I have reviewed Indian, Pakistani, and British material and exchanged ideas with South Asians in government and outside who are familiar with the Kashmir problem. But I have deliberately focused primarily on official and nonofficial U.S. sources to craft my account and reach my conclusions. I have also drawn on my own Kashmir experiences as a U.S. Foreign Service officer stationed in India and Pakistan in the 1960s and 1970s as well as my work in those years and later in State Department offices responsible for making American policy in the region. In the final chapter, I have recommended approaches to the problem in the context of broader U.S. policies on India and Pakistan and such pressing global issues as the proliferation of weapons of mass destruction and counterterrorism.

Many people have helped in the writing of this book. I am grateful to specialists in South Asian affairs who took the time to review all or some of the chapters in draft and let me know what I needed to do to make *The Limits of Influence* a more accurate and useful study. They include Walter Andersen, Stephen Cohen, Dennis Kux, Robert Oakley, and Ashley Tellis. I'm also in debt to the many people who played a role in the making of U.S. policies on Kashmir and were willing to share their experiences and views with me.

Margery Boichel Thompson of the Association for Diplomatic Studies and Training, who had been so helpful to me in the publication of my biographies of Chester Bowles and Ellsworth Bunker, once again provided enthusiastic support in moving this third book toward the light of published day.

I am delighted that the association has included it in its Diplomats and Diplomacy series, which it cosponsors with the Diplomats and Consular Officers, Retired.

My thanks also go to the Edmund A. Walsh School of Foreign Service at Georgetown University, led by Dean Robert Gallucci, and the school's Institute for the Study of Diplomacy, long headed by Casimir Yost. The institute gave me an academic home while I wrote the book and provided a succession of impressive undergraduate student interns who helped me in researching it. They include Aneesh Deshpande; Justin Douds; Andrew Griffin, now a U.S. Foreign Service officer; Kevin Grossinger; Arjun Pant; and Drew Tidwell.

My special appreciation goes to my friend Farooq Kathwari, the chairman, president, and chief executive officer of Ethan Allen Interiors and founder of the Kashmir Study Group, whom I met in Kashmir in 1964 when he was a student activist during one of the state's many times of trouble. He has helped keep alive the interest in the Kashmir issue that I first acquired in those distant days.

I also want to thank the many people at the Brookings Institution Press who agreed to publish the book and saw to its production. They include Larry Converse, Bob Faherty, Chris Kelaher, Mary Kwak, Susan Soldavin, and Janet Walker. Special plaudits go to Susan Woollen, the art coordinator of the press, and her colleagues for the stunning design they developed for the dust jacket.

While all these good people were helping me in a Washington busily in transition from the Bush to the Obama administrations, Marty Gottron was skillfully wielding her electronic blue pencil in the snows of the Berkshires editing the book to make it more readable and accessible. My warm thanks to her, too.

Finally, I want to express my gratitude to my wife, Ambassador Teresita Currie Schaffer. I can honestly say that without Tezi's loving support I could never have written this book.

Washington, D.C.
January 2009

THE LIMITS
OF INFLUENCE

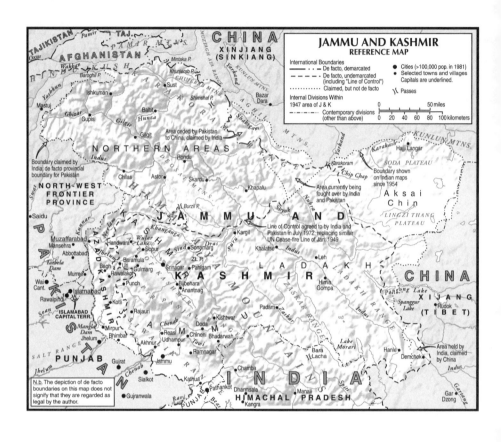

JAMMU AND KASHMIR
REFERENCE MAP

International Boundaries

—— · · —— De facto, demarcated

— — — De facto, undemarcated
(including "Line of Control")

· · · · · · · · Claimed, but not de facto

Internal Divisions Within
1947 area of J & K

— · —— · — Contemporary divisions
(other than above)

● Cities (>100,000 pop. in 1981)
■ Selected towns and villages
Capitals are underlined.

)(Passes

0   50 miles
0   20   40   60   80   100 kilometers

N.b. The depiction of de facto boundaries on this map does not signify that they are regarded as legal by the author.

Introduction

The dispute over Kashmir is the most central and intractable of the problems that have bedeviled India-Pakistan relations since the two countries won independence in 1947. For Indians and Pakistanis, Kashmir symbolizes the clash between their rival concepts of national identity. Pakistanis perceive Kashmir as the one Muslim-majority area of Britain's Indian empire that did not become part of Pakistan, conceived by its founders as the homeland for the Muslims of the subcontinent. Its possession by India makes Kashmir "the unfinished business of partition." For Indians, Kashmir's Muslim majority makes it a symbol of the country's secular identity. This sentiment has grown stronger with time despite the evident unhappiness of most Kashmiri Muslims with their tie to India. Losing Kashmir *because it is Muslim* would in India's view undercut its secular claims and confirm what has always been to most Indians the unacceptable view that Hindus and Muslims are "two nations" who should have separate states. Moreover, many Indians fear that if Kashmir or a part of it leaves the Indian Union in "a second partition," massive anti-Muslim communal rioting would break out in India proper. Muslims make up about 12 percent of India's 1.1 billion people.

Kashmir is also, of course, a territorial dispute, though Kashmiris bitterly resent the implication that they are pawns to be disposed of in a real estate deal. The extent to which Kashmiris should be allowed to govern themselves has also been an issue, much more so on the Indian side than the Pakistani. So has the quality of government (often bad) in the two parts of the state.

Any discussion of the Kashmir problem must begin with an understanding of the area itself. The pre-1947 princely state of Jammu and Kashmir, about the size of Minnesota, comprised five major areas (map 1).[1] The first three are now under Indian administration:

The *Valley of Kashmir* has a population of about 4.7 million, most of them Kashmiri-speaking Sunni Muslims. Its once prominent Hindu minority, the Kashmiri Pandit (Brahmin) community, now mostly lives outside the Valley following a mass flight after a still-raging insurgency broke out at the end of 1989. The Valley is the heart of Kashmir. It is distinguished from other regions of the state by its distinctive language and culture, known as *Kashmiriyat.* The Valley is the only part of the pre-1947 state in which the majority of the population is so seriously discontented with the status quo that it wishes to break its link with the country that administers it. Since 1947 the Valley's predominantly Sunni Muslim leaders have dominated the politics of Indian Kashmir, though almost always under New Delhi's strict supervision. Other Indian-held regions of Kashmir fear that if the state obtains greater autonomy within the Indian Union, they will become even more subordinated to the Valley, to their serious disadvantage.

Jammu, south of the Valley, has a Hindu majority but includes several Muslim-majority districts that adjoin the Pakistan-held parts of the old princely state. Many of its Muslim inhabitants fled to Pakistan and Pakistan-controlled Kashmir when India became independent. Its population is about 4.5 million.

Ladakh, on India's border with China, has only 200,000 people. They are predominantly Tibetan Buddhist but also include large numbers of Shiite Muslims concentrated in the Kargil district adjoining Pakistan-controlled Kashmir.

Pakistan administers the remaining two areas:

Azad (free) Kashmir in the western and southwestern reaches of the old state, has 3.1 million people, virtually all Muslim. It has strong ties to Pakistani Punjab. Its links to the Valley, once important, have withered over the years, though they are reviving somewhat now that the traditional route between the two areas has been reopened to a limited extent. Indians call the region Pakistan Occupied Kashmir, or POK.

The *Northern Areas* comprise a number of small principalities, once tributary to the maharaja of Kashmir, tucked away in remote valleys among some of the highest mountains in the world. Its 1.1 million people are close to 100 percent Muslim. Unlike the Valley and Azad Kashmir, which are predominantly Sunni, the Northern Areas include sizable groups of Shia as well as Ismaili followers of the Aga Khan. It is isolated from the surrounding regions, and there is no direct road connecting it to Azad Kashmir.

Equally important is an understanding of the rival claims. India's formal position is that all of Kashmir is an integral part of the Indian Union by virtue of the maharaja of Kashmir's accession to India in October 1947 and the confirmation, in 1954, of his act by the state's elected assembly. However, since the 1950s India has implied and at times explicitly acknowledged that it is prepared to give up to Pakistan the territories now administered by the Pakistanis and accept the line that divides the state between them as an international boundary.

Pakistan regards the whole state as disputed territory whose status is to be decided by the internationally supervised plebiscite called for in resolutions the United Nations Commission for India and Pakistan (UNCIP) passed in the late 1940s. In Pakistan's view, the provisions of these resolutions remain valid despite the passage of a half-century since they were adopted. However, like India, Pakistan has long acknowledged that it is willing to settle for less than the whole state. It will be satisfied with the transfer of the Valley to its control. In December 2006, Pakistan's president, General Pervez Musharraf, suggested that his government could accept the existing line as a permanent boundary provided India met other conditions regarding the governance of the state.

As noted, the Kashmir Valley is the only region of the old princely state in which a majority of the population is dissatisfied with the de facto situation. Unlike the Hindus of Jammu, the Buddhists of Ladakh, and the Muslims of Azad Kashmir and the Northern Areas, all of whom are content to remain under Indian or Pakistani administration, the Valley Muslims want to change their national status. Most objective observers, including Indian commentators, believe that in a free and fair vote, a majority of the population of the Valley would choose independence in preference to rule by either India or Pakistan. This "third option" was not included in the UNCIP resolutions, and India has always ruled it out. In recent years, Pakistan has softened its longstanding opposition to independence and has implied that it could accept separate status for Kashmiris of the Valley if they wanted it. Were Pakistan to agree to the independence option, it would almost certainly be in the expectation that the Valley would eventually decide to join it.

Diplomats sometimes find that they must make policy on the fly on issues new and strange to them. This was surely the case when Washington suddenly found Kashmir on its agenda in 1948. American policymakers had always regarded South Asia as a "British show." So when fighting broke out in Kashmir, and India brought the issue to the United Nations, probably only a few of them could have found the princely state on a map. But over the years they and their successors became very familiar with the problem and its many ramifications, if not with all the intricacies of Kashmiri politics and demographics.

American involvement (and noninvolvement) in Kashmir can be usefully divided into three phases:

Deep Washington engagement in efforts to bring about a settlement, 1948–63. The focus of America's diplomatic activity in these years was usually the United Nations, which it saw as the appropriate forum for resolving such disputes. The United States played a major role in drafting UN resolutions calling for an internationally supervised plebiscite that became the basis for multilateral consideration of the issue. An American, Admiral Chester W. Nimitz, was appointed to administer the plebiscite, which was never held. The United States did not enter the UN exercise with any biases or ulterior political motives. As negotiations foundered, however, American policymakers increasingly questioned India's goals and blamed New Delhi's intransigence for the continuing impasse. Washington kept up its efforts at the United Nations even after its security alliance with Pakistan in 1954 made Kashmir a cold war issue and ensured a Soviet veto of any Security Council resolution unacceptable to India. But it eventually recognized that the UN route was an exercise in futility.

The United States interspersed its bouts of multilateral diplomacy with efforts outside the United Nations, either alone or with Britain, to whom it looked for leadership and guidance as head of the commonwealth and recent imperial ruler of the subcontinent. President Harry S. Truman wrote to the leaders of India and Pakistan suggesting ways to deal with the problem, to no avail. His successor, Dwight D. Eisenhower, became personally involved in a more ambitious U.S. intervention. This called for simultaneous negotiation of Kashmir and two other pressing South Asian issues: division of the Indus Waters and the accelerating India-Pakistan arms race. India rejected Eisenhower's initiative.

These White House interventions climaxed in 1963 when John F. Kennedy played a major role in a long, intense U.S.-British–sponsored initiative to promote negotiations between the Indians and Pakistanis at a time when India's defeat in the Sino-Indian border war seemed to Kennedy's can-do administration to offer a window of opportunity for a settlement. This effort faced heavy odds that lengthened as the threat of renewed Chinese aggression against India diminished and the administration failed to use the leverage available to it. Like the earlier presidential intercessions, the intrusive and misguided initiative did not bring about a break in the deadlock. Instead, it fanned ill will toward the United States on both sides.

A quarter-century of American diplomatic quiescence, 1964–89. The failure of the 1963 negotiations and the continuing preoccupation of India and Pakistan with Kashmir and other bilateral disputes contributed to a growing questioning in Washington about the value the two countries had for the pursuit of broad U.S. foreign policy goals, especially as Vietnam increasingly became the focus of U.S. diplomacy. The attitude of "a plague on both their houses" intensified American policymakers' disinclination to play a role in efforts to resolve the Kashmir issue. The brief India-Pakistan war over Kashmir in 1965 was a serious setback for U.S. interests in South Asia. Outrage over the two sides' using against one another the arms the United States had supplied them to counter Communist aggression made Washington even more ready to disengage from South Asia.

Fed up, President Lyndon B. Johnson ruled out any unilateral American endeavor to end the fighting or work out a postwar settlement. His administration welcomed Soviet efforts to bring the two sides together, an astonishing development in light of the primacy the United States had long given to limiting Communist influence in South Asia. Washington applauded Moscow when it persuaded India and Pakistan to restore the status quo ante bellum. But the Johnson administration had no interest in stepping up to the plate again to help them reach a final resolution of the issue, and it sharply lowered the priority it gave South Asia on its political and security agendas. President Richard M. Nixon and his national security adviser, Henry A. Kissinger, tilted famously toward Pakistan in the 1971 India-Pakistan war over Bangladesh, the only conflict the two countries have fought that was not sparked by the Kashmir dispute. But that manifestation of renewed U.S. interest in the region proved a short-lived and ill-advised aberration.

Washington's determination to follow a hands-off policy was strengthened when the two antagonists pledged in 1972 to settle the issue peacefully and bilaterally. Delighted after years of frustration to watch Kashmir leave the international stage and the Kashmiris apparently accept the status quo, American diplomats concerned with South Asia, including myself, paid scant attention to the problem, now seemingly a nonproblem, for the rest of the 1970s and 1980s.

Focus on crisis management, 1990–present. The outbreak of a broadly based rebellion in the Valley against Indian rule at the end of 1989 returned Kashmir to American attention. Washington amended its position on a Kashmir settlement. It now added "keeping in mind the wishes of the Kashmiri people" to its call to India and Pakistan to settle the issue peacefully and bilaterally. It worried that the Kashmir upheaval could lead to another India-Pakistan war, especially since Pakistan could not resist fishing in the Valley's newly troubled waters. Both countries were by then well on their way to acquiring nuclear weapons. This made the prospect of another war even more alarming. In 1990 Washington sent a special envoy to the region on a successful mission to head off a potential conflict sparked by Pakistani support for the Kashmir insurgency. The Indians received the mission with unusual warmth, one of the first indications that they were beginning to see the United States as a potential asset rather than a threat to their interests in Kashmir.

When India and Pakistan conducted nuclear weapons tests in 1998, the Clinton administration launched a diplomatic campaign designed to head off a nuclear arms race in the subcontinent and restore the badly damaged global nonproliferation regime. With other major powers, Washington called on the two countries to resume their dialogue on the root causes of their mutual animosity, including Kashmir. President Clinton's personal involvement in efforts to bring about a withdrawal of Pakistani armed forces following their ill-conceived incursion into the strategically important Kargil area of Indian-held Kashmir reflected heightened U.S. fear of a potential nuclear war. Washington blamed the Pakistanis for instigating the crisis and successfully put heavy pressure on them to pull back.

The nuclear tests lessened the importance the United States had long given to the equities of the Kashmir issue. Maintaining the stability of the subcontinent became the guiding principle of American policy. The Kargil conflict strengthened this change in approach. As Clinton stressed when he visited Pakistan in 2000, the use of violence to change the status quo was an unacceptable option in nuclear-armed South Asia. Both the Clinton and the successor Bush administrations told India and Pakistan that they would help "facilitate" a Kashmir settlement only if both sides wanted U.S. intercession. As the stronger, status-quo power, New Delhi has opposed outsiders' involvement in South Asian affairs except on its own terms. As the weaker, irredentist one, Pakistan has sought to internationalize the Kashmir issue. The primacy that the Clinton and Bush administrations have given to stability in Kashmir—and hence to preserving the status quo on the ground—makes these positions outdated. The Indians now seem to be moving toward a more positive view of an American role.

Following the attacks of September 11, 2001, the United States renewed its security relations with Pakistan and looked to Musharraf's government for support in its efforts to quell terrorism and Islamic extremism. At the same time, it developed a serious strategic relationship with New Delhi and recognized India as a rising global power. The United States had never before simultaneously enjoyed such strong relations with both countries, though it promoted these ties for different reasons. Meanwhile, Pakistan's continuing sponsorship of insurgent activity in Indian Kashmir and its alleged role in terrorist incidents in India proper led to war-threatening crises in India-Pakistan relations. These prompted high-level, eventually successful U.S. efforts to defuse them. But these bouts of crisis management did not involve any initiative on Washington's part to resolve the basic problem. The United States continued to limit itself to cheering from the sidelines as India and Pakistan undertook a peace process that included dealing with Kashmir.

As this brief summary of the U.S. role indicates, Washington has been more effective at crisis management than peace building in Kashmir. The dispute has stubbornly resisted the diplomatic efforts of outside powers, even when the United States enjoyed great leverage with both claimants. The nature of the dispute has also shifted. The voice of the Kashmiris has become more prominent even as American concern for the stability of the nuclear-armed region has outstripped its interest in the rights and wrongs of the dispute. The broad outlines of a possible solution are starting to take shape. As a new administration takes office, the question before U.S. policymakers is whether this situation and the new salience of South Asia for American global interests makes advisable—even necessary—a fresh effort on Washington's part to help resolve the Kashmir dispute.

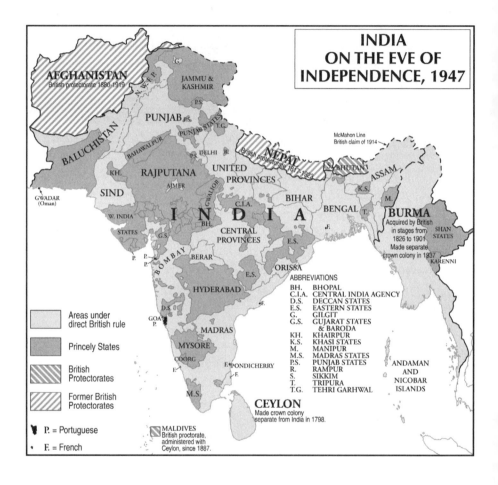

INDIA ON THE EVE OF INDEPENDENCE, 1947

AFGHANISTAN
British protectorate 1880-1919

JAMMU & KASHMIR

N.W.F.P.

PUNJAB P.S.

BALUCHISTAN

BAHAWALPUR

PUNJAB STATES

T.G.

DELHI R.

P.S.

McMahon Line
British claim of 1914

NEPAL
British protectorate 1817-1923

BHUTAN

KH.

RAJPUTANA

UNITED
PROVINCES

ASSAM

K.S.

GWADAR
(Oman)

SIND

AJMER

GWALIOR

C.I.A.

BIHAR

M.

W. INDIA

I N D I A

BENGAL T.

BURMA
Acquired by British
in stages from
1826 to 1901
Made separate
crown colony in 1937

STATES

BH.

CENTRAL
PROVINCES

F.

SHAN
STATES

G.S.

E.S.

P.

BOMBAY

BERAR

KARENNI

P.
P.

ORISSA

E.S.

ABBREVIATIONS

HYDERABAD

F.

BH.   BHOPAL
C.I.A. CENTRAL INDIA AGENCY
D.S.   DECCAN STATES
E.S.   EASTERN STATES
G.   GILGIT
G.S.   GUJARAT STATES
        & BARODA
KH.   KHAIRPUR
K.S.   KHASI STATES
M.   MANIPUR
M.S.   MADRAS STATES
P.S.   PUNJAB STATES
R.   RAMPUR
S.   SIKKIM
T.   TRIPURA
T.G.   TEHRI GARHWAL

D.S.

GOA
P.

MADRAS

MYSORE

COORG

E. PONDICHERRY

F.

ANDAMAN
AND
NICOBAR
ISLANDS

M.S.

CEYLON
Made crown colony
separate from India in 1798.

Areas under
direct British rule

Princely States

British
Protectorates

Former British
Protectorates

P. = Portuguese

F. = French

MALDIVES
British proctorate,
administered with
Ceylon, since 1887.

1

Impasse at the United Nations

Before the 1947 partition of India, few Americans knew or cared about the princely state of Jammu and Kashmir. Tucked away in the high western Himalayas, Kashmir, as it was commonly called, was an amalgam of territories widely varied in language, culture, religion, ethnicity, and economic development. Its disparate regions had been cobbled together by the dynastic ambitions of the state's rulers abetted by British imperial design. In the first half of the nineteenth century, these maharajas, Hindus of the Dogra ethnic group based in the Jammu area of the state, had with British backing created one of the largest states in Britain's Indian empire. Situated along India's border with China, touching Afghanistan, and close to the Central Asian regions of Czarist Russia and, later, the Soviet Union, it was also one of the most strategically placed.

What little American interest there was in Kashmir before rival Indian and Pakistani claims brought the state to international attention in late 1947 was confined to occasional private visitors. A handful of traders came to the state to purchase carpets, papier mâché, and other handicrafts for export to the U.S. market. American missionary activity was limited; the state was the preserve of mainly British church groups. A few American tourists interested in exotic places and wealthy enough to get to them visited the state. During World War II, U.S. servicemen operating in the China-Burma-India theater went to Kashmir on leave to lounge on houseboats and get away from the heat and dust of the Indian plains. Some of these boats still carry names, like the Mae West, that recall that era. But none of this limited exposure made any serious, lasting impact. As the British prepared to wind up their sub-continental raj and leave in its place the independent dominions of India and Pakistan, ignorance of Kashmir remained profound among U.S. officials and the American public.

The United States kept careful watch as the British negotiated with the contending Indian political parties—the Indian National Congress and the All-India Muslim League—about the form India would take when it became independent. American diplomats stayed in frequent contact with British officials and Indian political leaders. The United States fully supported British efforts to bring about a peaceful transfer of power on the basis of a federally united India rather than its partition into two separate states, as the Muslim League called for in its demand for a sovereign Pakistan comprising areas where Muslims were a majority. As these efforts failed and partition became increasingly likely, Washington strongly opposed any further breakup of the country and instructed American officials to be careful to avoid doing anything that might suggest otherwise.[1] This opposition to the balkanization of the subcontinent, which remained U.S. policy after India and Pakistan became independent in August 1947, led Washington to resist calls for support from advocates of a separate status for Kashmir and other areas unhappy with their lot within the Indian Union.

As they prepared to quit India, the British gave the rulers of the 565 Indian princely states the right to decide whether they wished to accede to India or to Pakistan. They encouraged these rulers to make their choice on the basis of the religious composition of their people and the contiguity of their states to India or Pakistan. With the lapse of British "paramountcy" over them, the princely states could theoretically remain outside both dominions. But the British strongly urged the rulers to avoid that option and told them they could not look to the crown for protection and support if they went it alone.

This formulation for the end of empire put Hari Singh, the autocratic maharaja of Kashmir, in a position that was unique, tempting, and fateful. A Hindu, he ruled a state with a large Muslim majority. His domains bordered both India and future Pakistan. Moreover, the most popular political party in the state, the secular National Conference led by Sheikh Mohammed Abdullah, was aligned with the Indian Congress Party and favored accession to India. Despite the machinations of Congress leaders urging him to accede to India and senior Muslim League figures calling for Kashmir to become part of Islamic Pakistan, the maharaja avoided making a choice. He had still not done so when the British raj ended.

Kashmir remained independent for more than two tumultuous months. The political situation in the state became increasingly unstable. Unrest among demobilized Muslim soldiers of the old British Indian Army angered by the maharaja's discriminatory, anti-Muslim policies soon turned into an armed uprising. With sympathetic help from across the Pakistan border, the rebellion spread to large areas in the heavily Muslim-majority districts in the southwestern part of the state. In the Jammu area in the southeast, where Hindus and Sikhs formed a majority, many Muslims were killed or forced to flee. The Kashmir Valley alone remained fairly quiet, though it was wracked by intrigue as contending Kashmiri, Indian, and Pakistani politicians and their agents sought to influence developments. Among them was Abdullah, whom the maharaja let free from his detention for political agitation against the state government.

Hari Singh's hand was forced in late October when a large contingent of tribal fighters from the North-West Frontier Province of Pakistan invaded Kashmiri territory. Pakistani and Indian interpretations of what happened differ sharply. The Pakistanis maintain that reports of atrocities committed against Muslims in the state impelled the tribesmen to come to their rescue. The Indians claim that Pakistani authorities instigated the invasion and gave it material support.

As the tribesmen swept aside state forces and advanced toward Srinagar, Kashmir's summer capital, the maharaja sent an urgent appeal for help to the Indian government. The sequence of events from the time the maharaja asked for this assistance to the airlifting of Indian troops to Srinagar airport three days later has been a subject of continuing debate.[2] What is most important and beyond dispute is that the Indian government told Hari Singh it could protect the state only if Kashmir became part of India. With the tribals already in control of the northwestern part of the Kashmir Valley and heading for Srinagar against limited opposition, the maharaja signed the accession document. In formally accepting it on behalf of the government of India, Lord Mountbatten, the last viceroy of the British India Empire and, since the transfer of power, the first governor general of independent

India, famously declared: "[I]t is my Government's wish that as soon as law and order have been restored in Kashmir and her soil cleared of the invader the question of the State's accession should be settled by reference to the people."

In the two months following the maharaja's accession to India, senior Indian and Pakistani leaders conferred, shot off angry cables, and issued statements denouncing one another's actions and proposals. Britain became involved through a series of messages Prime Minister Clement Attlee exchanged with Jawaharlal Nehru and Liaquat Ali Khan, his Indian and Pakistani counterparts. The British were understandably concerned about the possibility of all-out war between the two newest members of the commonwealth and believed they had an important stake in heading it off. The U.S. government followed the situation closely but played no role.

When these negotiations failed to make progress, reports reached Washington that India was considering referring the issue to the United Nations. Although the United States preferred that the Indians and Pakistanis resolve the problem by direct negotiations and was at best lukewarm to internationalizing the issue, it eventually decided to support the idea of a resolution requesting the United Nations to supervise a referendum in Kashmir if the draft of such a resolution was introduced by India or Pakistan and supported by Britain.[3] Concern that the problem might be dumped on the United States if the United Nations did not intervene helped prompt Washington to adopt this approach.[4] But U.S. policymakers worried that Indian recourse to the United Nations without a prearranged plan in place might lead to unnecessary complications and crystallize a pattern of India-Pakistan hostility.[5] Events would prove this concern amply justified.

On New Year's Day 1948, India requested the UN Security Council to ask the Pakistan government to prevent Pakistani civil and military personnel from participating in the invasion of Kashmiri territory or helping the intruders. The Indians made this request under Article 35 of Chapter 6 of the UN Charter, which calls on the council to recommend "appropriate procedures or methods of adjustment" for the pacific settlement of disputes. They did not cite Chapter 7, which deals with acts of aggression.

When the Kashmir dispute landed on the UN's doorstep, the world organization had only recently entered its third year. With only fifty-seven member states, it was much smaller and less diverse than it is today. The United States, which had been the driving force in establishing the organization in 1945, led the Western bloc, by far its largest group. The Communist bloc headed by the Soviet Union was much smaller. There were only a handful of Asian and African members. The great wave of third world countries whose membership dramatically changed the United Nations' composition and center of gravity in coming decades was just beginning. Independent India had inherited the seat of the British India Empire and was thus considered a founding member.[6] Pakistan was voted in soon after partition.

Although developments in the two years after the United Nations was formed had underscored its limited effectiveness in resolving or managing the growing confrontation between the Western and Communist blocs, Washington believed that the Kashmir issue, which was not then connected with the gathering cold war, was the kind of dispute that the United Nations could handle well. It seemed tailor-made for the fledgling organization's role as a crisis manager and problem solver. As the British historian Alastair Lamb has written, the dispute was seen in many quarters as a crucial experiment in the use of international mediation to settle quarrels between nations.[7]

In dealing with Kashmir at the United Nations and elsewhere, American diplomats worked closely with their British colleagues. Washington recognized that as the former imperial power and leader of the commonwealth, Britain was much more familiar than it was with South Asia. The British had close ties to Indian and Pakistani leaders, with whom they had negotiated the transfer of power just a few months earlier. The command positions that senior British officers continued to hold in the Indian and Pakistani armed forces strengthened London's awareness of South Asian military and political developments and its capacity to influence them.

This American deference pleased the British. Following a meeting with a U.S. embassy colleague in New Delhi as the Kashmir issue reached the United Nations, a British diplomat cabled London: "This is the first occasion on which we have been consulted formally by the American embassy and it may well provide a useful precedent."[8] At a higher level, Lord Inverchapel, the British ambassador in Washington, adopted an almost condescending tone toward American policymakers in informing the Commonwealth Office of his consultations with them: "We have been maintaining daily contact with the State Department on [Kashmir] and since they themselves admitted that they were short of background information have shown them freely material which you have prepared and kept them informed of your thoughts. In this way we have I think been able to help them in the briefing of the U.S. delegation at New York and to exercise some influence over the formulation of their policy."[9]

Washington's willingness to follow the British lead was exemplified on the eve of India's introduction of the Kashmir issue at the United Nations when the State Department, at London's request, sent a message to the Indian government urging it not to take provocative action. The department sent a similar message—which the British had *not* requested—to the Pakistanis.[10] When Howard Donovan, the U.S. chargé d'affaires, called on Nehru to convey American concern, the prime minister assured him that the Indian government had no intention of taking any steps against the government of Pakistan that would cause the situation to deteriorate further.[11] In Karachi, Chargé d'Affaires Charles W. Lewis Jr. received similar assurances from the Pakistanis.[12]

But at this early stage, the British apparently saw consultation as a one-way street. At a session of senior American officials dealing with South Asia held in Washington in late December, Henry Grady, the ambassador to India, told his colleagues: "The British have been friendly, but have made no attempt [in India] to consult with us on common problems or to ask our advice." In Ambassador Grady's view, the British were not happy with the strong position the United States enjoyed in India.[13]

Washington, the U.S. mission to the United Nations, and the American embassies in New Delhi and Karachi became deeply involved in the Kashmir issue once the Indians lodged their complaint. The point man for American efforts was Warren R. Austin, a former Republican senator from Vermont whom President Truman had named U.S. permanent representative to the United Nations in 1946. Guidance the State Department sent Austin a week before the Security Council began discussing Kashmir presaged the solution the United Nations would try to implement in this first phase of its efforts to resolve the dispute: "[T]he only solution acceptable to all parties concerned in the Kashmir problem will eventually be a determination, probably by plebiscite, of the wishes of the inhabitants of Jammu and Kashmir . . . , taking into account the possibility that some form of partition may be proposed. . . ."

The department told Ambassador Austin that although an effective solution required joint India-Pakistan action and cooperation, that should not preclude the Security Council's establishing machinery for observation and conciliation. The British should be assured that Washington wanted them to take the lead at the United Nations "insofar as it is reconcilable with the U.S. position." But the United States might sometimes have to get out in front when the "peculiar position Britain occupies vis-à-vis India and Pakistan" made it advisable for London to take a less prominent role.[14]

Some Indian commentators maintain that in dealing with the Kashmir issue, the Attlee government, and especially Philip Noel-Baker, its secretary of state for commonwealth relations, were consistently pro-Pakistan. In this view, London saw Pakistan as an important piece in its strategic calculations for South, Southeast, and East Asia following the windup of the raj.[15]

There is no convincing evidence, however, that Washington's willingness to defer to the British at this early stage was influenced by a shared partiality for Pakistan or an interest in the strategic role the Pakistanis could play in promoting Western objectives in South Asia and beyond. These factors would figure five years later, when Washington developed an alliance relationship with Karachi. They did not in 1947–48, a period in which the United States consistently rejected out of hand Pakistan's interest in developing such close ties. The Pakistanis, for their part, cited alleged Soviet activities in Kashmir to bolster their case with Americans. The governor general of Pakistan, Mohammed Ali Jinnah, warned Ambassador Paul Alling in March 1948 that Soviet agents were operating in Gilgit in the Pakistan-occupied northern part of the state.[16]

The limits to American willingness to accept British tutelage on Kashmir became evident when Noel-Baker and Lord Ismay, his principal adviser, hurried to the United States a few weeks after the issue reached the Security Council in a bid to influence the position Washington would take there. The British officials urged Robert Lovett, the American under secretary of state, to accept their proposal that the council itself work out a plan for stopping the fighting that would place Kashmir under UN control pending the holding of a plebiscite. The plan would include UN appointment of a neutral commander for all Indian and Pakistani troops in Kashmir and the division of the state into zones of military occupation, the Pakistanis in the north, the Indians in the south, and a mixed force of Indians and Pakistanis plus 1,000 international troops in the Valley. Noel-Baker and Ismay thought the end result might be "some kind of partition between Muslim and Hindu majority areas." They looked to the United States to take the lead in promoting this approach.

Lovett was cool to the British proposal, which he surely knew would have been unacceptable to the Indians had it been introduced at the United Nations. He claimed that the United States was too preoccupied with its commitments in Western Europe to play the role the British wished to assign it. Moreover, Lovett said, American involvement might prompt Soviet attention and make a solution more difficult. He also recalled that recent U.S. experience with the Indians and Pakistanis in the Security Council had not been promising. The British, in the U.S. view, "were perhaps setting their sights too high as to what could be done in a short time in the Council."[17] The British ruefully recognized that they had struck out.[18] In a subsequent message to Austin, the State Department again asserted that it wished to cooperate with the British but avoid taking the lead at the Security Council.[19]

Noel-Baker's setback in his discussion with Lovett did not deter him from further efforts to persuade the United States to support the proposals favorable to Pakistan that he promoted once the Security Council debate began. These included a draft resolution calling for a virtual UN mandate for Kashmir for an indefinite period, to be administered by an interim government superseding the existing pro-India state regime. The State Department correctly judged that the Indians would strongly oppose the proposal and questioned the advisability of the United Nations assuming the broad responsibilities of Kashmir's civil and military administration. But it wanted to avoid introducing a competing draft and instead called for efforts to develop a more widely supported resolution.[20]

Concerns about the implications of the British draft for other ongoing international disputes also prompted Washington to oppose it. The draft, American officials at the United Nations pointed out to their British colleagues, "recommend[ed] the use of foreign troops from one party to a dispute [Pakistan] in the territory of another party to the dispute [India]." In the

U.S. view, it was "difficult to deny the legal validity of Kashmir's accession to India." The UN-based Americans were willing to go along with the use of Pakistani troops, which they thought desirable, only if it was the result of an agreement between the governments of India, Pakistan, and Kashmir. Neither New Delhi nor Srinagar would have consented to such an arrangement.[21]

This virtual acceptance of the validity of the accession by American officials at the United Nations was not set in concrete, however. It was later superseded by a more authoritative State Department finding that backed away from that conclusion.

Formal Security Council debate on Kashmir began on January 15, 1948, when Indian representative Gopalaswami Ayyangar spelled out New Delhi's position. He was followed by the Pakistan foreign minister, Sir Mohammed Zafrulla Khan. Both diplomats claimed that their country was the aggrieved party. For Ayyangar, the tribal invasion and Pakistan's participation in it were the cause of the conflict. The immediate task before the council, he insisted, was the raiders' expulsion and an end to the fighting. Zafrulla put Kashmir into the broader context of India-Pakistan and Hindu-Muslim relations. He bitterly accused India of seeking to destroy the Pakistan state and of carrying out an extensive campaign of genocide against the Muslims of South Asia. The almost totally conflicting approaches the two representatives took made it clear that the council would face great difficulties as it sought to resolve the conflict.[22]

Overcoming its initial reluctance to play a leading role, the United States cosponsored with the United Kingdom and others all of the resolutions the council adopted over the next three months as it tried with scant success to bridge India-Pakistan differences. The first of these resolutions was a modest measure passed on January 20, only five days after the debate began, that established a commission to look into the situation firsthand and to use "mediatory influence" to "smooth away difficulties." This led to the formation of the United Nations Commission on India and Pakistan (UNCIP). Another, more comprehensive resolution, adopted in April 1948, dealt with three key, interrelated issues: how to end the fighting, bring about the withdrawal of outside armed forces from Kashmir, and conduct the free and fair plebiscite both sides claimed they wanted. With strong backing from its

American member, UNCIP later refined and expanded the provisions of this resolution in two landmark resolutions of its own. Adopted on August 13, 1948, and January 5, 1949, these UNCIP resolutions became the basis for all subsequent efforts to resolve the Kashmir problem through the United Nations. They are examined later in this chapter.

Like generations of American diplomats who dealt with Kashmir, Austin became increasingly frustrated. He criticized the form and scope of the Security Council's resolutions. They were unrealistic and ineffective because they depended on India and Pakistan cooperating with the council and failed to give it authority to impose sanctions if they would not, as seemed to him more and more likely. The two governments' negative attitudes got under his skin. He resented their having refused to accept council proposals after they had engaged the "very expensive machinery of the United Nations" and taken "the time of distinguished men from around the world." For Austin, these unbending Indian and Pakistani positions were out of line with the UN Charter and morally wrong.[23]

Reporting from the U.S. embassies in New Delhi and Karachi suggested that American diplomats there were as frustrated as their colleagues in Washington and New York. But like these U.S.-based officials, they continued to believe at this early stage of deliberations that the Kashmir issue could most effectively be handled at the United Nations. At times the embassies' reporting, analyses, and policy recommendations tended to favor their host countries' positions. This was particularly the case when Charles Lewis was chargé at Embassy Karachi.* At one point, the department felt it necessary to rap Ambassador Grady's knuckles when he accepted an Indian position that Washington had instructed him to oppose.[24] But as a whole, the two embassies' fidelity to State Department instructions and their objectivity in reporting and assessing the situation on the ground compared favorably with the way they conducted themselves in the 1950s and 1960s.

In a formal sense, the Kashmir dispute at this stage involved only two parties—India and Pakistan. The plebiscite the Indian government had promised and the United Nations had embraced offered the people of the disputed

---

*This is diplomatic shorthand for the United States Embassy in Pakistan. Similar shorthand is used in diplomatic language for American embassies elsewhere.

state one of two choices. Not included was what later would be called "the third option"—independence.

The possibility of a separate Kashmir was brought to Austin's attention only a couple of weeks after the debate began. Its unlikely source was Sheikh Abdullah, the articulate and personally impressive Kashmir Valley Muslim leader who had by then become head of the provisional administration that ruled the Indian-held part of the state.

The Indians had made Abdullah a member of their UN delegation, no doubt in the expectation that he would be an effective spokesman for India's cause. They could not have calculated that he would undercut their position by calling for Kashmir's independence in a private conversation with Austin. Apparently caught by surprise, the ambassador gave Abdullah no encouragement.[25] Nor could he have, knowing that Washington was firmly opposed to any further splintering of the subcontinent. In the U.S. view, such divisions would jeopardize and complicate South Asia's political and economic transition and create conditions of instability ultimately adverse to broad American interests in the area. This opposition to independence was not categorical, however. The State Department declared two months later in a message designed to guide the embassies in New Delhi and Karachi that if independence appeared to be a basis for an India-Pakistan settlement on Kashmir, the United States would probably not oppose the idea, although it would not take the initiative in promoting it.[26]

In later years, Abdullah was not consistent in his stated preference for the kind of relationship Kashmir should have with India. Whether in power or in opposition, his only constant theme was a demand for something less than the full integration of the state into the Indian Union. How much less ran the gamut from independence to limited autonomy.

The first direct American experience with Abdullah's inconsistent and often ambiguous approach came soon after his session with Austin. Meeting in New Delhi with Ambassador Grady, the sheikh retreated from the line he had taken in New York, telling Grady he wanted Kashmir to be independent as far as internal affairs were concerned. India and Pakistan should jointly administer the state's defense, foreign affairs, and communications. In a comment that must have pleased Washington, and was no doubt designed to do so, Abdullah said that a joint India-Pakistan defense arrangement for Kashmir would ensure the state's security against aggression "from the north."[27]

While the Security Council deliberated, fighting continued in the state. Indian forces advanced westward toward Kashmir's border with Pakistan, but large tracts of land in the western and southwestern areas of Jammu Province remained under Pakistan's control and were administered by what the Pakistanis called the "Azad [Free] Government of Jammu and Kashmir." The Pakistanis also held Gilgit and other areas in the northern part of the state that had broken away from Kashmir government control when the maharaja acceded to India. These mountainous tracts were never occupied by independent India's armed forces. Virtually all Hindus and Sikhs who had lived before 1947 in the parts of Kashmir that fell under Pakistani control were expelled or killed.

India completely controlled the Kashmir Valley both militarily and, through Sheikh Abdullah, politically. All significant opposition on the ground to Abdullah's provisional state administration had ended. Anti-Abdullah political leaders had crossed to the Pakistan side or were in jail. Organizations other than the sheikh's National Conference no longer functioned. Unlike Indian-held areas in the southeastern portions of the state, where the Muslim population had been decimated, the Valley remained remarkably free of communal violence. Only a relatively small number of Muslims left the Valley for Azad Kashmir or Pakistan proper.

Private U.S. citizens were involved in the Kashmir conflict at least twice. The Indians reportedly employed three American pilots to fly troops to Srinagar by commercial aircraft in October-November 1947 soon after the maharaja's accession.[28] A much more romantic tale is the compelling story of Russell K. Haight Jr., an American adventurer who served for two months as a brigadier general in the forces of Azad Kashmir.

Haight's story is as fascinating as it is improbable. A slim, blond, twenty-five-year-old ex-G.I. from Brooklyn, he had been a U.S. Army Air Force sergeant during World War II and saw combat in France. After the war he found his way to Afghanistan, where an American construction company employed him as a surveyor. Injured in a fall from a cliff, he decided to return to the United States. On his way home, he had a chance encounter in Rawalpindi with officials from Azad Kashmir. Learning of his military background (if only as a noncom), they offered him a captain's commission in the Azad Kashmir military forces. According to one contemporary account, Haight thought it a pity to miss a war and signed up. With no knowledge of either Urdu or Pushtu, but completely self-assured, he was put in charge of an Azad Kashmir unit on the Poonch front in southwestern Kashmir. When he caustically criticized the "Boy Scout tactics" of some of the other Azad Kashmir officers, he was promoted from captain to brigadier general, presumably because he was expected to do better.

According to a story Robert Trumbull wrote for the *New York Times* in January 1948, Haight learned how to handle unruly tribesmen—who were interested mainly in loot—by playing upon their vanities and tribal rivalries. But he decided to quit when he could not obtain either the supplies or the cooperation necessary for the tasks he was assigned. His departure was hastened when he got into a fight with some tribal warriors in a transit camp for Azad Kashmir rebels across the Pakistan border. Soon afterward, his romantic adventures as a mid-twentieth-century freebooter ended with his hurried departure from Karachi for America.

Haight's observations about the Azad Kashmir forces excited some interest, especially because of widespread speculation then current that the Pakistani military was involved in the Kashmir conflict. He told Trumbull that the Pakistani authorities provided the insurgents with plentiful supplies of gasoline, scarce and strictly rationed in Pakistan. Pakistan Army personnel operated the Azad Kashmir radio station, passed out matériel from army stocks, and organized and managed Azad military encampments in Pakistan. Although Haight was sympathetic to its cause, he characterized the Azad Kashmir provisional government as a Pakistani puppet and deeply implicated senior Pakistani government officials. Not surprisingly, reports of his activities in Kashmir prompted a Communist Party newspaper in India to denounce the young brigadier general as an American spy and won him some notoriety among other Indians suspicious of U.S. intentions in Kashmir.[29]

The five members of the United Nations Commission for India and Pakistan did not reach South Asia until early July 1948. Reflecting the composition of the United Nations at the time, they were drawn from Argentina (chosen by Pakistan), Czechoslovakia (picked by India), Colombia and Belgium (selected by the Security Council), and an initially reluctant United States (named by the president of the Security Council when the four original members could not agree on a fifth representative). The American delegate was Jerome Klahr Huddle, a career diplomat then serving as ambassador to Burma. Although Washington had insisted that UNCIP leave promptly for South Asia after the Security Council established it in February, it took its time before nominating Huddle, probably because it had problems finding a suitable candidate and was preoccupied by more pressing concerns.[30] Czechoslovakia was represented by Dr. Josef Korbel, whose book, *Danger in Kashmir*, often cited in these pages, remains one of the best accounts of the first phase of the effort to resolve the conflict. Korbel, the father of Madeleine Albright, secretary of state in the Clinton administration, later immigrated to the United States and became an American citizen.[31]

With its arrival in South Asia, UNCIP became the focus of international diplomatic efforts to resolve the Kashmir problem. At their first stop, in Karachi, the commissioners were stunned to learn from Foreign Minister Zafrulla Khan that three brigades of regular Pakistan Army troops had been in Kashmir since May. This shock could have been avoided. Reliable word of a substantial Pakistani military presence in Kashmir had been appearing for two months in American and British diplomatic messages, but the commissioners had not been informed. Zafrulla claimed that an Indian spring offensive in the western part of the state required Pakistan to reinforce the line Azad forces held there.[32] A few days later the commissioners conferred in New Delhi with Sir Girja Shankar Bajpai, the Indian secretary general for foreign and commonwealth relations. Bajpai did not spring any further surprises. But like Zafrulla, he reiterated the unyielding positions his colleagues had taken at the United Nations. The commissioners recognized that they would face hard negotiations.

For the next five weeks the UNCIP members shuttled between New Delhi and Karachi as they tried to draft a cease-fire proposal acceptable to both India and Pakistan. They also visited both the Indian- and Pakistani-held parts of Kashmir. Ambassador Huddle, who played a leading role in the commission's efforts, wisely resisted a bid to make him its permanent chairman. He recognized that his selection would inevitably lead to unwanted charges that the United States was dominating UNCIP's work. The ambassador kept in close touch with Washington through U.S. embassy facilities, sending the State Department appraisals and recommendations and receiving "advice" but not "instructions" about policies he should advocate. This distinction was apparently necessary because Huddle, like his four colleagues, was technically not a representative of his government. His status did not influence the way he carried out his assignment, however. Washington provided Huddle with a small military and civilian support staff, an advantage other UNCIP members did not enjoy.[33]

Despite the disdain the Indian and Pakistan governments had for UNCIP's efforts and their unwillingness to accept compromises on major points of disagreement, the commission successfully hammered out a fresh resolution on August 13, as noted. This called on India and Pakistan to agree to a cease-fire, which was to take effect within four days of the two governments' accepting its terms. Pakistan was to pull back its armed forces from the state and "use its best endeavors" to secure the withdrawal from Kashmiri territory of tribesmen and other Pakistani nationals. Local authorities under UNCIP surveillance would administer the areas within the state that Pakistan had held. Once the commission certified that the irregulars had departed and the Pakistani Army was being withdrawn, India would draw down the bulk of its forces. Pending a final settlement, India was to station on its side of the newly drawn cease-fire only the minimal force needed to help local authorities maintain law and order. India and Pakistan were to consult with UNCIP to decide on "fair and equitable" conditions for the plebiscite. Unlike the Security Council's April 21 resolution, UNCIP's did not recommend the installation of a broadly based state government in place of Sheikh Abdullah's pro-India regime, probably because the commission recognized that such an arrangement was no longer feasible, if it ever had been.[34] The Indians accepted the resolution subject to clarifications of a few points, most of them later resolved to their satisfaction. The Pakistanis were more difficult and hedged their acceptance with so many conditions that their position seemed to Korbel "tantamount to rejection."[35]

After further consultations with Indian and Pakistani officials and visits to both sides of Kashmir, UNCIP adopted another key resolution on January 5, 1949. This outlined a plebiscite process to begin with the UN secretary general's nominating a plebiscite administrator with sweeping powers.[36] Both India and Pakistan accepted the resolution with only a few reservations. Its adoption completed the basic structure for the resolution of the Kashmir dispute through UN mediatory efforts.

Just a few days earlier, the Indians and Pakistanis had agreed to a cease-fire in place. This took effect on New Year's Day 1949, exactly one year after

India brought the Kashmir issue to the Security Council.[37] Washington hailed the cease-fire and the resolution as "a demonstration to the world of how progress can be achieved in the settlement of international disputes by peaceful means."[38] The two achievements had very different outcomes. Despite the many troubles that continued to plague India-Pakistan relations, the cease-fire worked reasonably well for more than sixteen years before collapsing when another conflict broke out between the two countries over Kashmir in August 1965. By contrast, the January 5 resolution was never implemented and the plebiscite it called for never held.

When the commissioners returned to South Asia in early 1949 to negotiate the implementation of their resolutions with India and Pakistan, they could not resolve differences between the two governments on five key issues: disarming and disbanding the Azad Kashmir armed forces; withdrawal of Pakistani forces; the scope and timing of the withdrawal of the bulk of the Indian army; which local authorities would govern Azad Kashmir in the period before the plebiscite; and control of the remote, sparsely settled areas in the north and northwestern parts of Kashmir held by Pakistan. UNCIP's only success was in establishing a small, multinational force—the United Nations Military Observers Group in India and Pakistan, UNMOGIP—to patrol the four-hundred-mile-long cease-fire line that snaked across the state. At UN request, the United States provided the force's largest contingent. UNMOGIP carried out its monitoring responsibilities until the third India-Pakistan war in 1971. When, following the war, India and Pakistan signed an agreement replacing the cease-fire line with a new Line of Control drawn close to it, the Indians took the position that the mandate of the group had lapsed. Since then they have restricted the activities of UN observers on their side. UNMOGIP continues to operate on the Pakistan side but in light of the Indian position no longer plays a significant role.

Another seemingly favorable development was UN Secretary General Trygve Lie's nomination of Fleet Admiral Chester W. Nimitz as plebiscite administrator in March 1949. Nimitz had commanded American naval forces in the Pacific during World War II and was an internationally recognized figure. In a strong statement of support for the Nimitz nomination, Secretary of State Dean Acheson declared that the United States felt honored that India and Pakistan had agreed to repose their confidence in him.[39] The secretary's accolade proved premature. For the next five years the admiral cooled his heels in the United States and never got to South Asia to assume his responsibilities.

As UNCIP failed to make any significant progress in implementing its resolutions, American policymakers pinned the primary blame for the impasse on India. They became increasingly troubled by what they considered New Delhi's stonewalling of the commission's proposals and its outspoken expressions of animosity toward Washington's policy on Kashmir, which it alleged was tilted in favor of Pakistan. While the United States did not give the Pakistanis high marks for cooperation with UNCIP, it found their diplomacy less of a problem.[40]

This growing U.S.-India confrontation over Kashmir took place against a background of rising foreign policy differences between the two countries on a broad range of international issues. By 1949 the United States had made the containment of Communist designs for world domination the central tenet of its foreign policy. India rejected this cold war approach in favor of a policy of nonalignment, which Nehru devised, promoted, and personally implemented. Its concerns focused on what it regarded as the continuing menace of the colonialism and racism from which it had recently escaped. The mutual dissatisfaction that each country felt with the other's approach to Kashmir contributed to this downslide in their bilateral relations. By contrast, the United States had no similar foreign policy problems with Pakistan. Although Karachi also followed a nonaligned policy in 1949, this was more a matter of necessity than choice. The Pakistanis had not been shy in expressing their interest in joining the Western bloc if it would have them.

Two separate conversations Ambassador Loy Henderson had in New Delhi with Bajpai and Nehru in July and August 1949 illustrate the gap in the two countries' positions on Kashmir. Henderson, a top-ranking career diplomat who had succeeded Henry Grady as U.S. ambassador to India in November 1948, was a confirmed cold warrior. He had little use for Indian nonalignment and saw no reason to conceal his disdain. A strong personal dislike between Henderson and Nehru contributed to the difficult relations that quickly developed between them.

According to Henderson, Bajpai told him that Nehru and other senior Indian officials were disturbed that Washington thought the Indian government was using subterfuge and evasion to avoid a Kashmir plebiscite.

Bajpai said that he hoped that if the United States had such impressions, it would be candid in bringing them to India's attention.[41] The ambassador was characteristically forthright in his reply. He told Bajpai that U.S. officials' doubts about Indian intentions had been fueled by New Delhi's unwillingness to adopt the kind of conciliatory attitude that could help promote a prompt holding of the plebiscite. It was well known, he said, that in certain Indian official circles (which he did not identify), partition of Kashmir was preferred to a plebiscite. And because India held the most desirable portions of Kashmir, a postponement of the plebiscite would hurt Pakistan more than it would India. The State Department used more diplomatic wording in the message it asked Henderson to pass to the Indians a week later, but it told the ambassador that it was gratified by his prompt and forceful reply to Bajpai.[42]

Nehru waded into these troubled waters soon afterward. In an intemperate outburst, the prime minister informed Henderson that "he was tired of receiving moralistic advice from the United States. India did not need advice from the United States or any other country as to its foreign and internal policies. His own record and that of Indian foreign relations was one of integrity and honesty, which did not warrant admonitions. He did not care to receive lectures from other countries. So far as Kashmir was concerned he would not give an inch. He would hold his ground even if Kashmir, India, and the whole world would go to pieces." Although Nehru eventually calmed down, his message was a candid statement of how strongly he felt about the future of Kashmir and how inflexible India was likely to remain toward international efforts to resolve the issue in ways it found unacceptable.[43]

By the time Henderson had these two troubling conversations, Washington had reluctantly concluded that further UNCIP efforts would be useless. The only way to bring about a truce agreement, it now believed, was arbitration by a third party, with Indian and Pakistani consent. Henderson agreed and recommended that President Truman send a personal message to Nehru calling on India to accept arbitration should UNCIP request it. The White House accepted his advice. When UNCIP soon afterward confessed that it had failed and called for arbitration by Admiral Nimitz, the president sent identical messages to Nehru and Pakistan prime minister

Liaquat supporting the arbitration approach. British prime minister Attlee wrote similar letters to the two leaders the same day.[44]

The White House messages represented the first but not the last time an American president personally and openly involved himself in efforts to resolve the Kashmir issue. Explaining his unprecedented action to Nehru and Liaquat, Truman stressed the importance of an early Kashmir settlement to the peace and progress of Asia. Senior American officials told the press that U.S. interest in halting the spread of Communism in Asia had prompted the president's intercession.[45]

Nehru publicly expressed surprise and irritation with the proposal even before he wrote to Truman turning it down. He told the president he was not opposed to arbitration in principle but objected to the authority the proposal gave to the arbitrator to determine the points on which arbitration should take place. Liaquat accepted the proposal in a message that stressed his trust in Americans, an obvious play for Washington's sympathy that contrasted sharply with Nehru's reply.[46] His response reflected what was long to be Pakistan's basic approach to the Kashmir issue: encourage outside, especially American, intervention in the dispute to balance the advantage India enjoyed as the stronger, status quo power.

Truman did not repeat his appeal to Nehru when the prime minister visited the White House in October 1949. The two leaders agreed that the Kashmir issue should be settled by peaceful means. But their discussion of the problem was anodyne in content and noncontroversial in tone, and they made no effort to come to grips with the basic issues that stood in the way of a settlement.

Nehru's subsequent exchange with Secretary Acheson was much more pointed. The prime minister's official biographer, S. Gopal, has written that Nehru hotly defended India's position and criticized America's "equivocal attitude." Although Nehru's exposition seems by Acheson's own account to have been mostly a heated and angry repetition of familiar Indian arguments, his bottom line was new and important. According to Acheson, Nehru declared that if the people of Kashmir wished to question the state's accession to India—which he doubted—"the preferable way to ascertain their will would be through a constituent assembly of the natural leaders of the people elected to meet and discuss the future." This might lead to a Kashmir-wide decision or to division of the state. If Acheson recorded

Nehru's words correctly, they seem to represent a repudiation of India's plebiscite pledge. They also foreshadowed the later Indian argument that the ratification by the Kashmir Constituent Assembly in 1954 of the state's accession to India fulfilled India's commitment to self-determination for the Kashmiri people.[47]

While Nehru was visiting the United States, UNCIP members hammered out the commission's final report to the Security Council. Largely reflecting U.S. positions, the report called for appointment of a single individual as UN representative and consultation by the council with India and Pakistan to determine his terms of reference, including his authority to arbitrate on issues of demilitarization.[48]

Although the Indians were unwilling to accept arbitration, they were prepared to deal with a representative chosen by the Security Council. The first of these was General A. G. L. McNaughton of Canada, then council president. McNaughton's efforts spanned only a few weeks in December 1949 and were limited to negotiations with the Indian and Pakistani UN delegations. U.S. representatives in New York played an important role in helping him frame proposals designed to break the demilitarization impasse. India quickly rejected these proposals on what by then had become familiar grounds. These included the charge that they equated India with Pakistan. Pakistan accepted the proposals subject to minor changes in wording.[49] U.S. policymakers considered India's rejection the worst example yet of its intransigence.

McNaughton was followed early in 1950 by the prominent Australian jurist Sir Owen Dixon. Dixon was well known and respected in Washington, where he had served as Australia's ambassador during World War II. But his task was a thankless one, especially since he was instructed to negotiate demilitarization on the basis of the McNaughton proposals that India had already turned down. His difficulties were worsened by the outbreak of communal clashes in India and Pakistan that brought the two countries to the brink of war. The crisis completely overshadowed the Kashmir issue in the weeks following Dixon's appointment. The agreement the Indian and Pakistani prime ministers eventually reached to resolve it made no mention of Kashmir.

Dixon kept the United States informed about his progress but apparently received no advice from American diplomats about how he could best proceed. When he found that India would not accept any of his demilitarization formulas, he concluded that it was simply not possible to conduct a free and fair plebiscite covering the entire state. He then turned to other possibilities. The one he preferred was to limit the plebiscite to the Valley and to divide the other parts of the state between India and Pakistan according to the ethnic and communal character of their inhabitants. This proposal, still referred to as the Dixon Plan, continues to enjoy some support in Kashmir and elsewhere. But Indian unwillingness to agree to the plan or any of the other plebiscite proposals Dixon designed eventually doomed his mission.[50]

After McNaughton's efforts had failed and before Dixon undertook his, the State Department prepared for the first time an authoritative memorandum spelling out the main points in Washington's approach to the Kashmir issue. Drafted by two assistant secretaries, George C. McGhee, who was responsible for South Asia policy, and John D. Hickerson, who supervised the department bureau that dealt with international organizations, it was a remarkably candid and comprehensive document that is an important benchmark in the long U.S. effort to deal with the problem. For the balance of the Truman administration, the memorandum, which was approved by Secretary Acheson, remained the basic U.S. assessment of the Kashmir issue and how Washington should handle it.[51]

McGhee and Hickerson held that a resolution of the Kashmir issue was essential to South Asian peace and security and considered Indian intransigence primarily responsible for delaying a settlement.[52] They cited chapter and verse to support this conclusion. Assessing India's case, they quoted from a memorandum, prepared by the Office of the Legal Adviser of the State Department, in coming to the judgment that the maharaja's signing the instrument of accession did not settle the accession issue.[53]

McGhee and Hickerson found that India appeared determined to avoid an overall plebiscite despite its previous commitment. The United States would support any settlement acceptable to India and Pakistan, either an all-Kashmir plebiscite following which all of the state would go to one of the two claimants or a plebiscite that led to the partition of the state between them. McGhee and Hickerson rejected a partition of the Valley itself as infeasible.

The two officials also concluded that a settlement involving an independent Kashmir state would be unviable and dangerous and should be resisted. Their recommendations for ways to persuade India to modify its position included continued pressure by Britain and other commonwealth countries, statements by other Security Council members in council debate, friendly but firm and frank expressions of U.S. views on appropriate occasions, and some concession to "Indian aversion to an over-all plebiscite."

In a subsequent message to its London embassy, the State Department reaffirmed that Washington believed that Britain should take responsibility for promoting a settlement. The United States wanted that country to assume the leading role in consultations with Security Council members to work out a solution along the lines of the McGhee-Hickerson memo.[54]

The failure of the Dixon mission seems to have sharpened even further Ambassador Henderson's already deep suspicions of Indian motives and good faith. He concluded that growing resentment in India about the allegedly pro-Pakistan attitude of the United States on Kashmir—which he reported had been quietly stimulated by Nehru himself—made it desirable to have Britain and other commonwealth countries take the lead in working out a solution, as the McGhee-Hickerson memorandum had stipulated. No one in India had criticized Australia about the Dixon report, Henderson complained, but if Dixon had been an American citizen, the Indian press would have castigated the United States for playing great-power politics in Kashmir. Washington appears to have heeded the ambassador's advice. For the rest of 1950 it showed scant interest in taking part in another major international initiative on Kashmir.[55]

During this lull, Henderson became the first American ambassador to visit Kashmir. He found the military officers of the UN monitoring group and other foreigners in Kashmir almost unanimous in holding that the people of the Valley would prefer Pakistan to India if they had the opportunity to vote freely. Most thought that a majority would prefer independence if offered that option.

Henderson met twice with Sheikh Abdullah. By then the prime minister of the state, Abdullah promoted the independence option just as he had in his New York meeting with Warren Austin two years earlier. He claimed that the overwhelming majority of Kashmiris desired independence. Even the leaders of Azad Kashmir would be willing to cooperate with his National Conference party if there was a reasonable chance that such cooperation would result in independence, he said, and dismissed Dixon's partial plebiscite plan as impractical.[56]

Soon after his discussions with Henderson, Sheikh Abdullah had the National Conference pass a resolution calling for elections in Indian-controlled Kashmir to choose members of a constituent assembly who would determine the future shape and affiliation of the state. This body was expected to confirm the state's accession to India, thus providing the Indians with an argument of at least some plausibility that they had fulfilled their pledge to let the people of Kashmir determine their own political future. The United States and Britain drafted a Security Council resolution that called on India to reassure the council that such unilateral action would not prejudice the settlement of the problem, in accordance with past Security Council resolutions and the previous agreement of the concerned parties. But caught up in the far greater crisis of the Korean War, the council took no action on the resolution. The issue would return to haunt negotiations on Kashmir later in the decade and beyond.

A meeting of the commonwealth heads of government in London in January 1951 ushered in a fourth year of Kashmir diplomacy.[57] American hopes that progress could be made in informal discussions there were quickly dashed. The British told Washington that Nehru was to blame. This latest setback, which further eroded Pakistan's faith in multilateral diplomacy, led a politically weakened Liaquat Ali Khan to declare that his government would not participate in the defense of the Middle East or Asia until the Kashmir issue was resolved. Liaquat's decision was important to Washington, which looked to Pakistan to contribute to the American-led UN military effort in Korea, then at a critical point following Communist Chinese intervention. Concern about the Korean conflict and other dangerous confrontations with China, and the greater importance these developments gave to maintaining peace elsewhere in Asia, also helped prompt the United States and Britain to cosponsor another Security Council resolution on ways to resolve the plebiscite issue. The Indians quickly rejected it.[58]

Washington then decided to promote the selection of another special negotiator. Disregarding Ambassador Henderson's warning that Indian attitudes made it unwise to involve an American citizen in Kashmir efforts, it suggested senior UN official Ralph Bunche for the position.[59] When Pakistan vetoed Bunche, Washington turned to Dr. Frank P. Graham, a former U.S. senator and president of the University of North Carolina.[60] Graham was well known to Secretary Acheson for his success as an intermediary in negotiations between the Dutch and Indonesians. He took up his mission in September 1951, when India and Pakistan were preoccupied with another serious confrontation that had brought them to the brink of war—not an auspicious beginning. Although against the odds he developed good relations with Nehru and other senior Indian officials, Graham ultimately failed to win agreement between India and Pakistan on the disarmament issue.

Washington had been understandably pessimistic about Graham's prospects and had discussed alternative approaches with the British should he fail. These included establishing a temporary UN trusteeship or an India-Pakistan condominium over all or part of the state, both highly unrealistic ideas. More sensible were proposals to establish a joint India-Pakistan or UN authority to promote Kashmir's economic development, particularly through the use of water resources, and to set up a joint India-Pakistan water commission to resolve broader differences relating to water rights in Kashmir and neighboring Punjab. The idea of a joint commission had recently been suggested by David Lilienthal, a former chairman of the U.S. Atomic Energy Commission. Lilienthal's concept led a decade later to the World Bank–sponsored India-Pakistan Indus Waters Treaty. But it was only when they began their peace process in 2004 that India and Pakistan agreed to explore ways to develop other forms of economic cooperation between the two sides of Kashmir.[61]

Washington also considered asking the Security Council to request the International Court of Justice for an advisory opinion on the legality of Maharaja Hari Singh's signing the instrument of accession. A State Department memorandum argued that a court finding that the accession was invalid would "knock out" one of India's principal arguments supporting its occupation of Kashmir. The memo noted that the British Foreign Office and the department's legal adviser had tentatively concluded that the court would make this judgment but warned that an approach to the court had serious disadvantages. All initiatives on Kashmir would have to be suspended while it took its time coming to a decision. Moreover, the court might judge in India's favor. In the end, nothing came of the idea.[62]

While Washington and London pondered next steps, Sheikh Abdullah's government held elections in September and October 1950 for a state constituent assembly. These resulted in total victory for Abdullah's National Conference, which won all seventy-five seats. Since the state government disqualified all opposition and independent candidates or pressured them to withdraw, no actual balloting took place.[63] The election caused dismay in Washington, which feared that the Indians would use the assembly to wriggle out of their commitment to a plebiscite, as Nehru had suggested in his conversation with Acheson. This concern proved justified. In February 1954 the state constituent assembly unanimously ratified Kashmir's accession to India. It followed up this action in November 1956, when it adopted a state constitution that declared: "The State of Jammu and Kashmir is and shall be an integral part of the Union of India." Before either of these steps was taken, Abdullah had been overthrown and jailed.[64]

The Truman administration transferred Loy Henderson to Iran in mid-1951, no doubt to the ambassador's satisfaction. He was succeeded by Chester Bowles. Unlike Henderson, Bowles was determined to win Nehru's friendship and confidence. A highly successful advertising agency executive who had gone on to become wartime head of the Office of Price Administration and then governor of Connecticut, Bowles, more than any other senior official in the Truman administration, was convinced that India was important to broad U.S. interests extending well beyond South Asia.

Bowles tried hard to persuade Washington to judge the Kashmir issue in ways more sympathetic to India. He quickly drew conclusions about the problem that differed sharply from Henderson's. His interpretation of Nehru's position on Kashmir was far more positive. In an early message, he said he was convinced that the prime minister wanted a prompt settlement and was willing to explore ways to reach one either through the Security Council or in direct negotiations with Pakistan. Nehru, Bowles maintained, was confident that India would win a plebiscite in Kashmir because of Abdullah's consolidation of power, his popularity, and his ability to control the electorate.[65] The ambassador also reported that his fellow New Delhi–based chiefs of mission and locally assigned American reporters unanimously agreed that the Kashmiris would vote for accession to India.[66]

Bowles's controversial assessments and policy proposals on a broad range of issues often brought him into sharp confrontation with Washington policymakers, who regarded him as too pro-Indian. His conflict with them over Kashmir policy was especially contentious. Aside from faulting Bowles for trying with little basis to make India look good on the issue, Washington was troubled by his efforts to promote the partition–partial plebiscite plan Sir Owen Dixon had unsuccessfully proposed in 1950. Bowles quickly found that the idea enjoyed no support in Washington. Skeptical State Department officials suspected that the Indians were using it as a delaying tactic or a further pretext for obstructing a settlement. They also feared that encouragement given to the partition plan would undercut efforts to move forward with demilitarization and other aspects of the UNCIP resolutions.[67]

The State Department eventually became fed up with Bowles's relentless advocacy of the revived Dixon Plan and his freewheeling discussions about it with G. S. Bajpai and other Indians. In an unusually tough message, it instructed him "to avoid in conversations with [Indian] officials initiating any new substantive discussions of the Kashmir case, unless instructed by the Department. If the issue is raised, suggest you confine your remarks to stating your willingness to transmit Indian government views to the Department."[68] In a long follow-up letter, Assistant Secretary Hickerson pointedly recalled for Bowles that when Dixon floated his idea, India quickly made clear it was not prepared to accept conditions for a plebiscite in the Valley that in Dixon's opinion were the very minimum needed to ensure a free and fair vote. Hickerson believed that the Indians were being disingenuous in raising it again with Bowles. He said that Washington would continue to support Graham's efforts to work out a settlement based on the UNCIP resolutions but strongly opposed, as did Graham, a broadening of his mandate to include the partition–partial plebiscite approach.[69]

Despite this forceful rejoinder, Bowles continued to advocate the Dixon Plan until he completed his New Delhi assignment in March 1953. American policymakers and Graham himself remained unmoved. In Washington's view, the Dixon approach would be feasible only if India itself took the initiative in formally proposing it. The Indians were never prepared to do so.

Bowles's attitude toward Graham's efforts reflected his concern that Washington would regard New Delhi's position on Kashmir as an obstacle to the sharp, positive change in U.S. policy toward India that he ardently sought. Worried that continued failure to reach a settlement could damage bilateral relations, the ambassador argued that the United States should recognize that "we alone cannot solve every problem and [hence] restrict our role . . . to that of a friend to both countries which refuses to take sides but is anxious to help if at all possible." We should "pray for Graham's success, but, if he fails, keep our patience, refrain from moral judgments, and adopt a position in the Security Council which . . . will be best calculated to advance a settlement between India and Pakistan, without aligning the United States with one side or the other."[70]

Interestingly, Bowles himself briefly played a direct role in the negotiations on troop levels. En route from Washington to New Delhi, he met in Karachi with Pakistan prime minister Sir Khwaja Nazimuddin at the suggestion of Avra Warren, the career diplomat who had become American ambassador there. Nazimuddin disclosed to Bowles and Warren the substantial concessions Pakistan was prepared to make on its military presence in Kashmir provided the Indians agreed to the installation of a plebiscite administrator. The Pakistanis asked Bowles to sound out Nehru informally on their offer. With Washington's permission, Bowles then undertook what nowadays would be termed an exercise in shuttle diplomacy. Despite an emotional appeal from Bowles, Nehru rejected the Pakistani offer. Bowles was very disappointed but quickly sought to explain away the prime minister's rebuff.

A prominent Democrat, Bowles left his ambassadorship following Republican Dwight Eisenhower's victory in the 1952 presidential election. His departure signaled the end of any serious attempt to develop stronger and more confident U.S.-Indian relations, at least for the next four years. Graham gave up his effort at about the same time, when it became clear to him that the unbridgeable gap between the Indian and Pakistani positions on demilitarization and other provisions of the UNCIP resolutions ruled out any prospect for success. His exit—to which New Delhi and Karachi both agreed—brought to an ignominious conclusion the five-year effort to resolve the Kashmir problem through UN intervention.[71]

2

Impact of the Alliance with Pakistan

Like Truman's, the major foreign policy objective of the Eisenhower administration was to contain the threat of Communist aggression, especially in Europe and the Far East. John Foster Dulles, who had finally achieved his longtime ambition to become secretary of state, was a determined cold warrior who had scant sympathy either for India or for the nonaligned policies that Prime Minister Nehru favored. He would later famously label them immoral. The new administration ranked South Asia low on its list of concerns. Nonetheless, it recognized the potential danger the Kashmir dispute posed to American interests. Although the record of the previous five years must have tempted it to walk away from the issue, it looked for new ways to foster a settlement that both India and Pakistan could accept.

Senior State Department officials John Hickerson and Henry A. Byroade promoted the idea of partitioning the state. Hickerson, one of the architects of U.S. Kashmir policy in the Truman administration, had stayed on as assistant secretary for United Nations affairs under Eisenhower and Dulles. Byroade, a rising star in the department, had taken over George McGhee's job as head of the Bureau of Near Eastern, South Asian, and African Affairs. In a March 14, 1953, memorandum to Dulles, the two officials recommended that the administration send a private American citizen on a secret mission to South Asia to explore the partition idea and alternative proposals with the Indian and Pakistani prime ministers. They wanted someone who would be sufficiently prominent and politically influential to gain easy access. Although the envoy's mission should be made to appear informal, he should be able to tell the two leaders that he had the president's blessing and full support.

The man they had in mind was Paul Hoffman. A successful Republican businessman, Hoffman had won international acclaim as the first administrator of the Economic Cooperation Administration, the organization that directed the postwar Marshall Plan for European recovery. He had recently headed the Ford Foundation. In Hickerson's and Byroade's view, the remarkable success the foundation had achieved in India and Pakistan should help make him welcome in both countries.[1]

When he forwarded their recommendation to the White House, Dulles warned the president that an India-Pakistan war over Kashmir was "not a remote possibility." Partition seemed to be the only solution that offered any practical chance of success. Eisenhower quickly approved the Hoffman mission. "Our world simply cannot afford an outbreak of hostilities between these two countries," he told Dulles, "and I would risk a great deal to prevent any such eventuality." He wanted Hoffman sent out at once.[2]

Hoffman met Prime Minister Nehru soon after he arrived in New Delhi in early April 1953. According to Hoffman, they discussed several options, including a full plebiscite, a plebiscite limited to the Kashmir Valley, and joint India-Pakistan control of the Valley. Nehru would not commit himself to any particular solution but seemed confident that a satisfactory answer could be found. He was willing to meet with Pakistan prime minister Mohammed Ali Bogra to settle Kashmir and all other bilateral problems and authorized Hoffman to pass this word to Bogra when he saw him in Karachi.[3]

Hoffman's talks with Bogra and other senior Pakistani officials also went well. Bogra told him that he was determined to meet India more than halfway, and Hoffman passed this message on to Nehru when he returned to New Delhi. Nehru was condescending in talking to Hoffman about Bogra, a mediocre Bengali politician and recent ambassador to the United States who was much less powerful than Pakistan's military and civil service elite. But Nehru said he hoped to meet informally with Bogra when they were both in London in June for the coronation of Queen Elizabeth II. This would clear the way for a meeting in the subcontinent.

In the upbeat report he sent Dulles after returning to the United States, Hoffman said that the most significant development of his visit was the two prime ministers' agreement "to enter into negotiations on a 'neighbor to neighbor' basis for the resolution of all important issues in dispute." He was not sure if the United States could usefully take any further action to facilitate those bilateral negotiations. Oddly, Hoffman made no reference to the partition approach he had been recruited to promote with the South Asian leaders. He had evidently not pressed that option when he met them.[4]

Eisenhower was apparently pleased with Hoffman's efforts. According to Hoffman's biographer, the president offered to make him ambassador to India in 1954. Although Hoffman was interested in the assignment, his business commitments obliged him to turn it down.[5]

With bilateral negotiations in the offing, Washington did not undertake further diplomatic efforts on Kashmir. But before Nehru and Bogra conferred in July and August, Secretary Dulles made a historic three-continent journey that set the stage for Pakistan's joining the Western security system and profoundly affected America's role in the dispute.

Meeting with Nehru in New Delhi, Dulles promoted the partition proposal that Hoffman had neglected. The prime minister agreed that it might be a better solution than a plebiscite. But what Nehru had in mind was a division of the state on the basis of the status quo. This one-sided concept of partition, which would allow India to keep the Kashmir Valley, is still India's real objective despite its formal position that all of the state is an integral part of India. As Nehru surely knew when he met Dulles, partition defined that way would not be acceptable to Pakistan.

The Pakistanis made this clear to the secretary when he reached Karachi. Bogra told him that *any* partition amounted to selling the birthright of the Kashmiri people. In a separate conversation with Dulles, Foreign Minister Mohammed Zafrulla Khan said he was prepared to accept a UN-conducted vote in the Valley alone. But he said he had no hope that India would accept this approach, which he recalled Nehru had rejected when Sir Owen Dixon had suggested it. The foreign minister dismissed the notion of an independent Kashmir Valley. It would make the area an arena of international intrigue. But, he added sardonically, "if the people of the Valley wished to commit suicide Pakistan would not stand in the way."

Bogra and Zafrulla reacted dubiously to Secretary Dulles's expression of hope that the upcoming talks with Nehru would be fruitful. Bogra said that the Indian prime minister must make "a gesture" (which he did not specify). Zafrulla questioned Nehru's professed interest in moving forward. He added pointedly that "if Nehru feels that the United States is taking an interest and that this interest is likely to be continuous, he might possibly exert efforts to find a solution." The two ministers called for greater U.S. pressure to bring about a settlement. Dulles should "keep the heat on both of us [India and Pakistan]," Bogra declared.

General Muhammad Ayub Khan, the Pakistan army commander in chief, reiterated this call for U.S. action when he met with Dulles later the same day. As he did in the years when he ruled Pakistan following the 1958 military coup, Ayub argued that unless the United States brought pressure on Nehru, the prime minister would be quite content to bide his time on Kashmir because a delay was profitable for the Indians and extremely detrimental for the Pakistanis.[6]

Dulles resisted Pakistani suggestions that Washington use its economic assistance to twist India's arm on Kashmir. But he had already told Nehru, in carefully chosen but none-too-subtle words, that "it was difficult for the United States to justify before Congress the giving of economic aid when the economies of both India and Pakistan were being dragged down by the maintenance of military establishments made necessary by the possibility of hostilities over Kashmir." And in a telegram he drafted on his way home, he reported that he was not optimistic about the upcoming Nehru-Bogra talks and called for steady U.S. pressure on Nehru to get him to move on Kashmir.[7]

Dulles came away from his visit to Karachi much impressed with Pakistan's apparent martial prowess and anti-Communist credentials. He said he discovered a genuine feeling of friendship there for the United States that was much greater than he had found at his other stops in South Asia and the Middle East. In the secretary's view, Pakistan was one country that had the moral courage to do its part in resisting Communism and was a "potentially strong point for us."[8] He had found Nehru "an utterly impractical statesman" on broad international issues but very realistic on Kashmir and other matters directly affecting Indian interests.[9]

The secretary concluded that the best way to combat the Soviet Union's threats to the Near East was to establish a security arrangement on its southern borders that would include Pakistan. He strongly preferred this approach to the idea, long advocated by the British, of a defense pact that made Egypt its starting point, the Middle East Defense Organization. Dulles enthusiastically promoted his concept with Eisenhower and other senior administration officials.

As the staunchly Republican Dulles prepared for his hectic official trip, Democratic leader Adlai Stevenson was traveling at a more leisurely pace across South Asia as a private citizen. Defeated just a few months earlier in his bid for the presidency, the former governor of Illinois spent more than three weeks touring India and Pakistan. His itinerary included a visit to Kashmir, where he enjoyed the cool spring weather aboard one of the Valley's renowned houseboats. The visit sparked a serious contretemps in U.S.-Indian relations.

During his stay, Governor Stevenson was Sheikh Abdullah's guest at two long luncheons. According to Stevenson's biographer John Bartlow Martin, Abdullah greatly impressed him. Stevenson's own account suggests that what he said to Abdullah was unobjectionable: "I neither had nor expressed any views in my discussions with Sheik Abdullah, which were my first in Indian Kashmir. I recall perfectly his partiality for India and his casual suggestion that independent status might be an alternative solution. . . . I could not have given Abdullah even unconscious encouragement regarding independence, which did not seem to me realistic and made little impression."[10] In an article he later wrote for *Look* magazine, Stevenson said that the best solution might be a regional plebiscite, presumably confined to the Valley (that is, the Dixon Plan).[11]

Indian sensitivities about a "foreign hand" in Kashmir had been heightened at the time by concern that Abdullah had become dissatisfied with Indian control of the state and might have other arrangements in mind. The meetings the sheikh had with Governor Stevenson fueled speculation that the United States was encouraging him to plot for Kashmir's independence. In the weeks following Stevenson's visit, Abdullah's relations with New Delhi deteriorated sharply. His commitment to India was questioned as he began to equate India and Pakistan and distance himself from his earlier position that Pakistan had been the aggressor in 1947. Some of his colleagues in the Kashmir cabinet objected openly to his increasingly outspoken disavowal of the state's link with India.

Against this troubling background, some Indians alleged that Washington was seeking to influence Abdullah and other Kashmiri leaders to opt for independence by holding out hope for sizable U.S. economic assistance, possibly in return for American air bases. Stevenson was said to have played a major role in the conspiracy. According to some accounts, the Eisenhower administration had charged him with this mission. George V. Allen, the professional diplomat who had succeeded Chester Bowles as ambassador to India, reported that Nehru appeared to be convinced of Stevenson's involvement as an agent of the administration and may in fact have originated the allegations. Allen asked for and received State Department instructions to assure the prime minister that "the U.S. government is not interfering in Kashmir and that any loose talk by private Americans regarding independence is fully repudiated."[12]

The department also suggested that Allen might wish to instruct his staff to refrain from visiting Kashmir for the present in light of the current "misunderstanding" among Indian officials and the Indian public. This advice came too late to head off a trip to the Valley by a mid-level embassy officer, who reported that Abdullah dismissed as "a preposterous idea" the allegation that Stevenson or any other American had suggested financial aid on the basis of the independence of Kashmir.[13] But as Abdullah's relations with Nehru deteriorated and tension within the leadership of his ruling National Conference party grew, the embassy became convinced that he wanted a separate state.

The political crisis climaxed on August 10, 1953, when Abdullah was dismissed and jailed. The action was formally taken by Kashmir's titular head of state on grounds that the sheikh had lost the confidence of the state's constituent assembly. But few doubted that the Nehru government had a hand in his ouster. Abdullah's successor, Bakshi Ghulam Mohammed, pointed his finger at the United States. In his first public statement as head of the state government, Bakshi accused the sheikh of thinking in terms of carving out an independent state with the connivance of interested parties that had all along been resisting Kashmir's right of self-determination. After a month of allegations of U.S. interference, no one could have had any doubt about the identity of these "interested parties." Nehru made the situation worse by publicly commending the Kashmiri leader's statement.[14]

The embassy subsequently reported that the Indian government claimed to have documentary proof of American intrigues in Kashmir. These documents would not be used unless the United States demanded evidence. The embassy was told that Nehru had overcome his doubts about removing Abdullah when the documents were shown to him.[15] Ambassador Allen concluded that "the unfortunate feature of this nefarious scheme is that not only the Indian public at large but also practically every high Indian official and writer has become firmly convinced of a story manufactured out of whole cloth."[16] Assessing Nehru's own attitude toward the charges, Allen found that the prime minister "does not think the United States government has intervened officially but he believes private American individuals, notably Stevenson, influenced Abdullah."[17]

The Stevenson episode did not augur well for the Eisenhower administration's efforts to encourage a Kashmir settlement. Although the ill will it generated did not rank with the furor sparked by Washington's development of security links with Pakistan six months later, the baseless charges continued to figure for years in Indian suspicions of American motives and intentions in Kashmir and beyond. Even today, a half-century after his visit to Kashmir, Adlai Stevenson remains a contentious footnote in Indian history.[18]

The overthrow and jailing of Sheikh Abdullah went down badly in Pakistan, where the Kashmiri leader, earlier denounced as an Indian stooge, was now hailed as a hero and martyr. As tensions mounted, Nehru agreed to Bogra's request that they move forward their scheduled second meeting, to be held in New Delhi. The talks between the two prime ministers, which had begun badly with an unproductive session in Karachi, now assumed greater importance. The *New York Times,* which followed India-Pakistan relations closely, commented that "to describe the talks . . . as critical would be an understatement."[19]

To the surprise of many observers, the New Delhi talks produced apparent progress. Nehru and Bogra agreed that the Kashmir dispute should be settled in accordance with the wishes of the people of the state, to be ascertained by a statewide "fair and impartial" plebiscite conducted by a plebiscite administrator who would be appointed by April 30, 1954. While this formulation avoided the loaded word "partition," a proviso that the settlement should cause "the least disturbance to the life of the people of the state" was widely interpreted to mean that those areas that favored India in the all-state voting (that is, Jammu and Ladakh) would join the Indian Union while those that preferred Pakistan (Azad Kashmir and the northern areas) would join it. The practical effect of the plebiscite would be limited to the Kashmir Valley.

This was the farthest India had ever gone in offering concessions to Pakistan on Kashmir. In his official biography of Nehru, S. Gopal wrote that the agreement constituted a reversal of New Delhi's position that any Kashmir settlement must be broadly on the lines of the status quo. According to Gopal, the prime minister was prepared to give up the Valley if the people there voted for Pakistan.[20]

Nonetheless, the Nehru-Bogra agreement ran into immediate trouble in Pakistan. Embassy Karachi reported that deep and widespread disappointment with the agreement had diminished Bogra's strength and prestige. It warned that the fall of his government would be "extremely detrimental" to U.S. interests in South Asia, a somewhat surprising conclusion given the limited power the prime minister enjoyed in a regime dominated by the army and the bureaucracy.[21] Reacting to strong opposition to the agreement in his own cabinet, the media, and elsewhere, Bogra quickly called for substantial clarifications favorable to Pakistan. These included the withdrawal of all Indian and Pakistani troops from Kashmir and the installation of a nonpartisan administration during the plebiscite period. He also reneged on his agreement on replacing Admiral Nimitz as plebiscite administrator.

This Nimitz issue was of special concern to Washington. By the time he and Bogra conferred, Nehru had become outspoken in his determination that the admiral step down. Gopal attributed this to Nehru's desire to insulate Kashmir from cold war rivalries and his dismay with Washington's efforts to bar New Delhi from participating in a major international conference on Korea despite the important role the Indians had played in ending the war there. According to Gopal, Nehru was also angry with the United States for encouraging Sheikh Abdullah and instigating a revolt in Nepal.[22] The prime minister wanted a representative of a small, neutral country such as Switzerland or Sweden to succeed Nimitz. He categorically ruled out appointing another American.

Soon after he returned to Karachi, Bogra emphatically denied in a "fireside chat" radio broadcast that he had agreed to Nimitz's being replaced. He

was unaware when he spoke that the admiral had already submitted his resignation.[23] Frustrated by his inability to take up his responsibilities in Kashmir, Nimitz had wanted to quit for more than a year. He was convinced that
no mediation effort in Kashmir was going to succeed as long as Nehru maintained his present "unstatesman-like attitude."[24] Secretary Dulles and other
senior U.S. officials had persuaded him to stay on despite his unhappiness.
In their view, he was "a symbol of sustained interest and hope" in a Kashmir
settlement.[25]

Nimitz decided to resign following word that Nehru and Bogra had
agreed that he should go. By then the State Department's position had also
changed. Learning of Nimitz's decision, Dulles said that it was probably as
good a time as any for him to step down since an early solution of the Kashmir question did not seem likely. The secretary doubted that the United
Nations would be the means for settling the dispute. Bilateral negotiations
now seemed to him to offer the best chance of success, and he was encouraged that India and Pakistan were meeting directly.[26]

The surprised Pakistanis tried to head off Nimitz's departure. They were
strongly supported by Embassy Karachi, led since May 1953 by Ambassador
Horace Hildreth, a former governor of Maine and president of Bucknell
University. Hildreth worried that the admiral's departure would almost certainly be construed in Pakistan as U.S. surrender to Nehru's pressure. This
would have disastrous consequences both for prospects for a Kashmir settlement and for Pakistan's goodwill toward America.[27] Washington, for its
part, maintained somewhat disingenuously that the timing of the resignation rested with the UN secretary general. It was only in February 1954,
more than five months after he had given notice, that the Pakistanis finally
acquiesced in the admiral's departure. He was never replaced.

By then, U.S. diplomatic efforts on Kashmir had been overshadowed by
the Eisenhower administration's decision to make Pakistan a "key point" of
an anti-Communist bulwark of regional countries, as Secretary Dulles had
envisaged for it. Pakistan was eager to play this role, not because of any
serious concern about the threat of Communist gains in the Middle East or
South Asia but primarily to bolster the country's defenses against the threat
it perceived from India and to obtain American political and economic
support.

On January 5, 1954, Eisenhower agreed in principle to provide military assistance to Pakistan. The administration saw this arms package as part of a regional security project that would build on a U.S.-promoted and stage-managed Turkish-Pakistani mutual cooperation agreement then being negotiated. Already allied with Ankara in the North Atlantic Treaty Organization, Washington sought to design the regional grouping in a manner that would encourage other states in the area to join. It had in mind Iraq and Iran (but not Afghanistan). The decision to go forward with the U.S.-Pakistan agreement was announced on February 25, and the two countries formally signed it on May 19.[28] As the administration had hoped and planned, the Karachi-Ankara and Karachi-Washington agreements were eventually broadened to become the Baghdad Pact, which initially also included Iraq, Iran, and Britain. The United States chose to remain outside because of broader Near Eastern policy considerations. It feared that becoming a full pact member would worsen its already strained relations with the nationalist, anti-Western Nasser regime in Egypt. It was also concerned that membership could complicate its relations with Israel and American supporters of Israel. But it played a conspicuous role in the new organization's decisions and activities. Iraq dropped out after its pro-Western government was overthrown in 1958. The alliance was then renamed the Central Treaty Organization.

Perhaps the most vivid example of what Dulles's critics termed his "pacto-mania," the web of agreements made Karachi a major player in Washington's efforts to contain Communism.[29] Pakistan also became a member of the Southeast Asia Treaty Organization (SEATO), another regional grouping inspired by the United States. It soon came to term itself—quite correctly—"America's most allied ally in Asia."

Reports that Washington was seriously considering enlisting Pakistan as a cold war ally began to reach the subcontinent months before the administration had conclusively decided to proceed. Predictably, these stories ignited a firestorm in India.[30] Nehru was deeply angered. In public statements and diplomatic exchanges he warned of dire consequences for India's relations with the United States and Pakistan.[31] A central theme was his concern that American military assistance to Pakistan, which he considered an unfriendly act toward India, would destroy the neutrality of the subcontinent and seriously impair his efforts to develop a zone of peace comprising nations aligned with neither cold war bloc. It would bring the cold war to India's borders, make Pakistan an American satellite, and perhaps lead the United States to set up bases in Pakistan and the parts of Kashmir the Pakistanis controlled. The prime minister also feared that a U.S.-Pakistan security link could make Karachi more aggressive in dealing with the Kashmir issue.[32] He told the chief ministers of the Indian states that America's concern with Kashmir stemmed from its interest in establishing a military base "in the heart of Asia" and in exploiting the state's possibly rich mineral wealth, including uranium and other strategic ores.[33] He was not moved by Eisenhower's assurances of U.S. action against Pakistan should it misuse American-supplied arms or by the president's offer to entertain an Indian request for U.S. military aid.

The U.S.-Pakistan agreement brought to an end the last sustained effort to resolve the Kashmir issue through bilateral negotiations until the two sides tried (and ultimately failed) to come to terms in a series of talks they undertook at American and British prompting almost a decade later. Nehru retreated from the undertakings he had given Bogra and told him that the pact ruled out further progress toward bringing about a settlement. He said that American military assistance had a direct impact on the demilitarization issue because India would have to maintain a greater military presence in Kashmir to deal with the stronger forces that Pakistan could mobilize. Nehru refused to hold further meetings with Bogra. They would not confer again until May 1955, a gap of almost two years. Nor would India move toward selecting a new plebiscite administrator before the agreed April 30 deadline even after Pakistan had consented to Nimitz's replacement by a representative of a small, neutral country. The Kashmir dispute was back where it had been in January 1949 when the cease-fire came into effect—but with the important difference that the Indians had consolidated their position in the state.

The U.S.-Pakistan agreement also led Nehru to demand the withdrawal of American military officers from the UN observer force that monitored the cease-fire line in Kashmir. In his view, the United States had ceased to be neutral. Secretary General Dag Hammarskjöld declined to take any action, declaring publicly that UNMOGIP members owed their allegiance to the United Nations. He privately told an American official that "Nehru had taken a fantastic position."[34] But Nehru insisted that the American observers had become personae non gratae and would have to be removed.[35]

The prime minister's demand created both practical and policy problems. Eighteen of the forty-five observers were Americans. Washington agreed that they were agents of the United Nations and shared the UN Secretariat's concern that compliance with Nehru's position would impair the entire UN observer system. With good reason, it also feared that apart from establishing a harmful precedent, withdrawing American observers without replacing them would seriously damage the UN's monitoring ability along the cease-fire line.

But the administration did not want the issue to develop into a serious bilateral controversy. Nor, apparently, did the Indians. Three weeks after Nehru had issued his demand, they privately told American diplomats that they wished to find a way out. The United Nations and Washington concurred that the best solution was to have the American observers replaced by officers of other nationalities as their terms expired. The Indians consented to this arrangement, which worked well. U.S. participation in UNMOGIP eventually ended in early December 1954 when the last two American observers left Kashmir.

Several interrelated questions arise about the connection between the signing of the U.S.-Pakistan pact and the derailing of hope for an early Kashmir settlement that the Nehru-Bogra meeting seemed to offer. Was Nehru sincerely prepared to follow through with the concessions he had made to the Pakistan prime minister? If he was, would the Kashmir problem have been resolved had the United States *not* decided to supply arms to Pakistan? Did Nehru toughen his stand because he was genuinely concerned by the implications the U.S.-Pakistan agreement posed for Kashmir? Or had he used the pact as a pretext to retreat from his earlier flexibility, presumably because he had second thoughts?

Opinions differ. Some contemporary observers believed that by 1953 Nehru had concluded that the time had come for India to change its position in order to resolve the protracted, burdensome dispute. In this view, the tremendously warm reception he received in Karachi when he went there for his first round of talks with Bogra helped convince the prime minister that the people of Pakistan wanted friendly relations and that the constellation of political forces in the country offered the possibility of achieving them, perhaps for the last time.

But others, including at least some senior American officials, held that Nehru was not willing to run the risk of losing the Valley. The well-informed Canadian high commissioner at the time, Escott Reid, recalled in his memoirs that the heads of most diplomatic missions in New Delhi believed that Nehru never intended to agree to a settlement acceptable to Pakistan. After he had completed his assignment in India, Ambassador Allen told a senior Pakistani diplomat that Nehru had "seized on military aid to Pakistan as an excuse to go back on the Indian commitment for a plebiscite."[36] Reid and a few other chiefs of mission differed with that assessment. They believed, in the high commissioner's words, that "in August 1953 Nehru was for the first time prepared, in the interests of improving relations with Pakistan, to run the risk of losing the [Valley] but that his willingness to make concessions to Pakistan ceased to exist in or around December 1953 because of the negotiation for a [U.S.-Pakistan] military aid agreement."[37] We will never know whose assessment was correct.

Although the United States continued to be involved in Kashmir matters following Nehru's harsh reaction to the Pakistan agreement, it concluded that it could do little to help move the issue toward a settlement. Washington recognized that from the Indian perspective America had become part of the problem, not part of its solution. U.S. policymakers saw many costs and few benefits in returning to the Security Council, which had remained on the sidelines following the failure of Frank Graham's mission in early 1953. But the Pakistanis were eager to keep Kashmir on the world's agenda, and the Eisenhower administration searched for ways to stand with its new ally despite its awareness that Indian intransigence, now greater than ever, would doom any serious effort it could make or support.

One option was to take the issue not to the Security Council but, for the first time, to the UN General Assembly. Washington unrealistically hoped that Arab-Asian influence there might have a positive impact. Another possibility was to send Graham back to South Asia for a further round. The Graham option was hardly promising, but it might keep the Pakistanis satisfied at least for a short time. Washington also urged the Pakistanis to keep the bilateral approach in play. Pakistan, for its part, wanted to take the issue back to the council. But it eventually agreed to the U.S. request that it post-pone doing so.[38]

While American policymakers pondered what further steps Washington could usefully take, developments in Indo-Soviet relations made their delib-erations even less meaningful. Alarmed and angered by the new U.S.-Pakistan alignment, the Nehru government looked to Moscow as a balancing force. The Kremlin was keen to play that role. As Dennis Kux has pointed out, "At a time when the West was seeking to contain the Soviets—vigorously trying to limit Moscow's contacts with the newly emergent nations—the chance to expand relations with the largest non-aligned country was an opportunity the Russians eagerly seized."[39]

The red-carpet treatment the Soviets gave Nehru when he came to Moscow in June 1955 set the stage for the fifteen-day visit to India of Premier Nikolai A. Bulganin and Communist Party first secretary Nikita S. Khrushchev six months later. Replete with Falstaffian antics and total disregard for diplo-matic niceties, the visit turned into a barnstorming expedition in public diplomacy that was cleverly designed to exploit the Indians' anticolonialist sentiment at a time when they were especially sensitive about Western motives and intentions. The joint statement Dulles and his Portuguese coun-terpart had made only a few days earlier affirming that the enclaves Lisbon still controlled along the Indian coast constituted a "province of Portugal" had further inflamed Indian sensibilities on that score.

The Soviet leaders' most important stop was in Srinagar. Addressing a public meeting there, the self-styled "traveling salesmen" moved Moscow's position on Kashmir from an increasingly pro-Indian stance to a total endorsement of New Delhi's claims. Castigating the United States, Khrushchev declared that the people of Kashmir had already decided to join the Indian Union. The matter was settled, and the Kashmiris "do not wish to become a toy in the hands of the imperialist powers." He and Bulganin were not subtle in suggesting that Soviet hostility toward Pakistan caused by Karachi's new ties with Washington significantly influenced them to adopt this totally pro-Indian position.[40] Nehru welcomed the Soviets' support and took no exception to the diatribes they launched against the United States on Indian soil. His gratitude was widely reflected in the country, where the two leaders quickly achieved iconic stature.

Moscow's full backing for the Indian position on Kashmir meant that it would wield its veto power to kill any Security Council draft resolution New Delhi found unacceptable.[41] But the State Department took, or pretended to take, a cool view of the situation. When the Pakistanis, greatly alarmed by Bulganin's and Khrushchev's sharp attacks on them, asked for a public statement of American support, the department advised Embassy Karachi that the Soviet leaders had overplayed their hand. A formal U.S. statement would only save them from their folly. In Washington, a senior department official told the Pakistan ambassador that Khrushchev's intercession had actually weakened the Indian position. The official foolishly argued that Nehru could now be pictured as working for Soviet interests in Kashmir whereas Pakistan rested its case solely on the merits of the issue.[42]

The assessments the embassies in Karachi and New Delhi sent Washington were more realistic. Hildreth reported from Karachi that "the Soviet visit ha[d] strengthened the argument of those in Pakistan who contend that neutrality pays better than alignment."[43] Embassy New Delhi, where Kentucky Republican politician John Sherman Cooper had succeeded Allen as ambassador, found that the views the Soviet leaders had expressed "reinforce[d] Nehru's Kashmir policy and weakened prospects for third party mediation or a bilateral negotiated settlement." Their visit, the embassy said, "undoubtedly contributed to tensions in the subcontinent and made it more difficult for the United States to maintain a balanced position between India and Pakistan."[44]

Once it had joined the Western alliance system, Pakistan sought to use its membership in SEATO and the Baghdad Pact to put these organizations on record in support of its positions on Kashmir. When the SEATO Council met in Karachi in March 1956, the Pakistan foreign minister (with a major assist from Secretary Dulles) persuaded members to declare in their joint communiqué that the UN resolutions on Kashmir remained in force. The communiqué affirmed the need for an early Kashmir settlement through the United Nations or by direct negotiations. Dulles, who attended the meeting as head of the American delegation, reasserted Washington's longtime support for a plebiscite in a separate statement.[45]

The communiqué's reference to Kashmir drew a sharp rebuke from India, which charged that it showed that SEATO was being transformed into an instrument of pressure on states not party to the treaty to further the interests of individual member countries. Visiting New Delhi soon afterward, Dulles was told by an emotional Jawaharlal Nehru that SEATO was essentially a U.S. alliance with Pakistan against India. The prime minister was not amused by Dulles's presumably tongue-in-cheek suggestion that India join SEATO and change the character of the organization.[46]

The Eisenhower administration's Kashmir diplomacy now became a balancing act. Washington wanted to provide evidence to Karachi that its alliance with the United States would strengthen or at least sustain American resolve to push for a settlement favorable to Pakistan's position. Yet it knew that its efforts to move the issue forward at the United Nations, through bilateral India-Pakistan negotiations or by any other means, would fail. As Embassy New Delhi correctly warned, no pressure short of war would force India to relinquish the Valley.[47] So Washington needed to make Pakistan reasonably content while limiting Indian unhappiness, all the time recognizing that whatever it did would be futile. American policymakers found that this was not easy.

3

Eisenhower Tries His Hand

Prime Minister Nehru's visit to Washington in December 1956, a month after Dwight Eisenhower's landslide reelection victory, initiated a new and more positive phase in U.S.-Indian relations. The president had by then become more receptive to the nonaligned policies the prime minister had long advocated. A well-justified concern over the inroads the post-Stalin Soviet Union was making in India and in other important third world countries strengthened his interest in better ties with New Delhi.

For his own reasons, Nehru shared Eisenhower's desire for stronger relations. He recognized that it was not in nonaligned India's interest to drift too close to the Soviet camp, as it had increasingly done after the Baghdad Pact was broached in 1954. The contrasting actions of the two global superpowers in the weeks just before his visit to Washington—the Soviet military intervention in Hungary and U.S. opposition to the Anglo-French-Israeli invasion of Suez—may have helped persuade the prime minister that India should follow a more balanced line. India's need for American economic assistance for its ambitious Second Five Year Plan, launched in April 1956, also influenced him to seek more amicable relations with Washington.[1]

Eisenhower and Nehru developed a high personal regard for one another during the visit. Though they broke little new substantive ground, their candid and friendly exchanges produced a better understanding of one another's concerns. They discussed India-Pakistan relations at some length, Nehru focusing on what he considered to be Pakistan's unreasonable antagonism toward India and the importance of the United States in helping to curb this, Eisenhower seeking to reassure him that Washington would never allow Pakistan to use American-supplied arms against India. The Kashmir issue came up only marginally. According to biographer S. Gopal, Nehru spoke of the way Pakistan was exploiting American arms in its effort to bully India on the issue. Eisenhower replied that it would be unwise to take any steps in Kashmir that would upset the existing situation and create further difficulties. The much sketchier U.S. record of the Eisenhower-Nehru discussion includes nothing specifically on Kashmir.[2]

Soon after Nehru's visit, Eisenhower signed a National Security Council document (numbered 5701), which stressed India's strategic significance to the United States and for the first time accepted its nonaligned foreign policy. This document recognized that a strong, independent, non-Communist India would occasionally challenge U.S. programs and activities. Nonetheless, it concluded, such an India would be a successful example of an alternative to Communism in an Asian context. The report called for expanded U.S. economic and technical assistance to India, which its authors believed could counter Soviet activities there.[3]

In the course of the next four years, the United States under Eisenhower and India under Nehru would continue to have their difficulties and differences, as the National Security Council document forecast. But as Washington began to question the value of its alliance with Pakistan and as Sino-Indian relations deteriorated, the U.S. and Indian governments put their relationship on a firmer footing and made gradual if uneven progress in dealing with one another in a more constructive, less emotional manner.

Despite these promising long-term developments, the United States and India soon clashed again in the UN Security Council, where Pakistan had finally succeeded in reintroducing the Kashmir issue in early 1957. The United States was one of five cosponsors of a council resolution that reasserted the call for a plebiscite and declared that the Kashmir Constituent Assembly's vote in 1954 to reaffirm the state's accession to India was not internationally binding.[4] Washington understood that its position might well reverse the warming trend in U.S.-Indian relations that Nehru's visit had helped promote. But it probably concluded that it had run out of options for meeting Pakistan's demand for action.

In the heated debate that followed, the head of the Indian delegation, Defense Minister V. K. Krishna Menon, famously spoke for over five hours. The feat set a new United Nations record for the longest continuous speech at a single session. In this dramatic and vituperative effort, and in his almost three-hour-long presentation the following day, Krishna Menon mostly re-iterated—in some 80,000 words—familiar Indian arguments dating back to the council's initial consideration of the issue in 1948. Delegates were no doubt impressed by his stamina and bravura, but they voted 10-0 in favor of the resolution a few days later. Although the Soviet delegate reiterated Moscow's position that the Kashmiris had settled the issue themselves, the Soviet Union abstained, possibly because of Indian concern that a veto might open the way to General Assembly consideration of Kashmir.[5]

As the vote neared, New Delhi warned that U.S.-India relations would suffer dire consequences should the Security Council adopt an attitude critical of India. These could include Communist gains in the upcoming Indian parliamentary elections. (This was standard cold war rhetoric; Pakistan issued a similar warning about Communist gains in that country should the United States *not* promote a resolution.) At Eisenhower's direction, Dulles tried to soften the blow with a cordial message to Nehru on the eve of the vote, but to little avail. The prime minister and other Indian leaders reacted harshly when the resolution passed.[6] Not without reason, some saw U.S. support for the resolution as a payoff to Pakistan for its alignment with the West.

Mildly grateful, but hardly content, Pakistan then insisted that the Security Council go beyond the resolution's reiteration of past UN measures and pass another that would spell out further specific steps that should be taken. Over Embassy New Delhi's strong objections, Washington decided to cosponsor a second resolution that requested Gunnar V. Jarring, the president of the Security Council, to visit the subcontinent and examine, with the Indians and Pakistanis, demilitarization formulas and other measures that might contribute to a settlement. Jarring, who had served successively as Stockholm's ambassador to Pakistan and India, seemed ideally qualified for the task. The draft included a reference to Pakistan's proposal for the temporary stationing of United Nations troops in Kashmir, an approach totally unacceptable to India. The Soviet Union, which had unsuccessfully sought to amend the draft beyond recognition, used its veto to kill the proposal. A shortened, watered-down version that deleted all mention of a UN force and avoided the word *plebiscite* passed 10-0 on March 18.[7]

This time the Soviets abstained, presumably because the Indians had told them that they considered the milder revised draft less objectionable. Embassy Karachi reported that the Pakistanis were privately satisfied with the resolution, which they recognized was the best they could get.[8] Speaking on the election campaign trail in Bombay, Nehru castigated it as a move by the United States and Britain to support Pakistan because of its membership in the Baghdad Pact.[9]

During late 1956 and the early months of 1957, a chargé d'affaires led Embassy New Delhi. This situation no doubt reduced the embassy's clout in the State Department, but that changed in March 1957, when Ellsworth Bunker took over as ambassador. A retired businessman and longtime Democrat, Bunker was president of the American Red Cross when Eisenhower assigned him to India as part of an effort to win bipartisan support for the administration's foreign policy during its second term. Ambassador to Argentina and Italy in the Truman administration, Bunker used his superb diplomatic skill to good effect in his four years in New Delhi.

Like all other American ambassadors to India and Pakistan, Bunker tried to influence U.S. Kashmir policy. In a long telegram he sent to Washington six weeks after taking charge, he warned that no solution based upon a UN plebiscite would be either constructive or realistic. The Indian government was convinced that a plebiscite would jeopardize India's vital interests and stability. The United States had to face this reality. Recalling his experience in dealing with the Trieste dispute when he was ambassador in Rome earlier in the 1950s, Bunker recommended that Washington let tempers cool, await the arrival of governments in India and Pakistan able to agree to a settlement, and then undertake behind-the-scenes private and confidential negotiations.[10]

As Ambassador Bunker was sending Washington his initial recommendations on Kashmir, Gunnar Jarring reached the subcontinent to carry out his UN-mandated mission. Jarring's visit came only a few days after the ruling pro-India National Conference party had won the Kashmir state assembly election. Its candidates for most of the seats were elected unopposed because many of their potential rivals had been disqualified or jailed. The outcome, and the way it was arranged, echoed the state's badly flawed election five years earlier when Sheikh Abdullah was still in control. It was not a promising augury for the Swedish diplomat's efforts.[11]

Jarring shuttled between New Delhi and Karachi and met with the two prime ministers and other senior officials. Like earlier UN special emissaries, he did not visit Kashmir nor consult with Kashmiri representatives. With Washington's agreement, he avoided contact with the two U.S. embassies. He and the Americans feared this might be misunderstood.

In his report to the Security Council, Jarring offered no specific recommendations. He said that Nehru had told him that a plebiscite was unacceptable until the issue of Pakistani aggression was dealt with. So Jarring had suggested to both sides the possible use of some form of arbitration for the division of the state and the evacuation of troops. Pakistan had agreed to the proposal, but India had reiterated its long-standing position that such issues were not amenable to arbitration. Yet another mediation effort had gone nowhere.

Jarring's failure brought the issue back to the Security Council. The Pakistanis were eager to move forward right away. They urged the council to adopt a tough resolution that strongly favored their position. The Americans feared that the Soviets would veto such a draft. They preferred a blander version and were in no hurry to deal with the issue. After difficult negotiations, the United States cosponsored a draft resolution that requested Frank Graham to consult once again with India and Pakistan and then make recommendations on demilitarization. The council passed the resolution in early December by a 10-0 vote after it had been softened to avoid a Soviet veto. Moscow again abstained.[12]

Two months before the resolution passed, Krishna Menon had sarcastically remarked to Bunker that the council debate would have "the same agenda, the same people, the same arguments, and the same results."[13] The Indian defense minister was right. Like other Security Council initiatives that followed the U.S.-Pakistan security agreement, the exercise was essentially a charade. The Pakistan government wanted a Kashmir resolution in order to draw world attention to the problem, embarrass India, and mollify domestic critics. The Eisenhower administration felt it needed to satisfy an ally and demonstrate its fidelity to earlier UN resolutions. The Indians were determined to maintain what had become their official position: the United Nations had no role in determining Kashmir's future because the state was an integral part of the Indian Union. And all sides recognized that whatever the wording of the resolution and however overwhelming the vote in its favor, Security Council action would not break the impasse or help resolve the Kashmir problem either then or later. So no one could have been surprised when Graham once again made no progress when he visited South Asia.

In April 1958 the United States began a unilateral behind-the-scenes effort to break the impasse. This fresh approach, which the Bureau of Near East, South Asian, and African Affairs developed with Secretary Dulles's concurrence, envisaged a major personal role for President Eisenhower in launching summit discussions between the leaders of India and Pakistan. The proposed presidential intervention, the first specifically on Kashmir at that high level in almost ten years, reflected the second Eisenhower administration's interest in developing stronger relations with New Delhi while maintaining what was proving to be an increasingly difficult security alliance with Karachi. As the historian Robert McMahon has observed, Washington recognized that it could have friendly and productive ties with both countries only if they resolved their long-standing differences.[14] It would take four decades and a massive change in international circumstances before the United States, India, and Pakistan could surmount this zero-sum approach.

The initiative called for American mediatory efforts to persuade India and Pakistan to move forward with a negotiated package that dealt simultaneously with three major, interlocking problems—Kashmir, the division of the waters of the Indus River system, and the accelerating South Asian arms race. Proponents of the package saw it as a logical whole. In their very sensible view, the inability of the two countries to reach settlements on Kashmir and the Indus waters had generated in both a compulsion to build up their military power. This competition posed serious dangers to the subcontinent's stability and could significantly complicate U.S. interests in the South Asian region. Supporters of the approach reckoned that the high levels of economic assistance the United States was currently providing New Delhi and Karachi would give it the leverage it needed to win Indian and Pakistani acceptance. They also argued that considerably greater negotiating flexibility would become possible if the three problems were considered together. As Dulles succinctly put it in a memorandum to Eisenhower, "The essence of [the proposal] is to consider the Indus, Kashmir, and arms questions as clearly related so that a wider field for compromise will exist."[15]

Following the 1954 agreement, the Pentagon had developed an important stake in the U.S. security link with Pakistan, and it had to be convinced that the plan would not reduce the Pakistan Army's ability to carry out its Baghdad Pact obligations. The State Department brought it around with some difficulty. Because Washington still looked to London for advice and support on Kashmir, the British also had to be brought into the loop. Following a high-level meeting in Washington, they concurred in the concept. So did the World Bank, which for a decade had been working with India and Pakistan on the Indus waters problem and would necessarily be a major player if negotiations were launched. All of this took place in great secrecy while the administration was ostensibly focusing on Frank Graham's doomed efforts and seeking to influence his findings.[16]

President Eisenhower agreed to initiate the negotiations through a personal appeal to the leaders of both countries. The president was highly enthusiastic about playing a central role. He told Secretary Dulles that "if the progress of negotiations warranted the hope that a personal gesture might help assure success, there is no inconvenience at which I would balk. For example, I'd be ready to welcome and entertain the Prime Ministers simultaneously—I would even go out there."[17]

Eisenhower sent identical letters to Prime Minister Nehru and Iskander Mirza, the powerful military bureaucrat who had become president of Pakistan in 1956 after the country's republican constitution was promulgated. Eisenhower said he was convinced that "the peaceful, progressive economic development which each nation desires and which the foreign assistance program is designed to promote cannot succeed" if major outstanding issues remain unresolved.[18] If they thought it would help, he told Nehru and Mirza, he would be glad to designate a special representative to visit each country for further general talks. (The president's brother, Dr. Milton Eisenhower, had been mentioned for this role.) The three of them could then determine whether it would be useful for the United States to continue its good offices to help bring about more formal and detailed negotiations. In an unsubtle reference to American financial assistance, Eisenhower pledged that if negotiations were successfully completed, the United States would help in any way it could to make the settlement effective and ensure that it contributed to Indian and Pakistani economic development.[19] A couple of alternative formats were suggested to the two leaders: tripartite talks from the outset or initial shuttle diplomacy by the American special representative. British prime minister Harold Macmillan sent letters to Nehru and Mirza supporting Eisenhower's initiative.

As originally drafted, the Kashmir component of the package called for New Delhi and Karachi to agree that Azad Kashmir would go to Pakistan, Jammu to India, and a plebiscite in the Valley after ten years; or preferably— and even less realistically—a permanent partition of the state along the existing cease-fire line with minor, mutually acceptable adjustments in Pakistan's favor to compensate for India's retaining the Valley. Ambassador Bunker sharply criticized the delayed-plebiscite option. He wisely argued that because the package was based on the assumption that India was so eager to retain the Valley that it would be willing to "buy" a settlement by making concessions elsewhere, deferring a decision on the Valley's political future for ten years would defeat the purpose of the plan and keep tensions alive.[20] But both Bunker and the U.S. ambassador to Pakistan, James M. Langley, a New Hampshire newspaperman close to Sherman Adams, Eisenhower's powerful chief of staff, agreed to the initiative and helped refine it.[21]

The section on Kashmir had been substantially changed by the time the package was approved. The final text spoke at some length about the principles that should govern the partition of the state if this was a mutually acceptable solution. (Washington was convinced that it should be.) It stated that consideration of the partition line should not be related in any way to the existing military cease-fire line "but rather should provide a fresh approach to this dispute, divorced from its long and acrimonious history under the United Nations resolutions." This seemed to favor India, which had effectively long since written off the resolutions. But the criteria listed that were to be used in determining the new line were a mixed bag. Some could be read to favor Pakistan; others seemed pro-Indian.[22]

Pakistan immediately accepted the president's proposal in principle. The only jarring note in Ambassador Langley's discussion with President Mirza and Prime Minister Malik Feroz Khan Noon was the Pakistanis' insistence that because the talks would be kept secret, domestic political considerations stemming from the upcoming parliamentary elections required that Pakistan take the Kashmir and Indus waters issues to the Security Council while negotiations proceeded. Washington quickly instructed Ambassador Langley to shoot down this idea, which it recognized could jeopardize the initiative.

Bunker's opening session with Nehru was much less promising. The prime minister was prepared only to study Eisenhower's proposal. After consultations with key cabinet colleagues and a further meeting with Bunker to clarify points in Eisenhower's letter, he rejected the concept. Reasserting India's bilateral approach to Kashmir and other disputes with Pakistan, Nehru wrote Eisenhower that "if third parties intervene, even though that intervention proceeds from good will, . . . the aggressor country and the country against whom aggression has taken place are put on the same level, both pleading before the third party." The problems between India and Pakistan, he said, are the result, and not the basic cause, of Pakistan's hostility.[23] According to Gopal, Nehru wanted friendly relations with Pakistan but saw no hope for them in light of the policy of hatred for India pursued by every government of Pakistan since partition and Pakistan's aggressive intransigence encouraged by military and political support from the West. This had shaped his negative reaction to Eisenhower's proposal, Gopal believed.[24] The prime minister's assessment that the Pakistan government was weak and unstable and could not be counted on to follow through probably contributed to his decision to turn down the offer.

Bunker tried to put Nehru's rebuff in the best light possible. He reported that two senior Indian officials had told him that the prime minister "definitely" did not want to close the door. The best way to proceed, they said, was through regular diplomatic channels. Bunker hopefully concluded that "we should keep plugging away and not lose heart. . . . It may take a year or two years or even more to reach a desired solution, but . . . patience, perseverance, and the logic of events will ultimately bring us to success."[25]

In Washington, too, policymakers dealing with South Asia looked for ways to soften the blow. Some argued that the United States should assume that Nehru had not rejected the president's proposal but had only suggested different ways to carry it out.[26] For the next few months, American officials maintained that U.S.-Indian discussions about how to proceed were in fact implementing the proposal. It was only in October, after the Pakistan military overthrew the country's civilian government and established an authoritarian martial law regime, that Washington abandoned this state of denial and acknowledged the failure of its efforts to keep the package in play.

In the two and a half years that remained in Dwight Eisenhower's tenure in the White House after the package plan initiative failed, his administration made no serious effort to play a role on the Kashmir issue. Frustrated by Nehru's rejection of the president's offer of his personal good offices, Washington was in no mood to venture again down a dead-end street.

Nor did there seem to be any pressing reason to do so. In a message assessing the impact of the October 1958 coup on India-Pakistan relations, Embassy Karachi suggested that for some time to come the martial law regime would be so busy administering the country that it would largely shelve action on India-Pakistan disputes. Moreover, the military leaders of the new government headed by President Muhammad Ayub Khan, the commander-in-chief of the Pakistan Army, would recognize that its armed forces were inferior to India's.[27] This realization would dampen war-mongering tendencies. But the embassy cautioned that these positive developments were counterbalanced by the strategic importance the Pakistan military gave Kashmir and the "surprising degree of sentimental feeling" among members of the military toward their "Kashmiri Muslim brothers." The embassy's bottom line was that there was little the United States could or need do.[28]

Embassy New Delhi implicitly concurred. It reported that many Indians believed that the United States was involved in the Pakistani coup. In its view, this belief suggested that New Delhi would be even less receptive than before to Washington's playing an honest broker's role in resolving India-Pakistan disputes. The signing of another bilateral mutual security agreement between the United States and Pakistan a few months after the coup could only have strengthened this Indian conviction. Neither embassy suggested that there was any immediate danger of hostilities that would warrant UN or U.S. action.

Promising developments that would soon lead to a breakthrough in the Indus negotiations also lessened Washington's interest in again tackling the Kashmir problem. For the balance of Eisenhower's term, the Indus issue rather than Kashmir became the main focus of his administration's involvement in India-Pakistan disputes. Senior American officials met frequently with World Bank President Eugene R. Black and his colleagues to review the state of play in the bank-led negotiations and to discuss the nature and degree of American financial and political support for the massive canal waters project. At a meeting of the National Security Council chaired by Eisenhower, Douglas Dillon, the acting secretary of state, declared that "the Indus Waters question was the key to the Kashmir question; if the Indus Waters problem could be resolved, the Kashmir question could probably be settled on the basis of the status quo."[29] As developments in the subsequent four decades and more have demonstrated, he was wrong.

In September 1960, Nehru and Ayub signed the Indus waters pact, which divided the river and its five tributaries between India and Pakistan and provided for construction of extensive canals and barrages to redirect their flow. Eisenhower effusively praised the settlement. The two leaders, he said, had demonstrated to the world the highest statesmanship in accepting the compromises necessary to reach agreement.[30]

Eisenhower's handling of the Kashmir issue during his historic journey to South Asia in December 1959 reflected his opposition to further American involvement in settlement efforts. At their long meeting in Karachi, President Ayub argued that a resolution of the issue was needed to protect South Asia from the Communist powers, a theme he could expect would go down well with his American visitor. He urged Eisenhower to exercise the "tremendous influence" America had on India to encourage progress on Kashmir. He hinted broadly that what he had in mind was U.S. use of its substantial economic assistance program to bring India around. Ayub dismissed out of hand two suggestions Eisenhower made about how a settlement might be achieved: total demililitarization of Kashmir (the Chinese would move in) and Eisenhower's old idea of the division of the state on the basis of the status quo following an Indus waters agreement (it would put the Indians too close to important Pakistani territory). When Ayub pressed further, Eisenhower made it clear that he was not prepared to play a negotiating role.[31] He said he could do little more than urge Nehru to get together with Ayub to try to resolve the problem. It was not the kind of response the Pakistanis had wanted.[32]

When Eisenhower went on to New Delhi, he received what is still the most tumultuously joyous welcome the Indian capital has given a visiting foreign leader. Huge and enthusiastic crowds greeted him everywhere. As

Nehru famously observed at one public meeting attended by some 500,000 spectators, India had presented Eisenhower with a priceless gift—a part of her heart.

Eisenhower and Nehru spent some time discussing India-Pakistan relations and touched briefly on Kashmir. The president reported that Ayub had spoken heatedly about the Kashmir problem and had rejected any settlement on the basis of the cease-fire line. When Eisenhower asked the prime minister whether it would be feasible for India and Pakistan to act together against potential Chinese aggression, Nehru ruled it out. All India wanted was that Pakistan not stab it in the back in the event of major trouble with Beijing.[33]

The president considered Nehru's idea of a joint India-Pakistan communiqué or separate public statements by the two governments pledging to settle all present and future disputes by peaceful negotiations to be the "most outstanding point" that came up in his private discussions with the prime minister. He quickly instructed William Rountree, the American ambassador to Pakistan, to take up the proposal with Ayub. Rountree, a career Foreign Service officer, had come to Karachi in August 1959 after completing his State Department assignment as assistant secretary for Near Eastern, South Asian, and African affairs. He was well aware that there was nothing novel in this Indian initiative. Nehru had raised it with Pakistan prime minister Liaquat Ali Khan as far back as 1949. Then and afterward, successive governments in Pakistan had been unwilling to agree to the concept because the Indians would not spell out specific steps the two sides should take in the negotiations or commit themselves to arbitration should these fail. So it came as no surprise to Rountree when Ayub turned it down flat. Ayub told the ambassador bluntly that "what Nehru sought . . . was assurance that he could with impunity continue to hold vital areas of Kashmir without resolution of the problem in accordance with the UN resolution or otherwise, and with no concern that Pakistan would do anything about it."[34]

Rountree nonetheless struck a mildly hopeful note in his message reporting Ayub's rebuff. In his view, Eisenhower's visit and the resulting good will toward the United States in both Pakistan and India could offer unique opportunities for American intervention in their bilateral disputes. He urged the State Department to review all previous approaches to Kashmir and explore other avenues that might be open to Washington. But he did not offer any himself.[35]

Ambassador Bunker was more cautious. He warned Washington three weeks after Eisenhower's trip that India remained unwilling to approach a Kashmir solution except on its own terms, probably the status quo with minor adjustments. What was required was patience to let recent gains in India-Pakistan relations on such issues as the Indus waters generate public opinion favorable to a settlement. This, he said, would be an important factor in shaping Nehru's actions. Washington could play an indirect role by promoting greater U.S. cooperation with India and avoiding actions such as a proposed Central Treaty Organization air exercise that would stimulate India-Pakistan competition and estrangement.[36]

No one in the American foreign policy bureaucracy was inclined to call for a more robust approach than the embassies had recommended. With no apparent threat of an India-Pakistan armed conflict, the administration saw little reason to jeopardize the improvement in U.S. relations with both countries that Eisenhower's trip had advanced and celebrated. The president had been disappointed when Nehru had rejected his package plan. But in his pragmatic way he must have recognized that nothing was to be gained by yet another serious intervention. He was content to leave the Kashmir problem and the role the United States should play in resolving it to his successor, John F. Kennedy.

4

Kennedy Strikes Out

President John F. Kennedy, who entered the White House in January 1961, was even more determined to reorder U.S. ties with the South Asian countries than Eisenhower had been in his second term. He gave special importance to India, which he had strongly backed and praised as a senator and presidential candidate. The new administration quickly raised economic assistance to New Delhi to a level well above the generous amounts reached during the Eisenhower years. Although it castigated India for its seizure of Portuguese Goa in December 1961, it fully accepted Indian nonalignment. It believed that, if handled skillfully, the Nehru government could be persuaded to play a constructive role in the international arena. It took a concerned and sympathetic though not yet active interest in New Delhi's confrontation with Beijing over their disputed Himalayan border.

This favorable view of India's potential contrasted with a widely held assessment in the upper tiers of the new administration that Pakistan's value as a cold war partner had peaked. While it did not wish to dismantle the security pacts that had bound Washington to Karachi for more than six years, the administration was not fully persuaded that these agreements were as important for American interests as they had seemed earlier. Nor did it have the same emotional attachment to Pakistan and the U.S.-Pakistan alliance that many senior diplomats and military officers held in Eisenhower's time. At the same time, it recognized that progress in South Asia—and American interests there—would be crucially influenced by the ability of India and Pakistan to find a way to live together without conflict.

Jammu and Kashmir, after 1947

The problem the new administration faced as it considered its South Asia policy was how to develop better relations with New Delhi while retaining reasonably strong ties with Karachi. Pakistan's dismay with the more even-handed policy the Eisenhower administration had begun to pursue in the region suggested that this exercise would not be an easy one.

During its first six months in office the Kennedy administration followed a noninterventionist approach to Kashmir. India-Pakistan relations had improved with the signing of the Indus waters treaty in September 1960, and Prime Minister Nehru's offer to President Ayub to discuss Kashmir suggested, at least to sanguine observers, that India might be prepared to be more accommodating. Although the Pakistanis still called for a settlement based on the plebiscite stipulated in UN resolutions, they suggested at times—always in low key—that they might be ready to resolve the dispute on other terms. William Rountree, who carried on as ambassador to Pakistan in the new administration, continued to argue that American unwillingness to make a serious effort to find a Kashmir solution was a major source of Pakistani disillusion with the United States. But State Department officials who dealt with South Asia concluded that any progress made toward a settlement would come about through bilateral negotiations. In their view, U.S. involvement would be counterproductive.[1] Their assessment was accepted and probably welcomed by the Kennedy White House. The administration had a great deal on its foreign policy plate and was reluctant to take on more.

Ayub Khan tried to encourage greater U.S. involvement when the new American vice president, Lyndon B. Johnson, visited Karachi in May 1961. Indeed, in its postmortem of the visit, Embassy Karachi found that "the Pakistan government and press were determined to send Johnson back to Washington fully aware that nothing mattered so much for Pakistan's continued orientation toward [the United States] as some progress on the Kashmir issue."[2] Taking a line that he knew would be attractive to an American, Ayub told Johnson that a Kashmir settlement would permit Pakistan to concentrate its armed forces entirely against potential Communist aggression and make possible India-Pakistan cooperation in the defense of the region. He was critical of what he said was America's failure to support its friends. Nor was he persuaded by Johnson's contention that the United States could do little to move Nehru on the issue. American power was greater than Washington thought, Ayub maintained, and Nehru would be compelled to heed it because "India's flexibility . . . was gone." Facing Chinese Communist pressure, New Delhi had no alternative but to rely even more heavily upon the United States.[3]

Dissatisfied by the administration's unwillingness to offer even lip service, Ayub told Rountree later that only the United States could prevent the disastrous consequences of a failure to arrive at a Kashmir solution.[4] The ambassador, who sympathized with this view, worried that America's aloof attitude was leading increasing numbers of Pakistanis to conclude that the Ayub government needed to adopt a stronger line on Kashmir. Although Pakistan's president was "a man of patience and moderation," Rountree told Washington, Pakistani public opinion, combined with Ayub's own personal belief in Pakistan's cause on Kashmir, might lead him to take whatever action he thought necessary to bring the dispute to world attention.[5]

John Kenneth Galbraith, the Harvard professor and Kennedy confidant who became American ambassador to India in April 1961, saw things differently. An outspoken and domineering intellectual determined to use his close ties with the Kennedy White House to promote his own policy agenda, Galbraith did not believe that a fresh U.S. initiative would serve any purpose. In his view, India was inflexible on the Kashmir issue. Its hard-line position was consistent with the unyielding stand it took for similar reasons in rejecting the Chinese demand that it renegotiate the Himalayan border. India-Pakistan relations needed to be considerably transformed before Kashmir could be usefully tackled, he argued. Calling Washington's attention to the Indian parliamentary election scheduled for early in 1962, he concluded that it was doubtful that Nehru could gain parliamentary approval for any kind of Kashmir solution even in the unlikely event he wanted to. In Galbraith's view, a settlement based on the UN resolutions was no longer a practical possibility.[6]

Washington pondered these conflicting recommendations as it prepared to welcome Ayub on a state visit in July 1961. By then in power for almost three years, the military president was giving Pakistan its first extended stretch of stable government in a decade. He was highly regarded in the Pentagon, and although State Department officials were not enthusiastic about him, they could perceive no realistic alternative national leader.[7]

Spelling out prospects for Pakistan and Ayub on the eve of his arrival, a special National Intelligence Estimate highlighted the frustration Pakistanis felt about their country's failure to achieve any progress on Kashmir and their dismay that Pakistan's alliance with the United States had not led to the American support they had expected. The intelligence estimate predicted that Pakistan was likely to seek greater independence in foreign policy within the framework of its pro-Western orientation. Echoing Rountree, it concluded that Ayub would try to focus attention on the Kashmir issue again "perhaps even by provocation or agitation in the disputed area."[8]

Ayub used his American visit to stress the reciprocal responsibilities the United States and Pakistan had to one another. Addressing a joint session of Congress, the high point in his remarkably effective public diplomacy effort in Washington, he declared: "The only people who will stand by you are the people of Pakistan, provided you are also prepared to stand by them." Kashmir figured prominently in Ayub's exchanges with his American hosts. He stressed again and again that if the United States wanted a stable South Asia it needed to use its influence to persuade India to adopt a more reasonable position.[9]

When Ayub made this point to Kennedy at their White House meeting, he did not ask the president to threaten to withhold economic aid to India to bring about a fair settlement. Washington, he said, merely needed to tell Nehru that it was concerned about the waste of its money that occurred because the issue remained unresolved. As he had in his conversation with Johnson, Ayub maintained that the Indian confrontation with the Chinese had left Nehru without maneuverability and had increased U.S. leverage. He also suggested obliquely that Pakistan might have to turn to China for support.

Kennedy reacted in a forthright but friendly way. He told Ayub that the United States provided economic support to India not in the expectation that New Delhi would back American policies but because it was in everyone's interest that India not collapse. He declared that resolving the Kashmir dispute was a vital U.S. interest. But as Johnson had, Kennedy repeatedly downplayed Washington's ability to influence Nehru, for whom he said Kashmir was a "bone-deep issue."

Despite these misgivings, Kennedy agreed to make a major effort with Nehru when the Indian prime minister visited the United States that November. He promised Ayub that if this failed, and Pakistan again raised the issue at the United Nations—as Ayub said his government would be compelled to do under those circumstances—the United States would vote with Pakistan.[10]

Nehru followed Ayub to the United States four months later on a visit that Kennedy described as "a disaster . . . the worst head-of-state visit I have had." For the most part, the aging Nehru remained withdrawn and unresponsive to the president's probing questions on major foreign policy matters.[11] On Kashmir, the problem was different. The prime minister discussed the issue emotionally and in great detail, staunchly defending India's position and adopting a patronizing, almost contemptuous attitude toward Pakistan as a country and Ayub as its (unelected) leader. Aside from citing long-standing Indian claims, Nehru argued the case in terms of Indian domestic political realities. It would be difficult enough, he contended, to get the Indian Parliament to accept the status quo. MPs would certainly not accept a revision of boundaries to India's detriment. The prime minister gave no indication that he would yield anything in Kashmir other than minor modifications of the cease-fire line. He was coldly negative when Kennedy asked him if the United States could do anything for India-Pakistan relations.

Kennedy, for his part, stayed mainly in a questioning mode. He told Nehru that he hoped the U.S. role on the Kashmir issue could be helpful but made no serious effort to persuade the prime minister to adopt a more flexible position. While the president volunteered the hardly surprising information that he had discussed Kashmir with Ayub, he understandably did not mention his pledge to support Pakistan at the United Nations if his own efforts to move Nehru failed and the Pakistanis raised the issue there.[12]

Sitting in on the White House discussion, Ambassador Galbraith offered a different "nonterritorial approach" to a Kashmir settlement. India and Pakistan, he said, should retain the territory they currently held but permit greater movement between the two sides of the state. In his view, this concept offered the only way to resolve the dispute given competing and irreconcilable Indian and Pakistani demands for the Valley. Galbraith had floated the idea earlier with Nehru and had received a noncommittal response. At the White House, the prime minister was more positive. He said that if territorial claims were dropped, all other questions could be resolved without difficulty. It was easy enough for him to take this position since Galbraith's formula let India retain the Kashmir Valley.

Galbraith's proposal foreshadowed what came to be called the "soft-borders solution." Over the years many varieties of this idea have been put forward. Most recently, the opening of bus service between the two sides of Kashmir and the development of other intra-Kashmir confidence-building measures have given it fresh currency. In Galbraith's version, residents of the Valley or perhaps a larger area would move freely between this designated territory, India, and Pakistan. The cease-fire line would no longer inhibit family, cultural, economic, and religious ties. Military forces would be reduced and eventually withdrawn along the line itself. A joint India-Pakistan constabulary would act as a border control force in place of the United Nations. Galbraith continued to promote this approach during much of his tenure in New Delhi.[13]

In January 1962, two months after Nehru's visit to Washington, Pakistan asked the United States to support its request for a Security Council meeting on Kashmir. Ayub told Ambassador Rountree that he was taking this action to keep pressure on the Indians. He said the Indians' seizure of Goa and other Portuguese possessions the previous month had heightened his distrust of the Nehru government and made another approach to the council even more necessary. Ayub probably also calculated that the strongly negative international reaction to the Goa takeover had made India more vulnerable at the United Nations.[14]

Washington found itself in an awkward position. It continued to recognize that Security Council deliberations would be an exercise in futility. The Soviets would once again veto any resolution that put pressure on the Indians. A State Department assessment concluded that the Pakistanis understood that. "But they seem to feel that drawing UN attention again to the problem would at least draw world attention to India's intransigence and might serve as a form of pressure towards concessions in eventual bilateral talks."[15] Galbraith cabled that raising Kashmir again at the Security Council would inevitably harden lines and prejudice progress toward a solution.[16] This assessment was widely shared in Washington.

Yet at the same time the administration was painfully aware of President Kennedy's White House promise to Ayub. It sought to deal with this dilemma by once more encouraging the Indians and Pakistanis to engage in bilateral talks. It did not believe that the talks would lead to a settlement, but they were better than another barren and counterproductive UN exercise. To encourage a favorable response, Washington proposed that a private American citizen be appointed mediator.

Kennedy became deeply involved in this exercise. He persuaded Eugene Black, the head of the World Bank and principal negotiator of the Indus waters treaty, to take on the assignment and personally requested Nehru and Ayub to agree to the role he proposed that Black play. Despite this presidential intercession, Nehru turned down the proposal. Kashmir's sovereignty rested with India, he said, and his government could not accept arbitration or mediation on matters of sovereignty. Ayub cleverly deferred replying to Kennedy's proposal until Nehru had reacted, then accepted it.

At American request, Pakistan had delayed further calls for Security Council action while Washington promoted bilateral talks. When the administration eventually recognized that it could no longer avoid biting the bullet, it adopted a damage-control position. Its objective now was to ensure that the council deliberations did not further impair the possibility of a peaceful settlement through bilateral means and to minimize Indian and Pakistani irritation with the limited role the United States was willing to play.[17]

Washington eventually supported an effort by five nonpermanent Security Council members to develop a compromise resolution it hoped would be acceptable to both parties. This "Little Five" group soon began to crumble under Indian pressure despite vigorous U.S. efforts to stiffen its resolve. Ireland became the sole member of the original five to sponsor the resolution, and it took a personal phone call from Kennedy to the Irish ambassador to persuade Dublin to stand fast. The draft resolution referred to earlier UN resolutions on Kashmir and urged India and Pakistan to enter into direct negotiations. The Indians strongly opposed this compromise draft because of its references to resolutions they no longer considered relevant. The draft resolution won majority support when the Security Council voted on June 22, but Moscow vetoed it.

Washington had been reluctant to sponsor the resolution, and Kennedy's persuasive phone call to the Irish ambassador spared it from having to do so. But this did not save the United States from Nehru's wrath. The prime minister declared that the Kashmir debate had "hurt and angered" India and had caused "doubt in our minds about the goodwill" of America and Britain.[18] Galbraith was not surprised by the prime minister's angry self-righteousness, which he thought had been heightened by Nehru's resentment over pressure the Kennedy administration was currently putting on India on several other important issues. These included New Delhi's prospective purchase of MiG fighters from the Soviet Union, a move Washington stoutly opposed. (India had always purchased its military aircraft from Western sources.)

Galbraith was disgusted by the futility of the UN exercise and the damage he believed it had inflicted on U.S. interests. He told Kennedy that the action had done nothing practical for Pakistan, given the United States a bad press in India, and left the Pakistanis still complaining about the Americans while Pakistan went on negotiating with China about territory in dispute between the two countries in the Kashmir area.[19] Fed up with continuing U.S. support for the UNCIP resolutions, Galbraith requested Washington's approval to state publicly that "as a practical matter, and without reference to the merits of the case, [the United States] considers the plebiscite question dead and that any Kashmir settlement will obviously have to be found in other directions." Kennedy himself shot down the ambassador's proposal.[20]

Walter McConaughy, who had succeeded Rountree as ambassador to Pakistan in March 1962, was one of the few American officials who did not find the UN exercise totally useless from the U.S. viewpoint. An experienced diplomat, Far East specialist, and dedicated cold warrior, McConaughy was on his first assignment to South Asia. He became renowned among his staff at Embassy Karachi for his accurate, almost verbatim accounts of his conversations with Pakistani officials. His reporting of conditions and issues in Pakistan was considered solid in the State Department. According to Phillips Talbot, then assistant secretary for Near Eastern and South Asian affairs, "As Indo-Pak differences escalated, [McConaughy] reported the Pakistani positions fairly and recommended that we support some of them. [But] gradually—as Embassy New Delhi began hammering for support of Indian positions—he became an advocate of much of what Ayub demanded on the basis of what Pakistan considered our prior commitments and our 'sense of fair play.'" McConaughy never attained anything approaching the standing in Washington that Galbraith had there.[21]

McConaughy told Ayub that the debate at the United Nations had been helpful in reaffirming the UNCIP resolutions (the same resolutions Galbraith wished disowned) and exposing Soviet misuse of its veto power.[22] Galbraith, for his part, was typically caustic in discussing Pakistani attitudes and intentions. In his view, Pakistan "would prefer to have the [Kashmir] issue continued ad infinitum, ad nauseam even with no affirmative gain if it provides the negative return of worsened U.S.-Indian relations."[23] Although Ayub formally expressed his gratitude for U.S. support, the State Department concluded that the exercise had produced a definite feeling among Pakistanis, government officials and private citizens alike, that the United States had not fully lived up to Kennedy's commitment to support Pakistan at the United Nations.[24]

While the Security Council fruitlessly debated the Kashmir issue, relations between India and China worsened. Their border confrontation in the Himalayas had intensified in November 1961, when New Delhi adopted a foolhardy "forward policy" of infiltrating its forces into areas in the Ladakh province of Kashmir. These included the strategically important Aksai Chin plateau, which India claimed and the People's Liberation Army controlled. The Nehru government thought these tactics could improve India's bargaining position in future negotiations leading to a diplomatic settlement. Some in Washington understandably feared that Pakistan might take advantage of a further escalation of the Sino-Indian conflict to make trouble for India in Kashmir and elsewhere. The triangular India-China-Pakistan character of the Kashmir dispute was underscored in early May 1962 when the Pakistanis declared that they and the Chinese would negotiate the line separating the areas they controlled in the mountainous northern part of the state.[25] This announcement provoked an outraged Indian reaction. The Indian government maintained that because the area Pakistan and China disputed and now planned to divide was Kashmiri territory, the Pakistanis had no right to be there, let alone negotiate its ownership with the Chinese. Nor did it welcome the prospect of broader collaboration between China and Pakistan in ways inimical to Indian interests that their decision to negotiate suggested.

As a former head of the department's Near East–South Asia bureau, Under Secretary of State for Political Affairs George C. McGhee continued to take a strong interest in India-Pakistan relations. McGhee suggested to his colleagues that it might be useful to ask Ayub to assure New Delhi that Pakistan would not stir up Kashmir if India became involved in a major clash with China. Phillips Talbot, an experienced "old South Asia hand" and academic who held McGhee's former job, argued against this initiative. In Talbot's correct view, a U.S. request to Ayub to give guarantees to India without an Indian quid pro quo on Kashmir would be unproductive and probably strongly resented by Pakistani leaders. They would interpret it as further evidence that the United States was shifting its policies in favor of India. Moreover, Talbot added, because no significant escalation of fighting was likely during the balance of 1962, such a U.S. initiative was unnecessary. McGhee did not press the matter, and no action was taken.[26]

The concerns Under Secretary McGhee had expressed became more salient when, to the Nehru government's surprise, clashes between Indian and Chinese forces developed into a full-scale border war in October 1962. Provoked by Indian army advances in Ladakh and the North East Frontier

Agency (NEFA, now Arunachal Pradesh), the Chinese struck with great force in both areas. Their army, substantially larger, better equipped, and more easily supplied than India's, quickly won a stunning victory in NEFA, where they forced the Indians to retreat to the plains of Assam. The Indian army fought more effectively in Ladakh. But there too the Chinese rapidly advanced, overwhelming the small outposts the Indians had established as part of their forward policy.

Faced with these military disasters, New Delhi jettisoned its long-standing nonaligned policy and turned desperately to the West for help. Kennedy quickly let the Indians know that the United States was sympathetic to their plight and would provide prompt support. Nehru asked for military assistance soon afterward. Within days U.S. transport planes carrying arms and other supplies were landing at Indian airfields.

The decision to arm India, which the Pakistanis bitterly resented, brought into sharp focus the fundamental flaws in the U.S.-Pakistan alliance. For America, military assistance to India was part of a global effort to contain the same challenges from Communist aggression that had prompted it to bring Pakistan into the Western security camp. For Pakistan, the aid undercut the very different purpose it had in allying with the United States—to bolster itself militarily, economically, and politically against the threat it perceived from India.

The American action further strengthened the widespread Pakistani belief that the Kennedy administration preferred India to Pakistan and found little value in the U.S.-Pakistan alliance. Ayub's bitterness at what he considered Kennedy's failure to honor his pledge to consult with Pakistan before going ahead with arms shipments to India heightened the strain it produced in bilateral relations. Ayub and other Pakistanis were convinced that India would use the arms that America and other Western powers gave it not against China but against Pakistan, even though these weapons were primarily useful for fighting in the mountains rather than on the plains of the Punjab. They continued to give lip service to the importance of strengthening "free world" resistance to the Communist threat but made no effort to conceal their delight at India's misfortunes.

The Kennedy administration's immediate goal in dealing with India-Pakistan relations during the war in the Himalayas was damage control. It tried hard and ultimately successfully to head off Pakistan's natural inclination to take advantage of India's military defeat. It recognized that Pakistani moves to stir up trouble inside Kashmir or along the cease-fire line would be a disaster for America's South Asia policy and for its broader cold war strategy of containing Communist aggression.

Immediately after the People's Liberation Army launched its initial offensive, Washington instructed Ambassador McConaughy to urge Ayub to avoid any action that would inhibit India from concentrating on the Chinese attack and to suggest that Ayub propose a mutual understanding with Nehru to keep the India-Pakistan border calm during the crisis.[27] President Kennedy followed this up with a personal letter to Ayub. The two men had met only a few weeks earlier at the Kennedy family home in Newport, Rhode Island. At that time, Kennedy had again rebuffed Ayub's renewed call for the United States to exert economic pressure on the Indians to bring about a Kashmir settlement. Such action, Kennedy firmly told Ayub, would not only undermine India's prospects but might seriously injure the security and stability of all of South Asia.[28]

In his letter, sent under radically changed circumstances, Kennedy urged Ayub to send a private message to Nehru assuring him that he could count on Pakistan's making no moves on the ground that would alarm India. Specifically mentioning Kashmir, he told the Pakistan president that action taken by Karachi now in the larger interests of the subcontinent would do more in the long run to bring about a sensible resolution of India-Pakistan differences than anything else.[29] The administration formally and, in a watered-down version, publicly reiterated the pledge the United States had made earlier to come to Pakistan's assistance in the event of Indian aggression against it.[30]

In his reply to Kennedy and in conversations with Ambassador McConaughy, Ayub was unsympathetic to India's plight. He maintained that India had brought its disaster on itself. Moreover, China's goals were limited. Ayub wanted India, not Pakistan, to make the initial gesture. Pakistan could then reciprocate. He continued to insist that Washington bring pressure on India to move on Kashmir. He was not reassured by Kennedy's pledge that the United States would see to it that the arms it supplied to India were used only against China and that America would come to Pakistan's assistance should India attack. "The answer to the problem," Ayub wrote the president, "lies in creating a situation whereby we are free from the Indian threat, and the Indians are free from any apprehensions about us. This can only be done if there is a settlement of the question of Kashmir."[31]

Assessing this reaction, National Security Council staff member Robert Komer, who had scant regard for the value of the U.S.-Pakistan alliance, found that the Pakistanis "were going through a genuine emotional crisis as they see their cherished ambitions of using the United States as a lever against India going up in the smoke of the Chinese border war." But Komer was convinced, as were others in the administration, that the Pakistanis would not risk their relationship with the United States.[32] In the event, Ayub assured the United States orally and privately that Pakistan would not take military action against India, and the Pakistanis did not do so. But he refused to make any public statement. And, not surprisingly, he turned down Kennedy's highly unrealistic request that he send a message to Nehru promising him that Pakistan would not take advantage of India's parlous situation.[33]

If the administration's immediate goal was securing assurances from Pakistan that it would not cause problems for India, its broader, more ambitious objective was to make use of what Kennedy called "the fleeting . . . one-time opportunity" the Sino-Indian war offered for a reconciliation between the two countries.[34] Such a historic development could lead New Delhi and Karachi to devote their military resources to providing security for the whole subcontinent against the Communist threat rather than using them against one another. To Washington's thinking, it would bolster the U.S. position in the cold war and strongly serve the interests of India and Pakistan as well. It would also justify America's sending military assistance to India while maintaining its security ties with Pakistan. And if U.S. intervention proved successful, the administration could claim credit for a major foreign policy achievement, further evidence of the diplomatic skill it had recently demonstrated in its deft handling of the Cuban missile crisis.

The decision to pursue this interventionist course also reflected the administration's strong preference for activism. The Kennedy White House put a premium on boldness and innovation. It prized a tough, can-do attitude. As David Schneider, a State Department officer who worked on South Asian affairs in the early 1960s, put it, "Those were the days [when] every international problem had its solution and the safe policy was the activist policy regardless of what reasonable analysis might have told us about the prospects for success."[35] A more cautious and reflective leadership would have paid greater heed to the formidable, well-known obstacles involved. But in its determined way the administration concluded that the effort was worth making and it hurried forward without worrying much about the long odds against success.

The administration recognized that progress toward its ambitious goal would crucially depend on the willingness of India and Pakistan to reach an agreement on Kashmir. Its own experience in dealing with the two countries on the issue made it painfully aware of the daunting difficulties that had to be overcome to reach a resolution of the issue acceptable to both sides. But it believed that despite this unpromising background, the United States could play a major role in engineering a settlement. For the first time America was in a position to exert substantial leverage on both countries. India's nonalignment policy was in tatters, and it desperately needed U.S. support against China. And despite its "near hysterical state" over American military assistance to the Indians and its flirtation with the Chinese, Pakistan was dependent on U.S.-supplied arms and appeared to recognize that it would ultimately be Washington, not Beijing, that could help bring about a Kashmir settlement it could live with.[36]

Washington believed that it was particularly important that India adopt a more accommodating position. As Secretary of State Dean Rusk observed, "The United States cannot give maximum military support to India while most of India's forces are engaged against Pakistan over an issue where American interest in self-determination of the peoples directly concerned has caused us since 1954 to be sympathetic to Pakistan's claims."[37] President Kennedy made this even more explicit when he told the Indian ambassador that "whether we like it or not, the question of Kashmir is inescapably linked to what [the United States] can do to assist India militarily."[38]

But Pakistan also had to cooperate and to recognize how radically the Sino-Indian border war had altered the situation on the subcontinent. Kennedy put this forcefully in spelling out talking points he wanted used with Ayub: "We have had to look at the situation in terms of free world security and we regard it as a major test of our alliance [with Pakistan] as well as Ayub's statesmanship whether he does so too." He instructed American diplomats to stress to the Pakistan president that the Chinese threat created a recognized community of interest between India and Pakistan and a new basis for resolution of their differences. Should Ayub be forthcoming, Kennedy said, "We are prepared to tell Nehru that if we give him major military aid he should agree to negotiate at a suitable point on Kashmir."[39] The president accompanied this carrot with a stick—a warning of the dire consequences to U.S.-Pakistan relations should the Pakistanis draw closer to China.

Galbraith, for one, worried that Washington might squander its opportunity if it tried to force unrealistic conditions on New Delhi. China's announcement of a unilateral cease-fire and the withdrawal of its troops within ten days to a line twenty kilometers north of the starting point of the fighting in the Assam Himalayas and twenty kilometers east of the Chinese border claim in Ladakh bolstered India's reluctance to compromise, as American officials quickly recognized. Although the possibility that the People's Liberation Army would return could not be dismissed, the Indians would not feel as pressing a need to offer concessions to Pakistan in their less-beleaguered state. Their reluctance to take an accommodating position was probably also bolstered by an improvement in their relations with Moscow. The Soviets moved to a position on the Sino-Indian border dispute that was more evenhanded than the line they had taken while the fighting in the Himalayas raged and the dangerous Cuban missile crisis remained unresolved. The missile crisis had discouraged them from causing further trouble for themselves with the Chinese, whose sympathy they needed. Moscow was now prepared once again to offer MiG fighter planes to the Indian Air Force, an important consideration for the Nehru government both for its real and symbolic value.

Kennedy decided to send to South Asia a high-level mission led by veteran diplomat W. Averell Harriman, the assistant secretary of state for Far Eastern affairs, to get a better understanding of the situation. Harriman's State–Defense Department team was charged with both military and diplomatic responsibilities. The president instructed the Harriman team to determine the Indian military's arms requirements in its confrontation with China and recommend what Washington should do to help New Delhi meet these. He also told Harriman to deal with the Kashmir issue. Kennedy did not expect quick results on Kashmir but hoped to set in motion a trend that would result, "with nursing from us," in a settlement.[40]

Commonwealth Secretary Duncan Sandys headed a parallel British political-military team. As on many earlier occasions, Washington wanted London to take the lead because of its commonwealth ties with New Delhi and Karachi. But as negotiations progressed, the United States came to play a somewhat more important role.

Harriman had several difficult exchanges on the Kashmir issue with Prime Minister Nehru in New Delhi. Nehru maintained that the Indian public would not tolerate concessions on Kashmir. He claimed that these could trigger anti-Muslim disturbances. Harriman ultimately got him to consent to bilateral India-Pakistan negotiations, but Nehru indicated that all he was prepared to concede in those talks were some adjustments to the cease-fire line. After considerable further effort by Harriman, Nehru agreed that he would enter the negotiations with an open mind and without preconditions.[41]

Harriman's discussion on the Kashmir issue with President Ayub in Pakistan seemed to go better. Harriman told Ayub that although a further period would be needed to bring the Indian cabinet and public opinion along, he believed that time was running in the right direction. It was essential, he said, to start negotiations. These would focus public opinion on the issue. Harriman and Sandys made it plain to Ayub that a plebiscite was not possible, nor could the Kashmir Valley be transferred to Pakistan. Despite the hard line that Nehru had taken, which they did not mention, they claimed they had found an understanding in India that it had to make certain concessions beyond adjusting the cease-fire line.

According to Harriman, Ayub acknowledged that negotiations might take considerable time. But the Pakistan president said that if Nehru agreed to the draft communiqué he, Harriman, and Sandys had worked out, it would be possible to continue discussions even though the first rounds might not reach a satisfactory conclusion. Nehru eventually consented to a text that, among other things, declared: "The President of Pakistan and the Prime Minister of India have agreed that a renewed effort should be made to resolve outstanding differences between the two countries on Kashmir and other related matters so as to enable India and Pakistan to live side by side in peace and friendship."[42]

As so many others had before him, Harriman concluded that only a resolution of the Kashmir problem could change Pakistan's attitude toward India. He told Kennedy that a settlement on terms acceptable to Pakistan was Ayub's price for forming a joint front with India against the Communists. The problem, he recognized, was that terms acceptable to Pakistan were unacceptable to India. He argued nonetheless that though prospects for a settlement were remote, the United States (and Britain) should continue to press India and Pakistan to move toward each other even if both resented this pressure.

Harriman said he had no concept of what form a settlement could take, but it was evident to him that the two sides would both have to give up much more than they then believed possible. He commended, with good reason, Ayub's remark that any fair solution would be unpopular with both the Indians and the Pakistanis.[43] Assessing the results of Harriman's efforts, Washington recognized the obvious: what was needed was India's willingness to make concessions greater than those it had been previously prepared to consider and Pakistan's acceptance of solutions likely to fall well short of its objectives.[44]

Harriman and Sandys were still in Pakistan when to their dismay Nehru told the Indian parliament that upsetting the existing arrangement in Kashmir would be very bad for the Kashmiri people. The two envoys knew that this comment could derail the bilateral talks even before they began. Sandys rushed back to India and persuaded the prime minister to declare publicly that the talks would be without conditions. The episode was not a good augury for the success of the negotiations.

Bilateral negotiations began in Rawalpindi on December 29, 1962, and dragged on through six sessions before petering out ignominiously five months later. Senior U.S. officials were deeply involved throughout the negotiating period, and President Kennedy himself sent personal letters to Nehru and Ayub at crucial points. The American ambassadors in New Delhi and Karachi and their senior staffs haunted the negotiation sites "like the ghost of Banquo," in Galbraith's colorful phrase. So did their British counterparts. Washington constantly monitored and assessed developments and sent the ambassadors an extensive flow of instructions and analyses. The envoys, Galbraith in particular, but McConaughy too, were not shy in offering their own thoughts. When the negotiators failed to make progress, and the exercise seemed on the verge of breakdown, Washington introduced its own detailed proposals. Throughout the negotiations, India and Pakistan importuned U.S. officials to pressure the other side to make concessions. The intervention was by far the most intensive and extensive the United States government has ever undertaken to help resolve the Kashmir issue. If the talks failed, it was not for lack of effort or attention on the part of the Kennedy administration.

Initially, at least, Washington was determined to exercise its influence from the sidelines and confine itself to a watchdog role. It instructed the resident ambassadors and their staffs to focus on helping to build a positive negotiating environment in which progress could be made. The substance of the negotiations should be left to the Indians and Pakistanis. American diplomats were to refrain from making specific proposals but were not precluded from exploring and discussing types of settlements that seemed to have an appeal to the two sides. Washington admonished them to take special care that settlement formulas were perceived as spontaneous India-Pakistan concepts; they should not be identified as American proposals. If the talks were obviously foundering, however, the embassies, preferably in concert with the local British high commissions but alone if necessary, were to inform the two governments that they would have concrete proposals to suggest in the near future. Public comment was to be kept to a minimum at all times.

The discussions opened on a decidedly unpromising note. President Ayub had already welcomed the Indian delegation, led by Minister of Industries Swaran Singh, a Punjabi Sikh politician known for his imperturbability, when the visitors heard on Pakistan radio that China and Pakistan had reached an agreement on the location of the line dividing the parts of Kashmir each controlled. The Pakistanis were well aware that the Indian government strongly objected to China and Pakistan parceling out territory that India considered its own. Ayub's failure to tell the Indian delegation that an agreement was imminent made the negative impact of the announcement even greater. Ambassador McConaughy berated Ayub for the timing but accepted his claim that the blame rested with the Chinese: the president told him they had skillfully mouse-trapped the Pakistanis in order to create a formidable roadblock to the India-Pakistan negotiations.[45] Washington was furious about the agreement but also chose to go along with Ayub's benign interpretation. The Indian delegates seriously considered scrapping the talks and returning home. Fortunately, McConaughy and Sir Morrice James, the skillful and experienced British high commissioner to Pakistan, persuaded Ayub and Swaran Singh to take conciliatory positions, and the discussions went forward. Zulfikar Ali Bhutto, Ayub's ambitious and politically savvy minister of commerce and industry, headed the Pakistan delegation in the absence of Foreign Minister Mohammed Ali Bogra, who was gravely ill.[46]

As Washington had anticipated, the first round of negotiations made little progress. Each side spent a good deal of time reasserting long-standing positions, which the other then refuted using equally familiar arguments.[47] According to High Commissioner James, the possibility of Kashmir's partition was raised toward the end of the conference. But it is not clear who did so or what precisely they had in mind as the location of an international frontier. The delegations then agreed to hold another session in New Delhi January 16–19.[48]

At this second round of talks, diplomatic dueling continued as the two sides seriously discussed the principles on which a boundary in Kashmir could be drawn. The Pakistanis suggested that these should include the composition of the population, security requirements, and control of the rivers, factors they thought would give them the most territory. The Indians, for their part, said that any territorial adjustment considered necessary should take into account geographical, administrative, and other considerations, and involve the least possible disturbance to the life and welfare of the Kashmiris. This last point was very much to India's advantage; it was widely expected that transfer to Pakistan of Indian-held areas in the Valley and elsewhere would lead to the wholesale flight of their non-Muslim residents. The Indians also warned, as they had before, that such a transfer would lead to serious anti-Muslim violence in India proper. In a joint statement that was not made public, the two sides agreed that a settlement should include the delineation of an international border between India and Pakistan in Kashmir. The disengagement of the two countries' forces in and around Kashmir would be an essential part of such a settlement. The delegations undertook to present maps showing their sides' concepts of the boundary at the next session, to be held in Karachi in early February.[49]

American policymakers believed that the third negotiating round would be crucial. They became increasingly convinced that if India and Pakistan failed to make a breakthrough at that session the United States and Britain would have to develop a proposal of their own. Galbraith welcomed this prospect. Both before the negotiations began and while they were in progress, he had urged Washington to adopt a more active role, only to be rebuffed. He found that the current approach of "urging the Indians to be forthcoming and the Pakistanis to be patient and backing this with an appeal to their self-interest plus the awe and majesty of the United States" was wearing thin. McConaughy agreed with his assessment.[50]

By then Washington had concluded that the best way to resolve the problem was to partition the Valley. A couple of weeks before the third negotiating round the administration quietly developed a proposal to divide the state along a precisely drawn line that transferred to Pakistan substantial territory in the northwestern part of the Valley and the western portion of Jammu Province. India would receive a sliver of Pakistani-held territory above Kargil to provide it with a buffer area north of the vital road connecting the Valley with Ladakh.[51] Robert Komer told Kennedy that the partition scheme would be thrown into the breach if talks seemed about to break down.[52]

Provisions designed to soften the newly delineated international border were also included. There was to be free movement of people and goods between the Indian- and Pakistani-held portions of the Valley, and Indian and Pakistani citizens from outside the Valley would have access to the other side. A joint Indian-Pakistani board would be organized to promote the Valley's economic development.

Finally, the proposal mentioned approaches to other issues that could be usefully added to broaden this package. India and Pakistan might be persuaded to offer one another mutual diplomatic support for their boundary claims against third powers. This meant Karachi's backing New Delhi's claim to its version of the British-negotiated McMahon Line as the Sino-Indian border in the Assam Himalayas in return for Indian acceptance of Pakistan's claim to the Durand Line, also British-negotiated, as its boundary with Afghanistan. Augmented transnational transit arrangements were also included. To strengthen the defense of India's North East Frontier Agency, Pakistan would give the Indians greater land and air transit rights across

East Pakistan. Pakistan would receive in return increased transit rights across India between its eastern and western wings. A joint India-Pakistan transit board would be established to implement and supervise these arrangements.

It was all very heady stuff. In the event, none of these imaginative if wishful ideas ever got off the ground.

Ambassador Galbraith contended that if the proposal to partition the Valley were put to Nehru, he would reject it out of hand. (When the ambassador raised the idea with the prime minister later, he reported that Nehru was willing to talk about it "though his face did not brighten perceptibly.") But Galbraith also acknowledged that reasonable Indians did not exclude a settlement similar to the department's proposal. Although he was not sanguine about the possibility of selling partition to the Indian government, he thought it worthwhile to develop a conversation along these lines. He warned, however, that "unleashing" the map could have great and probably adverse consequences.[53]

Ambassador McConaughy held that partition was totally unacceptable to Pakistan at that point. (Ayub and Bhutto both told Assistant Secretary Talbot soon afterward that it was not feasible.) He said that the slim chance of selling the partition formula had been reduced by the leak of a State Department message instructing Embassy Karachi on tactics for promoting it. He warned that difficult questions would be asked about the plan, such as its acceptability to the Kashmiris. He did not rule out serious consideration of the case for partitioning the Valley. But he said the plan did pose issues that Washington needed to think about.[54]

Galbraith and McConaughy had an opportunity to make their arguments directly to Talbot when the assistant secretary visited South Asia in late January. Meeting in New Delhi, the three of them agreed that a specific U.S. proposal should not be offered to the two parties yet. This decision echoed the view in Washington that "Indian and Pakistani noses should be kept to the grindstone a while longer" before the United States made an ostentatious move that would both enable India and Pakistan to shift responsibility and relax their own efforts. The three American officials also concurred that despite all of Washington's recent mapmaking, it was probably premature to draw a full partition line for later submission to the two governments. The United States should encourage them to continue their efforts to reach a partition agreement. Only if they were unsuccessful should internationalization of the Valley be raised as a basis for a settlement. This was the solution the British favored.[55]

On his way back to Washington, Talbot cabled Galbraith to ask him whether he saw any sense in suggesting consultations with representative Kashmiri leaders during the negotiation process. This appears to have been the first time the United States considered having the Kashmiris play a role in the discussions that would determine their future. Galbraith, looking ahead to the terms of a settlement, feared that the Kashmiris would oppose partitioning the Valley if they were allowed to express their views freely. Nothing ever came of the idea of bringing the Kashmiris into the act.[56]

As forecast, the third round of negotiations, held February 8–10 in Karachi, proved critical. Urged on by Kennedy, who wrote to Nehru and Ayub on the eve of the talks to promote a settlement that included drawing an international boundary through the Valley, the two sides finally grappled with the details of partition. Their opening positions indicated that the gap between them was almost certainly unbridgeable. Neither was willing to offer the other any territory within the Valley. The Indians suggested partition along the cease-fire line, with some mutual swapping of real estate. The Pakistanis demanded the whole state excluding only a small corner in the southeast that was overwhelmingly Hindu. They even wanted Ladakh and the responsibility for defending it against the Chinese. Both sides were shocked by the other's proposals, which seemed to offer no possibility for an acceptable compromise. (Galbraith, who called the proposals outrageous, wryly recalled predictions that the Indian line would run though Damascus and the Pakistani line just short of Tokyo.) Despite the enormous differences, the delegates agreed to hold a fourth round.[57]

The State Department found the Pakistanis more to blame for the deadlock and told them so. In its view, the Indians had made a proposal that seemed to invite the Pakistanis into the marketplace; the Pakistanis had replied with such a ludicrously inadequate offer that it was surprising that the Indian delegation had not turned it down out of hand. Nonetheless, Assistant Secretary Talbot continued to be optimistic. He held that if the United States and Britain exerted pressure, the bilateral sessions could still produce progress. In Talbot's opinion, dividing the Valley continued to offer the best prospect for a settlement. Internationalizing it could be a fallback if partition was rejected. At his direction, elaborate instructions were sent to the embassies detailing the tactics they should use with the Indians and Pakistanis.[58]

As the fourth round approached, President Kennedy again became directly involved. At a February 21 White House meeting, he authorized greater American engagement in the negotiations. This meant exerting more muscle on India and Pakistan to agree to the Valley's partitioning and the setting up of special joint arrangements there. As Secretary Rusk quipped, we would now get in from "up to our ankles" to "up to our knees."[59]

Following this presidential decision, the administration pressed India to show a greater willingness to give Pakistan a "position" in the Valley and to be responsive if Pakistan made a new offer. At the same time, it vigorously urged the Pakistanis to modify their outlandish demands. Kennedy sent forceful letters to Nehru and Ayub giving his personal support to these pleas.[60] The value of these frequent presidential messages was at best debatable, however, and Galbraith was probably right when he complained that "letters from the president have been issued like Confederate currency and with similar results."[61] The State Department prepared detailed partition plans that included provisions for local autonomy and a major role for an outside third party in administering the Valley and in settling disputes that would inevitably arise there between India and Pakistan. Despite their continuing preference for internationalizing the Valley, the British accepted the U.S. partition approach, and American and British diplomats in India and Pakistan closely coordinated their efforts to promote it.[62]

All to no avail. The fourth negotiating round, held in Calcutta March 12–14, made no progress. Although Ayub had confessed to McConaughy that Pakistan's earlier proposal on how the Valley should be divided had been "damn nonsense" required in the haggling process and had privately spelled out a more forthcoming position, all his representatives did in the Calcutta negotiations was to hint that Pakistan might be prepared to give India more territory in Hindu-majority districts in the southern part of the state.[63] But the Pakistanis never tabled such a proposal. Galbraith had also found some evidence on the eve of the negotiations that India, too, might be more accommodating. The Indians made no further territorial offers, however. Instead, they used much of the session to complain angrily about the recently signed Sino-Pakistan Kashmir border agreement.

The way the Pakistanis handled the signing of that agreement had also infuriated the United States, especially since the administration had urged them to treat the event in low key and they had said they would do so. Washington protested forcefully when Bhutto, by then foreign minister following Bogra's death, went to Beijing with great fanfare to sign the pact. At State Department instructions, McConaughy told Bhutto bluntly that if the talks failed because of the Pakistanis' dealings with the Chinese, the United States would pay less heed to their concerns about its arming India. Nor would Washington support any further initiatives on Kashmir. To some American analysts, the timing and handling of the border accord suggested either that Pakistan did not really want an agreement with India on Kashmir or that the Chinese were seeking to torpedo one, or both.[64]

Despite the failure at Calcutta, a fifth round was scheduled. Washington regarded the session as a key test of the two sides' genuine interest in seeking a compromise settlement. Convinced that they would have to develop more concrete proposals of their own, the United States and Britain produced four "elements" outlining what they considered a practicable solution. This was the farthest Washington and London had ever gone in offering a formula for a settlement.

These elements were: (1) both India and Pakistan must have a "substantial position" in the Valley; (2) they must have assured access to and through the Valley for the defense of their positions to the north and east; (3) outside the Valley, India's interest in Ladakh and Pakistan's interest in the development of water storage facilities on the Chenab River should be recognized; and (4) the position of the two countries in the Valley must be such as to permit clearly defined arrangements for sovereignty and the maintenance of law and order, political freedom and some measure of self-rule for residents, the free movement of Kashmiris throughout the Valley and their relatively free access to other parts of Kashmir as well as to India and Pakistan, rapid development of tourism, and effective use of development funds available from external sources.[65]

Walt Rostow, the chairman of the State Department's Policy Planning Council, could not have been optimistic about the fate of these "elements." In a perceptive report he sent Kennedy following a week's visit to India and Pakistan between the fourth and fifth rounds that was designed to reemphasize to both countries the importance Washington attached to a Kashmir settlement, Rostow saw a stone wall rising ahead. In his pessimistic—and accurate—view, "Indian minds run into a real block in surrendering any substantial part of the [Valley]; and Pakistani minds run into an even greater block in ceding any part of the [Valley] to India. Quite apart from political pressures, the issue is so charged and men's minds have run so often over the tracks which rationalize their respective present positions that it is literally painful for them to visualize a change in the way things are (for Indians) or anything short of the fulfillment of their dream and crusade (for Pakistanis)." Rostow concluded that before giving up any part of what they held, the Indians would need very firm assurances that they would in fact obtain a better relationship with Pakistan as a result. American pressure and exhortation at the right moment could prove useful but only if there were a workable negotiating track that Nehru and Ayub could perceive. "Right now the central fact . . . is that they do not see such a track embracing the full complexity of the problem—and neither does anyone else on the subcontinent."[66]

Rostow's pessimism soon proved justified. On the eve of the fifth round, held in Karachi April 22–25, Ayub told McConaughy that partition of the Valley was "1000% out of the question." He insisted that Pakistan was openminded and flexible on the type of settlement that would preserve the Valley as an undivided whole. But by this he meant its cession to Pakistan immediately or arrangements that would give it to Pakistan within a year. He blamed the Americans and the British for failing to insist on a Kashmir settlement as the price for military aid to India.[67]

Nehru, who by then had made it abundantly clear to Galbraith that partition was a nonstarter, sent a message to Kennedy the following day in which he called the U.S.-British "elements" proposal "ill-considered and ill-conceived." He told the president that the proposal made it impossible to reach any Kashmir settlement for the present.[68] According to Nehru's biographer, S. Gopal, the prime minister believed that Pakistan had no real desire for a settlement, only a wish to take advantage of India's poor relations with China.[69] Galbraith reported that "Nehru had been uniquely angry, in part at my presence, much more at the fact that I have translated his vague talk of wanting a settlement into firm concessions he didn't want to make."[70]

With both sides taking uncompromising positions, to no one's surprise the Karachi negotiations failed. Galbraith wrote in his journal: "We succeeded in bringing the Indians and Pakistanis into new opposition to ourselves. Nothing else was accomplished."[71] Another round was scheduled for New Delhi in May. India agreed to this only after much American and British pleading. It was not expected to fare any better than earlier bouts.

Before that sixth session took place, a team of top U.S. and British policymakers came to India and Pakistan. Secretary Rusk led the American group. Both the Americans and the British came away from their visit deeply discouraged about prospects for a breakthrough. Rusk reported that he found no evidence of a desire in either India or Pakistan to work hard toward reconciling their differences. Because the terms of any Kashmir settlement that could be negotiated would cause serious domestic political difficulties to both governments, it would need to be cushioned by far-reaching agreements on other matters. "Nothing less than a Franco-German type of reconciliation is likely to work," he cabled Washington. India was more ready for this than Pakistan, which was reluctant to ease pressures on the Indians on Kashmir by resolving other issues first. (This has been Pakistan's consistent approach over the years.) "The absence of such a settlement," the secretary concluded, "leaves the two parties in an atmosphere of unreasoning hostility which militates against good results on other issues." It was a classic chicken-and-egg problem.[72]

With prospects bleak for any progress at the sixth and, so it proved, final negotiating round scheduled for New Delhi on May 15–16, Washington revived the idea of mediation. As noted, the Indians had dismissed a similar U.S. proposal in early 1962 when Kennedy had urged Nehru to accept Eugene Black as mediator. This time they were more enthusiastic. Indeed, Brajesh Kumar Nehru, India's ambassador in Washington and a cousin of the prime minister, seems to have had an important hand in persuading the United States to put mediation back on the table. But the Pakistanis, who had been sympathetic to the projected Black mission, proved recalcitrant. They made demands that they surely knew the United States could not accept. These included imposing a freeze on long-term military assistance to India during the mediation period. They were impervious to Washington's veiled threat to wash its hands of the Kashmir issue if they did not accept mediation. But the United States would not take "no" for an answer and continued for months to try to sell the idea to Karachi and to keep it alive in New

Delhi, where initial favor for the proposal soon waned. It was only in August that a firm and formal Pakistani rejection led Washington to give up.

By that time the bilateral negotiations were long over. There was no bang, and hardly a whimper, when they finally ended in New Delhi on May 16 following two more days of fruitless discussion. At that sixth round, the Pakistanis proposed the internationalization of the Valley for six months, after which the wishes of its inhabitants would be ascertained. This was no more than a thin cover for its cession to Pakistan: the Pakistanis were confident that with the pro-Indian state government and the Indian army no longer present, the Muslim majority in the Valley would support union with their coreligionists in Pakistan. The Indians rejected this proposal. They suggested instead that the two sides agree to use only peaceful methods to settle their differences on Kashmir, an idea they had floated many times in the past. Pakistan recognized that such a "no-war" agreement would consolidate Indian control and turned it down. The two sides then issued a mildly worded joint communiqué stating that they had regretfully concluded that agreement could not be reached.

The U.S.-British effort to break the Kashmir impasse foundered for several reasons. Probably the most important was the revival of Indian self-confidence as it became increasingly evident that another Chinese military attack was unlikely, at least in the near term. This sharply reduced the value to India of a compromise settlement that included painful, politically perilous concessions.

As Rusk and Rostow found, the long-standing bitterness the two sides felt toward one another placed further hurdles in the negotiating track. The Indians were never persuaded that concessions on their part would lead to a new, much improved relationship with Pakistan that would justify their making them. Nor did they share the American and British belief in the compelling importance of India and Pakistan agreeing to the joint defense of the subcontinent, which the United States regarded as the most significant benefit of a Kashmir settlement.

Pakistan, of course, was a member of pacts specifically designed by their sponsors in Washington to contain Communism. But its professed interest in finding common cause with India against threats from the north was at best doubtful. The Pakistanis did not in fact believe that such threats existed, a conviction that the unilateral withdrawal of Chinese military forces from Indian territory only strengthened. Pakistan was eager to bolster its ties with China as a counterweight to both India and the United States. The border agreement with Beijing, an important step in the Pakistani effort to play this China card, further diminished prospects for a settlement.

Domestic political circumstances in both India and Pakistan were also unpromising. The Indian debacle in the border war had seriously weakened the aging Nehru. Always emotionally attached to Kashmir, he was neither in a mood nor in a position to risk further damage to his political standing by making concessions likely to cause him serious difficulties both within and outside the Congress Party—possibly to the point of losing power—even had a palpable Chinese threat persisted. (This did not mean, however, that post-Nehru leaders were likely to offer greater concessions, as Ayub and others including some American analysts hoped.) In Pakistan Ayub too faced political inhibitions as the country returned to civilian government. Although he remained very powerful, he did not have the same free hand he had enjoyed during the 1958–62 martial law period.

But perhaps the most daunting problem Washington faced in its long, ultimately failed effort to facilitate a Kashmir settlement was finding a way to bring its influence to bear on India and Pakistan in a manner that did not damage other compelling U.S. cold war interests. Secretary Rusk tersely spelled out the problem in April 1963, when the United States had come to understand the limits to the leverage it could use to persuade Nehru and Ayub to reach a compromise resolution involving painful concessions neither thought worth the likely end result. "Our overriding purpose," Rusk said, "is some accommodation between India and Pakistan. The question is how to achieve it. If we back India against the Chinese, we may drive the Pakistanis off the deep end. If we abandon the Indians, they might move toward the USSR and China again."[73] The fact that India and Pakistan were well aware of this American dilemma and knew that they had options aside from U.S. support—China for the Pakistanis, the Soviet Union for India—made the problem more acute.

The major source of American leverage was the prospect of military assistance to India. As noted above, Washington had rushed aid to New Delhi when Nehru desperately pleaded for it following the Chinese victories in the

Himalayas. At their meeting in Nassau in December 1962, Kennedy and British Prime Minister Harold Macmillan pledged $120 million to help India arm. But New Delhi needed more assistance. From then on, as political scientist Timothy Crawford has pointed out, "The fulcrum of U.S. leverage lay in the distinction between a limited infusion of emergency aid and a larger commitment" in the future. The idea was that India would have to earn the further substantial assistance it sought by good behavior on Kashmir.[74]

But, to phrase it crudely, Washington was never willing to put its money where its mouth was. Countless high-level meetings were held to consider how pressure could be effectively applied. Yet no satisfactory plan was ever accepted that successfully related forward movement on arms aid packages to progress in the negotiations. Instead, there was a disconnect that could only have led the Indians to conclude that the United States had no serious intention of using the military aid lever. U.S. government delegations visited India to develop programs for joint American-British-Indian projects and announcements were made of new agreements, all in total disregard of New Delhi's current behavior at the India-Pakistan negotiating table.

American officials from Kennedy down exhorted the Indians. They asserted that a Kashmir agreement, or at least a conciliatory Indian posture on the matter, would ease the problems the administration would face in selling Congress on further military assistance to India. But they never resorted to anything approaching an ultimatum, nor were they prepared to use this aid to bring about specific moves by the Indians in the negotiations. Meanwhile, Chinese restraint, Soviet friendship, and the passage of time bolstered Indian self-confidence, seriously reducing the efficacy of this form of leverage had the United States chosen to wield it.

Galbraith challenged this cautious approach between the fourth and fifth negotiating rounds by recommending a "plain political bargain." He proposed that Washington provide substantial support for the development of Indian defense production and give the Indians backup air support in return for substantial Indian concessions to Pakistan on the drawing of the partition line through the Valley. If India accepted, it would be up to the Pakistanis to respond. If the Pakistanis did not, the United States would go ahead with the military aid. "The Pakistanis will have lost their right to complain," he argued.

At a later stage of the deal, Galbraith went on, Washington should tell the Indians that although it recognized their need for transport planes, high-performance fighters, and advanced pilot training, it had no choice but to go slow because of the danger of an adverse and damaging Pakistani reaction. The Indians would be given to understand that these items would be provided as soon as a Kashmir settlement was reached.[75] But both the State and Defense Departments opposed this "crude bazaar level" approach, as Galbraith called it, and although Kennedy seemed initially attracted to the idea he ultimately judged it premature.[76]

So U.S. military assistance programs moved ahead without any diplomatic quid pro quo even when it became apparent that the Chinese would not renew the war. Nor was India punished for its bad behavior: the programs continued even after the talks had failed.

The Indians must surely have concluded fairly early in the negotiating cycle that there was no serious risk to them in calling America's bluff on Kashmir. During the balance of 1963 and beyond, they further strengthened their ties with Moscow and became increasingly bold in challenging Washington on issues important to the United States. Galbraith and Komer were right to conclude acidly that the outcome of American intervention on Kashmir was that the United States was left "with no progress in Kashmir and no Indians either."[77]

If India was not impressed with Washington's vague and heavily veiled threats, neither was Pakistan. Ayub was not moved by the suggestion that it was to Pakistan's advantage to make a deal before U.S. military assistance made India stronger. Like Nehru, he saw how reluctant the United States was to lean on the Indians, either by the crude use of the military assistance pressure point that he favored or by less drastic measures. He was not swayed by Washington's insinuation that if India was willing to compromise and Pakistan was not, it would pay less heed to Pakistani concerns when it provided arms to India and might even walk away from the Kashmir negotiations, to Pakistan's detriment. (There is no evidence that Washington ever seriously considered threatening to reduce, let alone cut off, the sizable flow of weaponry and other military assistance it had provided to Karachi since 1954 if Ayub was not accommodating.) The Pakistan president's disappointment with Washington's evident willingness to move forward with aid to New

Delhi no matter what the Indians did on Kashmir strengthened his inclination to turn to the Chinese. The expanding Sino-Pakistan entente became an increasingly serious problem for the United States.

Ayub may not have "gone off the deep end," as Rusk had feared. He did not withdraw from the pacts binding Pakistan to the United States, although both Washington and Karachi increasingly questioned their value. Nor did the continuing U.S.-Pakistan alliance deter Pakistan from drawing closer to America's sworn enemy in Beijing. Although there is no record of their having said so, Galbraith and Komer might well have come to the further conclusion that the United States was left with no progress in Kashmir and no *Pakistanis* either.

Historians and American South Asia policy practitioners disagree about the wisdom of the Kennedy administration in seeking to bring about a Kashmir accord in 1963.

As President Kennedy did, those who believe the long-shot effort was worth making point to the "unique opportunity" the Sino-Indian War offered Washington to engineer a historic change in India-Pakistan relations at a time when the bad blood between them was increasingly complicating America's role in Asia. Proponents argue that a breakthrough could have brought about gains for U.S. interests and the subcontinent itself that significantly exceeded the potential penalties of failure. To their way of thinking, Washington would have supplied arms to India in any event: under prevailing international conditions it could not have ignored the seeming Chinese threat to India and the apparent opportunity to enlist New Delhi on the right side in the cold war. So Ayub would have turned toward Beijing, probably even more eagerly, had Washington not promoted Kashmir negotiations. They conclude that the administration was right to give diplomacy a chance, even against long odds.

Critics of the U.S. intervention make more compelling points, however. In their view, governments should undertake major diplomatic initiatives only when there is a reasonable chance for success. Their basic contention, which I share, is that the Kennedy administration ought to have been aware that the "unique opportunity" it fancied was a chimera. It should have taken into advance account the reasons cited above, many of them foreseeable, that led to the failure of the negotiations. Perhaps most important, it should have understood that even had the Chinese threat to India remained as menacing as it had seemed to be in the fall of 1962, the Nehru government and any conceivable successor would not have agreed to make the concessions necessary to bring about a settlement acceptable to Pakistan.

As Dean Rusk and Walt Rostow discovered—too late—the Indians could not be persuaded that such concessions were worth making even had their domestic political equation offered an opening, which it did not. Washington should also have recognized that had Nehru been driven from power because he offered concessions on Kashmir—a possibility not to be dismissed—the result might have been political instability in India harmful to American interests. Ayub was in a stronger position in Pakistan. But the administration should have anticipated before it made its decision to intervene that he too would be unwilling to settle for anything less than absorption of the Kashmir Valley into Pakistan, as the negotiations later demonstrated.

Rostow was right in his observation that Washington's influence could have been effective only if the Indians and Pakistanis could perceive a working negotiating track. The administration should have foreseen that there was nothing it could do to set up such a track and to persuade the contenders to stay on it. It should have stifled its activist preferences, limited itself to damage control and crisis management, and recognized that in the circumstances prevailing in late 1962 and early 1963, it did not serve the purposes of the United States to undertake such a mission impossible.

5

"A Plague on Both Their Houses"

After the failure of the Kennedy administration's sustained high-level effort to promote a Kashmir settlement, Washington lost its appetite for intervention. Like Kennedy's, the Johnson administration that came to power in November 1963 regarded the Kashmir issue as a serious danger to peace and stability in the subcontinent and a major complication in U.S. relations with India and Pakistan. But most American policymakers had concluded that there was little the United States could do either on its own or at the United Nations to help resolve the problem, which by 1964 was in its seventeenth year.

Washington was also beginning to question whether either of the rival claimants could play a useful role in promoting broader American political and security objectives. The deterioration of U.S.-Pakistan relations from the giddy heights they had reached in the mid-1950s had accelerated following the breakdown of the 1962–63 negotiations. The Pakistanis resented the U.S. decision to provide arms to India even more than before. Washington had its own complaints. It was angered by President Ayub Khan's growing ties with Beijing, part of his effort to free Pakistan from what he regarded as its overdependence on America. Increasingly doubtful about the value of the alliance, the United States was less inclined than before to go to bat for Pakistan on Kashmir and other issues.

American relations with India were also heading downhill from the high point they had reached in late 1962, when Washington had come to New

Delhi's rescue in the Sino-Indian border war. The Nehru government's unwillingness to join U.S-led efforts to contain Communist expansion in Southeast Asia had become a sore point, especially for those Americans who had mistakenly thought that India's conflict with China would lead it to play a more helpful role there. The Johnson administration's growing dissatisfaction with India's economic performance, which remained unimpressive despite substantial assistance from the United States and other donors, added to the negative mix. So did a series of other nettlesome bilateral problems that prompted Indians and Americans to accuse the other side of letting them down.

Washington's opposition to Pakistan's early 1964 bid to bring the Kashmir dispute to the UN Security Council once again reflected its unwillingness to become involved. The administration reassured Pakistan of its continuing support for the 1948 and 1949 UN resolutions. But it concluded that going back to the council might retard a solution, not advance one.[1] When Pakistan persisted in its initiative, the United States declined to assume the active role it had played earlier. It sought instead to dissuade its fellow Security Council members from introducing any resolution at all during the council's sessions. In Washington's view, moving forward with a draft would prove unnecessarily provocative to India. It would also be futile, since the Soviets would again veto any text New Delhi did not accept. The administration preferred an innocuous consensus statement by the council calling on India and Pakistan to resume their negotiations with some sort of undefined assistance from the UN secretary general.

In 1964 and 1965, as at many other times, the U.S. embassies in India and Pakistan often disagreed on the significance for American interests of developments in South Asia and made very different recommendations to Washington about how to deal with them. Walter McConaughy continued to lead Embassy Karachi. Still a strong supporter of the U.S.-Pakistan alliance and of policies that would help preserve it, the ambassador admired the Ayub government and tended to disdain India and discount its value to the United States. The embassy in New Delhi was again headed by Chester Bowles, a man of almost totally different background, temperament, and policy preferences. A prominent figure in the liberal wing of the Democratic Party, Bowles had been a forceful opponent of close U.S.-Pakistan political and security ties since they were first talked about when he was President Truman's ambassador to New Delhi in the early 1950s (see chapter 1). He continued to consider the alliance with Pakistan a major blunder that should be undone, not least because it handicapped the development of the strong U.S.-India relationship he relentlessly advocated. The scant professional and personal regard the two ambassadors had for one another further complicated their relations.

McConaughy and Bowles did agree that the United States should not support another sure-to-fail effort on the Kashmir issue at the Security Council. But the focus and tone of the arguments they made about the proper position America should take on the issue itself differed. McConaughy stressed that Washington needed to avoid any weakening of its long-standing support for the UN resolutions. Otherwise, he warned, the United States would undermine its whole position in Pakistan. In his view, Karachi's dissatisfaction with Washington's role in the failed negotiations had weakened its confidence in the United States. New Delhi's recent moves to integrate its portion of the state more fully into the Indian Union had further heightened Pakistan's worries about Kashmir. (Washington had pointedly expressed its concern to the Indians about these constitutional and political changes, to no avail.) McConaughy reported that consequently the Ayub government had been "thrashing about for alternative courses of action which will keep pressure on the Indians until they accede to meaningful negotiations of the Kashmir issue."[2] Washington called this Pakistani policy "leaning on India."[3] Bowles, for his part, highlighted what he considered Pakistan's error in seeking to raise the issue at the Security Council. For him, Karachi's initiative was "an act of folly, least calculated to serve Pakistan's own interests or promote the settlement of problems facing India and Pakistan." It could only worsen a clearly explosive situation.[4]

Meanwhile, widespread disturbances in the Kashmir Valley following the December 1963 theft from a major religious shrine near Srinagar of a holy relic said to be a hair of the Prophet Muhammad further roiled India-Pakistan relations. The turmoil, which led to the collapse of the repressive and corrupt pro-Indian state government, caused considerable concern in New Delhi about the loyalty to India of Kashmir's Muslim majority, eventually prompting the Nehru government to liberalize the political environment of the state and free Sheikh Mohammed Abdullah, the charismatic, independence-minded Kashmiri leader who had been dismissed from office and jailed a decade earlier. The theft and subsequent civil commotion also sparked serious Muslim-Hindu disturbances in East Pakistan and eastern India.

Pakistan cited these troubles to justify its approach to the United Nations. But its basic objectives remained the same. It still wanted to focus world attention on Kashmir, highlight India's failure to carry out UN resolutions designed to resolve the issue, win reaffirmed support for those resolutions, and remind the Kashmiris that there was hope for a change in the status quo. For all these reasons, India strongly resisted further UN consideration of the issue.

For weeks following the theft of the holy relic, *Washington Evening Star* correspondent Richard Critchfield provided the only objective reporting of the turmoil in the Valley, where he developed excellent sources. He found that almost everyone he interviewed wanted Kashmir to become independent or to join Pakistan.[5] Later, Ambassador Bowles succeeded after some effort in persuading the Indian government to sanction what became the first official visit of an American embassy political officer to the state.[6] Embassy officers vacationing in the Valley sometimes reported their observations and informal interviews to Washington, but these private initiatives were sporadic and had limited value. Bowles argued that it was important to have a trained political observer provide a firsthand report on developments in the troubled state. He chose me for this assignment.

In the week I spent in the Valley and the Jammu area, I met a broad range of political leaders including the newly installed state prime minister, Ghulam Mohammed Sadiq, most of the ministers in his government, important opposition personalities, and other prominent and ordinary Kashmiris. I was struck by the widespread opposition among all classes of Muslims in the Valley to Kashmir's remaining a part of India. "The most fundamental cause for this acute dissatisfaction," I wrote, "is the Kashmiri Muslims' feeling of separateness. They do not consider themselves Indians."[7]

Phillips Talbot had carried on as assistant secretary of state for Near Eastern and South Asian Affairs in the Johnson administration. Talbot had lived as a student in a Kashmiri village for six months in the early 1940s and continued to have a lively interest in the state. Visiting South Asia in March 1964, he found a "grave deterioration" in India-Pakistan relations. He recommended that Washington adopt a position of "limited diplomatic, but, so far as possible, no public activity." He doubted that any external enticement or pressure consistent with U.S. interests in the region could soon loosen India's grip on Kashmir or that President Ayub could afford to give up the political dividends he got from challenging the status quo. He was convinced that Ayub believed that for reasons of national identity Pakistan could not abandon its goal of winning the state.

Talbot suggested that Washington encourage secret India-Pakistan talks outside South Asia. These would have the advantage of keeping the heat on India but would not be a "public circus."[8] Robert Komer, the South Asia specialist on the National Security Council staff, challenged Talbot's analysis and recommendations. He contended that active preventive diplomacy might at least minimize the likelihood of "a galloping crisis in which our interests almost inevitably suffer." He also saw an opportunity in the current situation to end "the overcommitment [to Pakistan] we slid into in 1954–60." But Talbot's more restrained approach carried the day.[9]

Talbot's visit to South Asia had been marked by widespread media speculation that he was bringing with him an American proposal to resolve the Kashmir dispute. According to a typical report in the *Hindustan Times*, this "Talbot Plan" called for the creation of an autonomous entity comprising the Kashmir Valley and the Pakistan-held areas of the state. Hindu-majority Jammu and Buddhist-majority Ladakh would remain with India. A joint India-Pakistan guarantee together with some form of UN participation was reportedly being considered to ensure the viability of the arrangement.

The stories prompted considerable interest and hope among Kashmiri dissidents, I found, as I traveled in Kashmir at the time. When I reported this to Talbot in New Delhi, he chuckled. There had never been a Talbot Plan, he told me.[10] And just as well. For Embassy New Delhi was on the mark when it stated: "Much as we share the view that some form of autonomy with or without partition [of the state] is the ultimate way out of the Kashmir impasse, . . . official American association with the concept could be the kiss of death, at least in India."[11]

Embassy Karachi also threw cold water on such an idea. It doubted that the Pakistan government would accept Kashmiri autonomy should India move in that direction. In its view, Pakistan would eventually be prepared to depart from its longtime position only if the degree of autonomy was essentially complete and the Kashmiris wanted that solution. Moreover, Pakistan would insist on having a role equal to India's in providing guarantees.[12]

While uninformed parties argued over the nonexistent Talbot Plan, Pakistan's efforts to win UN backing for its Kashmir initiative went nowhere. Faced with an almost total lack of enthusiasm in the Security Council, where the United States and other members tried unsuccessfully to persuade them to drop the issue entirely, the Pakistanis eventually abandoned their hope of getting a resolution or even a consensus statement adopted. In mid-May they settled for a statement by the council president that merely noted that some members supported and others opposed the UN secretary general's involvement in facilitating India-Pakistan negotiations. For their part, the Indians continued to insist that Kashmir was an integral part of India. They held to this hard line throughout the proceedings.

The outcome pleased Bowles. He had warned in almost apocalyptic terms of the damage American backing for another council resolution on Kashmir would have on relations with India. It would be read there, he said, as "total capitulation to Pakistani pressures to support an action which the Indians know we deplored."[13] Bowles's pro-India reputation probably led Washington policymakers to pay limited attention to this alarmist forecast.

As UN consideration of the Kashmir issue stumbled to a close, attention shifted to the activities of Sheikh Abdullah and the possibility that he could play an important role in progress toward a settlement through a bilateral India-Pakistan agreement. Following his release from jail in April 1964, Abdullah was the New Delhi house guest of Prime Minister Nehru. The two had been good friends before Nehru had approved Abdullah's dismissal and arrest in 1953, and the sheikh was seemingly prepared to forgive if not forget. Abdullah then returned to the Valley, where he was wildly acclaimed. As I found when I visited the state a few weeks before his triumphal progress, he was still the "Lion of Kashmir."

The embassies in Karachi and New Delhi drew different conclusions about the significance for U.S. policy of Abdullah's return to the center of the Kashmir political stage. Ambassador McConaughy considered it one of several factors that made the status quo on the subcontinent virtually impossible to retain. (The others were the gradual decline of the ailing Nehru's leadership, heightened communal tensions in both India and Pakistan, and New Delhi's projected five-year military buildup.) McConaughy said that while the Ayub government had officially welcomed Abdullah's release in anticipation of a basic change in Kashmir's status, it recognized that the unpredictable sheikh might come up with a Kashmir proposal acceptable to the Kashmiris but unpalatable to some elements in Pakistan—and without Pakistan's participation in preliminary negotiations. Concern that it might be frozen out of what is now often called the "New Delhi–Srinagar dialogue" has been a recurrent theme in Pakistan's appraisal of Kashmir developments, especially in recent years.

McConaughy worried that such a unilateral Kashmir settlement by India with a "softened-up Abdullah," along with a major Indian military expansion and further deliveries of U.S. equipment, especially sophisticated aircraft, were likely to lead Pakistan to opt out of the Western alliance system. This was not the first time, nor would it be the last, that Embassy Karachi warned Washington about the danger of Ayub's being driven to defect from Pakistan's free-world alignment. The embassy's apprehensions were not shared by Chester Bowles, who would have welcomed Pakistan's breaking its military ties with the West.

McConaughy argued for a more muscular U.S. policy to deal with the unraveling of the subcontinental status quo that he feared. He preferred indirect pressure to direct American involvement in Kashmir negotiations and recommended a temporary slowdown of long-range U.S. commitments to economic and military programs for India and Pakistan until Washington could judge their effect on prospects for a Kashmir settlement triggered by Abdullah's return.[14] By contrast, Bowles called for a hands-off approach. His embassy reported that Abdullah's release had strengthened chauvinist forces in India. The embassy detected only slim prospects for early reconciliation and maintained that outside pressure would be counterproductive.[15]

In late May Abdullah went to Pakistan with Nehru's encouragement and met with Ayub. Talbot recalls that at the time there were many questions in Washington and the subcontinent about Abdullah's goals and strategy.[16] After his meetings in Pakistan, in which he greatly impressed President Ayub, Abdullah stated that he expected that Nehru and Ayub would meet in New Delhi in June to discuss Kashmir. Popular hopes for a breakthrough (which

American officials did not share) reached new highs. They were dashed by Nehru's death on May 27. Abdullah returned to India empty-handed soon after the news reached him in Pakistan-administered Kashmir.

Nehru's passing from the Indian political scene he had dominated for so long sparked great speculation about its possible impact on the Indian government's position on Kashmir, especially since many believed that his Kashmiri heritage had significantly influenced his approach to the issue. Lal Bahadur Shastri, a key member of Nehru's cabinet from Uttar Pradesh in northern India, was quickly elected prime minister as the consensus choice of a "syndicate" of top Congress Party leaders. Embassy New Delhi reported that he was "by far the best bet as successor to Nehru from the point of view of bringing flexible conciliatory influence to bear on the Indian position toward Pakistan."[17] But everyone understood that as a fledgling prime minister with a limited political base, Shastri could not be expected to move boldly on such a sensitive and controversial issue as Kashmir even if he wished to, which was by no means certain. It was also evident that Abdullah, whose relations with Shastri were at best tenuous, would have a sharply reduced role in New Delhi's strategy for dealing with Kashmir.

Prospects for the helpful U.S. role on Kashmir that Ambassador McConaughy sought were not improved by President Johnson's growing dissatisfaction with Pakistan. Annoyed by Karachi's incessant carping about American military assistance to India, which Ayub claimed had eroded Pakistan's ability to meet its obligations to its CENTO and SEATO allies, Johnson pointedly asked the Pakistan ambassador if that was why Ayub had failed to respond to U.S. requests for assistance to Vietnam, an increasingly dominant issue in his administration's foreign policy. In a subsequent discussion with McConaughy, Johnson questioned what America was getting from its assistance to Pakistan (and India). Johnson instructed McConaughy to tell Ayub that while he regretted Ayub's feeling that it was necessary to reevaluate the desirability of the U.S.-Pakistan alliance, he recognized Pakistan's right as a sovereign nation to do so. "Regrettable as it might be," Johnson added, "we would have to reexamine ours also, if Pakistan did so." In his view, neither side would settle the Kashmir dispute. He saw the issue as another example of foreign countries repaying America for its efforts by involving it in their own feuds.[18] Johnson's outburst foreshadowed the "plague on both your houses" approach to India and Pakistan (and Kashmir) that became the dominant theme in U.S. South Asia policy a year later.

Following Johnson's harsh criticism, Washington's limited diplomatic activity on the Kashmir issue diminished further. Although Rusk and others at the State Department became concerned by reports of an increase in the frequency and scale of violations along the cease-fire line, the secretary saw no advantage in another airing of the issue at the Security Council. The administration moved away from this noninterventionist approach briefly in December 1964, when India announced major moves to integrate Kashmir more fully into the Indian Union. But even then Washington confined its diplomatic activity to expressions of disapproval. Talbot reaffirmed that the United States did not recognize any Indian action to settle the Kashmir dispute unilaterally and warned that the moves might induce Pakistan to call for yet another Security Council meeting. He observed that this would benefit neither India-Pakistan nor U.S.-India relations. Undeterred by Washington's rebuke, India not only declined to change its integration policy but accelerated it.[19]

The Kashmir issue remained a secondary matter on Washington's South Asia agenda in the first half of 1965. But other important concerns heightened the sense of disillusion with South Asia that Johnson had expressed. These inevitably influenced the way his administration would deal with the India-Pakistan war over Kashmir that broke out in August.

Pakistan's warming relations with the two major Communist powers figured importantly in these concerns. Ayub's visit to Beijing in March highlighted his efforts to strengthen his government's ties with the People's Republic. Embassy Karachi ruefully reported that Ayub's repeated expressions of admiration for Chinese leaders as models for other Afro-Asian countries "created an unfortunate image of a close and increasingly amicable Pakistani relationship with the Chinese in an Afro-Asian context."[20] Ayub's subsequent visit to Moscow, where he assured Soviet leaders that his government would not serve as an instrument of American policy in South Asia, heightened the administration's questioning of Pakistan's value as an ally.

Angered by Pakistan's growing ties with China and its continuing unwillingness to help in Vietnam, Johnson further complicated bilateral relations by abruptly canceling Ayub's scheduled April visit to Washington. At

Johnson's insistence, the administration adopted a tougher policy on American economic assistance to Pakistan and forced a two-month postponement of the annual World Bank–chaired aid-pledging session. According to Harold Saunders of the National Security Council staff, "The postponement was designed to show Ayub that American aid was far from automatic, and to be a forceful reminder that his relations with Communist China and other U.S.-Pakistani difficulties could endanger his nation's economy."[21]

U.S.-India ties were less strained but far from good. When Johnson cancelled Ayub's state visit he also decided, over Ambassador Bowles's frantic objections, to cancel one by Prime Minister Shastri that was to have followed. The sudden, inadequately explained action rankled the Indians for a long time. The administration also declined to provide high-performance aircraft and assistance for their production in India. The Indians instead acquired MiG-21s from the Soviet Union.

As he had with Pakistan, but for different reasons, Johnson also took a hard look at U.S. economic assistance to India. The president and others in his administration and in Congress were dissatisfied with Indian economic policies and performance, especially in the food and agriculture sector. (By contrast, Washington was pleased with Pakistan's economic progress. This had made it a poster child for American aid programs.) The P.L.-480 food grain program, which had failed to deliver the boost in Indian farm production its supporters had hoped for, came under particular presidential fire.

An outbreak of fighting in April between Indian and Pakistani military forces in the contested wastes of the Rann (marsh) of Kutch near the Arabian Sea further roiled American relations with both countries. Although Washington deferred to the British in the effort to bring about a cease-fire and eventual settlement of the dispute, it gave the conflict a good deal of attention, especially because Pakistan was evidently using U.S. Military Assistance Program (MAP) equipment contrary to bilateral agreements.

Some Washington policymakers feared that the Kutch fighting might lead the Indians to retaliate where the odds were more in their favor, perhaps in Kashmir. As the British peacemaking effort faltered, Bowles urgently warned that unless India was immediately given some realistic alternative, the situation could spin out of control. He feared that their 1962 defeat by China put the Indians under heavy political and emotional pressure to "let fly at a place and time of their own choosing if only to prove that they are not doormats."[22] Assistant Secretary Talbot shared the ambassador's concern. In his view, an Indian counterstrike in Kashmir or elsewhere would be madness, but "fear of flabbiness and humiliation seems to have struck so deep that such a catastrophic decision cannot be ruled out."[23] Looking for ways to head it off, Ambassador McConaughy recommended that Washington warn the Indians that it would regard a retaliatory attack as unwarranted aggression calling for assistance to Pakistan in accordance with U.S. commitments.[24]

Indian seizure of two Pakistani picket posts along the cease-fire line in the Kargil sector on May 17 suggested that New Delhi had in fact chosen Kashmir as the site for a countermove. (Ironically, the Pakistanis selected the same area for an offensive operation thirty-four years later.) Although Washington was understandably troubled by this military escalation, it was relieved that a fortnight after the seizure of the posts, the two sides both continued to maintain publicly that the fighting along the cease-fire line was a familiar game with tacitly recognized ground rules. The administration was more concerned by the call some in the Pakistan government were making for the infiltration of irregulars across the line to stir up violence in the Valley.[25]

Washington wondered whether the reputedly docile Kashmiris would be willing and able to contest Indian control if Pakistan tried to foment an uprising. The situation in the Valley had changed since the heady days following Sheikh Abdullah's return to the state little more than a year earlier. With New Delhi's obvious approval, the government of Chief Minister G. M. Sadiq had cracked down on anti-Indian elements, ending a brief period of political liberalization. This was a tacit admission by Sadiq and his Indian sponsors that their efforts to confront Sheikh Abdullah and his supporters on the political plane had failed.

Abdullah himself was again in detention. Outraged by his meeting with Chinese Premier Chou En-lai at an Afro-Asian summit conference in Algiers, the Indian government had arrested him when he returned from his foreign travels.[26] The sheikh's jailing led to widespread demonstrations in the Valley that were harshly suppressed with considerable loss of life. When I visited Kashmir a few weeks later, I found that Srinagar had returned to normal. While the quelling of the disturbances had increased Muslim bitterness toward India and its Kashmiri political designees, it seemed to me that prospects for any large-scale violence in the Valley, Pakistani-inspired or otherwise, were remote absent some unforeseen incident similar to the theft of the Prophet's hair a year and a half earlier. What appeared more likely was that the Kashmiri Muslims would continue to live unhappily with India and the government it had imposed on the state without becoming reconciled to them.[27]

Washington's concern about escalating activity along the cease-fire line mounted when a senior UN military observer reported to Embassy Karachi on June 9, 1965, that the Indian Army had occupied a large salient of high ground west of Kargil and refused to give up the territory.[28] Talbot saw the Indian move as a symptom of the very serious deterioration of India-Pakistan relations evidenced by the fighting in Kutch and the subsequent forward deployment of the armies of both countries at key points along the border.[29] But this anxiety subsided when the Indians withdrew later in June from the areas they had seized and the British succeeded in working out a Kutch settlement. Following their acceptance of the U.K.-brokered pact, Shastri and Ayub agreed to withdraw troops from forward positions along the entire India-Pakistan border, to Washington's satisfaction.

This respite proved short-lived. On the night of August 5–6, Pakistan began a large-scale infiltration of armed personnel across the cease-fire line (Operation Gibraltar) that was designed to spark a Kashmiri popular uprising against Indian rule. Embassy Karachi sent Washington a long and insightful cable assessing the move. In the embassy's view, the Pakistanis had concluded that direct action was the only way to bring the Indians to the conference table. They feared that Indian moves to integrate Kashmir into the Indian Union would confront them with a fait accompli. The disturbances following Sheikh Abdullah's arrest had persuaded them that the situation in Kashmir was unusually favorable. They had been encouraged by their military success in Kutch but feared that the buildup of India's armed forces that began following the Sino-Indian war would soon reach the point where Pakistan faced overwhelming Indian superiority. Although the drafters of the embassy message did not say so, they and other American officials surely recognized that enhanced U.S. assistance to India had contributed to Pakistan's concern that time was running out.

Embassy Karachi held that evidence of internal Indian weakness such as food shortages, economic difficulties, and riots over language policy probably contributed to Pakistan's decision. Pakistani perceptions of Chinese and American reactions might also have figured. The Pakistanis may have concluded that fear of a Chinese attack had been important in the Indian decision not to widen the Kutch conflict and would have the same inhibiting effect in Kashmir. They might also have estimated that American preoccupation with Vietnam would lead the Indians to conclude that Washington would not aid them against Chinese intervention.[30]

The embassy argued it was likely that the Pakistanis had calculated that they could carry out the infiltration without seriously risking a dangerous escalation. It thought that they might also have reckoned that a skillful propaganda campaign could keep the Kashmir issue at the forefront of domestic and international attention for some time even if the situation on the ground proved disappointing. In a later cable, the embassy added that in the Pakistanis' view a full-blown revolution was neither necessary nor desirable for achieving their objectives, which could be to establish an effective underground or carry on open guerrilla warfare, or something in between.[31]

The results of Operation Gibraltar failed to fulfill the Ayub government's hopes and expectations. The Kashmiris did not rise; some even cooperated with the Indian authorities against the infiltrators. The Pakistanis could not develop an effective underground, let alone guerrilla operations. And while the infiltration did indeed bring the Kashmir issue to greater world attention, it did so in ways that did not help Pakistan.

After warning the United States and other major powers that it would have to take "strong countermeasures" if the infiltration did not stop, India again launched attacks across the cease-fire line.[32] Although Komer told President Johnson that "this could be the Rann of Kutch all over again, with each side alleging that the other is using MAP arms," Washington seemed only moderately concerned.[33] On August 19, the State Department advised that it was not necessary to go beyond the current position of urging restraint and using UN machinery while continuing to watch the direction of Kashmir events.[34] Komer's memos became more pressing, but he stopped well short of ringing alarm bells. Kashmir was still regarded in Washington as less important than other aspects of what some saw as a crisis in U.S.-Pakistan relations sparked by the two countries' mutual dissatisfaction with each other's political and security policies. A decision on economic assistance and, closely related to this, the rescheduling of Ayub's visit to Washington, still topped the administration's immediate South Asia agenda.[35]

On August 28, Ambassador Bowles reported that although Pakistan's military activity in Kashmir was generating pressures for escalation, the Shastri government could satisfy Indian public opinion simply by mopping up infiltrators—provided the Pakistanis backed off. Calling for measures that would help ensure that Pakistan stopped the infiltration and reinforce Indian restraint, Bowles urged Washington to warn Karachi that if Pakistan significantly escalated military operations, the United States would suspend arms shipments should it find that Pakistani forces were using MAP-supplied matériel to conduct them.[36]

By the time Bowles sent in this evaluation, the situation on the ground had become even more dangerous. Claiming that its attack was designed to interdict infiltration routes, India moved across the cease-fire line in south-western Kashmir on August 24. On August 30 its forces captured a key mountain pass, eliminating a major Pakistani salient. The following day the State Department told Arthur Goldberg, the U.S. permanent representative to the United Nations, that it was beginning to prepare the groundwork for formal Security Council consideration of the deteriorating situation should that prove desirable or necessary.[37] Bowles argued against this course. He feared it would "likely open Pandora's box, raising temperatures even higher[,] further reducing any leverage we might have in the situation with both parties and probably coming up with little more than admonitions to both sides."[38]

With Indian troops advancing into Azad Kashmir and the Kashmiris in the Valley largely ignoring Pakistan's call for an uprising, the Pakistanis launched the second part of their operation, a major armored thrust (Operation Grand Slam), on September 1. This offensive was designed to cut India's main supply routes to the Valley and to its forces on the southern end of the cease-fire line. Alerting Johnson, Komer accurately noted that the rationale for the attack was that the Pakistanis, having failed to spark a "war of liberation" in Kashmir, might now feel that they had to move in directly to head off a humiliating failure. He wanted the administration to push the

United Nations and perhaps Britain to intervene. Washington should supplement this with "private blasts" at both India and Pakistan.[39]

At a meeting with President Johnson and other officials on September 2, Secretary Rusk stated that the United States would support UN Secretary General U Thant's appeal for an immediate cease-fire and withdrawal of forces. He called for a limited American démarche, principally to query the Pakistanis about their use of U.S.-supplied military equipment. Johnson was cautious in his reply. He said he had found out over the last few months how little influence the United States had with the Pakistanis and the Indians. He wanted U Thant or British prime minister Harold Wilson to take the lead. He did not wish to intervene personally himself and would "like to sit it out a bit."[40] Reflecting the president's position, the State Department instructed Embassies New Delhi and Karachi to reiterate urgently to their host governments the administration's strong concern about use of MAP-supplied equipment in Kashmir. But "at this immediate point," it told them, "we do not believe we should make any démarche to either side as to what we might have to do if fighting escalates, but rather restrict our position essentially to full support for the efforts of the UN secretary general."[41]

In New Delhi Ambassador Bowles watched developments with mounting alarm. Recognizing only too well that his efforts to improve U.S.-Indian relations would fail if India and Pakistan went to war, he made desperate pleas for restraint to Prime Minister Shastri and other senior Indian officials. At the same time, he urged Washington to tell Shastri that if India accepted U Thant's appeal and Pakistan did not, the United States would cut off all military assistance to Karachi. A parallel approach should be made to Ayub. Bowles was told in reply that a decision had been made at the highest level not to engage in direct pressure on either country for the time being but to place primary reliance on the United Nations, where the United States had joined all other Security Council members in passing a resolution calling for restraint.[42]

In Karachi McConaughy agreed with this multilateral approach. But he also wanted Washington to inform India and Pakistan that it would examine its assistance programs in light of their response to U Thant's call, and that once peace had been restored the United States would be ready to assist in "any feasible way" to find a viable solution to the Kashmir problem."[43]

Indian Ambassador to the United States Brajesh Kumar Nehru warned Rusk on September 3 that India would launch an attack across the international border if Pakistan did not withdraw.[44] Three days later, in the early hours of September 6, the Indian army opened a major offensive toward Lahore, the provincial capital of West Pakistan located only a few miles from the border. The previous evening Washington had instructed McConaughy to tell Ayub that American public opinion was likely to force it to cut off military supplies to any country that did not respond positively to U Thant's appeal, essentially Bowles's recommendation. By the time the ambassador called on the Pakistan president, the Indian army had struck.

At their meeting, Ayub told McConaughy that the United States had obligations to Pakistan that it must now fulfill. Uncharacteristically blunt, the ambassador replied by charging that Pakistan was using in Kashmir American military equipment that had been provided to counter Communist aggression, not for local wars. He called on Ayub to accept the secretary general's cease-fire call. Ayub said that Pakistan could not accept a cease-fire unless it was part of a wider agreement on Kashmir.[45]

At this same crucial session, Foreign Minister Bhutto handed McConaughy an aide-memoire calling on the United States to fulfill the terms of the U.S.-Pakistan bilateral security agreement of 1959. This agreement stated that the United States would view any threat to the security, independence, and territorial integrity of Pakistan with the utmost gravity and would take effective action to assist Pakistan to suppress aggression.

Washington subsequently rejected this Pakistani demand. It said the United States was acting to meet the common danger, as called for in the 1959 agreement, by fully supporting immediate UN action to end the hostilities. It did not agree that Pakistan had been the victim of Indian aggression. Citing a report the UN secretary general had issued, it maintained that the immediate crisis had begun with Pakistan's infiltration of armed men across the cease-fire line. Although Washington conceded that the Indians had been the first to send regular forces across the line, Pakistan's response had struck at points India considered vital. The Pakistan government should have been well aware of the risks involved in its action. When McConaughy conveyed this response to Bhutto, the foreign minister retorted angrily that if the only reason for the bilateral agreement was to refer matters to the United Nations, Pakistan might as well not have it. As Ayub had, he rejected a cease-fire unless it was part of a package agreement that ensured a plebiscite in Kashmir.[46]

The escalation of the fighting into a full-scale war created a firestorm on Capitol Hill. Senators and representatives angrily demanded to know why the United States was supplying arms to India and Pakistan that they were using against one another. Within a few days, the administration cut off all military deliveries to both countries. Economic assistance shipments, including P.L.-480 food grain, continued in accordance with existing agreements, but no new economic loans or grants were made.

Although rival claims in Kashmir had sparked the war, American policymakers recognized that the crisis could have much broader implications for U.S. interests. High on their list of potential dangers was the threat of an attack on India by China, which soon began to make ominous noises along the disputed Himalayan border. Rusk in particular became anxious. In a grim message that spelled out a series of nightmare scenarios, he told President Johnson that "if Kashmir were the only issue, the United States could reasonably hope to stand aside. But the whole Western power position in Asia may be at stake."[47] The secretary seemed to be edging toward a more interventionist stand. However, at Johnson's direction the administration continued to look to the United Nations as the primary instrument for bringing an end to the fighting. As president of the Security Council for the month of September, the United States played a major role in UN handling of the crisis. But Johnson, who remained deeply involved in developing policy during the crisis, continued to flatly rule out a unilateral U.S. strategy.

As it pursued this multilateral approach, Washington stayed in close, high-level contact with the Indian and Pakistan governments. Both tried hard to influence U.S. thinking and to explain in a favorable light their positions on U Thant's cease-fire call. The Pakistanis continued to insist that they would not stop fighting until there was a self-executing agreement providing for Kashmiri self-determination. Ayub asked McConaughy: "After all the sacrifices that have been made, how can I explain a decision to throw it all away with nothing but another UN resolution to show [the Pakistani people]?"[48] Responding to Washington's warning about the danger to bilateral relations that Pakistani collusion with the Chinese would arouse, Ayub claimed that he had discouraged Beijing from intervening. Only later did reports emerge that he had briefly visited China, where his calls for military assistance were rebuffed.

Meanwhile, the war on the ground continued. In what was called the biggest tank battle since World War II, the Pakistanis failed to break through into Indian Punjab. The tide began to turn in favor of the Indians, who had the advantage of numbers. The Pakistan army's use of U.S.-supplied tanks and other military equipment despite American assurances to New Delhi that this would not be permitted caused an uproar in India. Embassy New Delhi officials believed that had Pakistan's "U.S. Patton tanks" (as the Indians called them) advanced farther, anti-U.S. demonstrations could have endangered the American community in the capital and elsewhere in India. The embassy dispatched officers to urge private American citizens living north of New Delhi to come to the embassy compound, where temporary housing was arranged for them. Many did. In Pakistan, disillusion with alleged U.S. failure to honor its security commitments became acute, and violent mobs damaged official American installations in Karachi and Lahore.

Rebuffed by the Chinese and under intense international pressure, Pakistan agreed to a cease-fire in place at a dramatic Security Council session in the early hours of September 23. Ayub phoned President Johnson later that morning and expressed confidence that Johnson, "as a man of honor and a gentleman," would see to it that an honorable settlement was reached on Kashmir to prevent "such unfortunate happenings" from occurring again. Johnson assured him that the United States believed that settling the underlying problem was essential. But he added that he could not give Ayub "any assurance of any particular form of settlement." This empty statement was the best the Pakistanis could get from the disgusted American president.[49]

The war was a serious setback—some called it a disaster—for U.S. interests in South Asia. It left the Johnson administration's policy there in tatters. Washington now faced strong antagonism in both Pakistan and India. The overwhelming sentiment in Pakistan was that in failing to honor its treaty obligations, the United States had betrayed a friend and ally in its hour of need. This belief that America was an unfaithful partner, which their dissatisfaction with American policies in later years reinforced, continues to be a powerful influence in shaping Pakistanis' assessments of Washington's reliability in its dealings with them.

In India the United States lost ground for other reasons. Leaders and ordinary people alike angrily asserted that Washington had failed to fulfill its pledge that arms it supplied to Pakistan would not be used against India. Indians were also outraged by the evenhanded policies the United States pursued during the war. Though knowledgeable people recognized that the cutoff of American arms deliveries hurt Pakistan more than it did India, many Indians contended that Washington was wrong in equating the two countries when it made its decisions on military assistance and other issues. Recognition that as the status quo power India in effect won the war—by not losing it—eventually reduced this bitterness toward the United States.

As Washington sought to deal with the unpromising situation the war had caused, the UN-crafted cease-fire remained tenuous. This state of suspended animation in Kashmir and the Punjab was dangerous. Each side still occupied territory that the other had held before hostilities began. Pakistan continued to insist that withdrawal go hand in hand with the creation of machinery for a Kashmir settlement. India hinted that the prewar cease-fire line was no longer valid. Embassy New Delhi reported a surge of nationalist fervor in India. In this mood, it said, the Indians were highly unlikely to compromise on Kashmir. No Indian government could yield to Pakistan by negotiations what the Pakistanis had tried and failed to gain by force.[50] In Pakistan, where Ambassador McConaughy found U.S. prestige at an all-time low, the atmosphere was no better.[51]

Johnson was of no mind to try to broker a peace agreement. At the United Nations and elsewhere, Washington preferred to use deliberately fuzzy language in dealing with Pakistan's continuing demand that any settlement had to provide a specific, workable formula for the resolution of the Kashmir dispute. No one in the Johnson administration seems to have objected to this hands-off approach. At the National Security Council, McGeorge Bundy and Robert Komer reinforced it when they told the president in early October: "We should not kid ourselves about an early Kashmir settlement. American fidgeting over Kashmir will only make us trouble with India and arouse false hopes in Pakistan." The two men found that

"Kashmir fixers are a plentiful and dangerous commodity." In their view, the United States should limit itself to calling on both sides to accept a political process.[52]

On September 18, while fighting was still going on, Soviet prime minister Alexei Kosygin offered Shastri and Ayub Moscow's good offices to set up a meeting between them to work out a Kashmir settlement. He suggested Tashkent in Soviet Central Asia (now the capital of independent Uzbekistan) as its venue. Both New Delhi and Karachi told Moscow that they appreciated this initiative but did not find the timing propitious. The Indians sounded out Ambassador Bowles informally on U.S. reaction to the Kosygin approach. Bowles reported to Washington that although it was difficult to assess Soviet objectives, Moscow might have taken the gambit to counter the Chinese. But he judged the proposal a dead-end street because the Pakistanis were likely to refuse.[53]

When Kosygin renewed this offer after the cease-fire, the administration reacted favorably. Bundy and Komer gleefully told Johnson that the Soviets would find themselves in the same box the United States had been in. They thought that "if by remote chance" Moscow did work out a Kashmir deal, Washington would gain as much from it as the Russians would.[54] When Ayub finally made his postponed visit to the United States in December, acting secretary of state George Ball told him that Washington welcomed the Soviet initiative. Ball urged him to approach Tashkent "with the hope of accomplishing something."[55] In a private session, Johnson encouraged Ayub to do his best and told him that if Tashkent failed "we would try something else." But Johnson also warned Ayub that he should not be under any illusion that the United States could force a settlement. "If we were able to do so we would have done so already," he said.[56]

Reviewing the U.S. attitude toward Tashkent in an oral history statement he made for the Johnson Library, Dean Rusk recalled: "We encouraged the Russians to go ahead with the Tashkent idea, because we felt we had nothing to lose. If they succeeded we would gain from that fact. If the Russians failed at Tashkent, at least [they] would have the experience of some of the frustration that we had had for twenty years in trying to sort out things between India and Pakistan. As a matter of fact, in a semi-joking way, I told the Russian ambassador that if he wanted them we would be glad to give him all our old memos on efforts that we had made over the past twenty years to try to solve things between India and Pakistan as a part of their preparation for Tashkent, but that did not prove necessary."[57]

At a difficult six-day conference at Tashkent in early January 1966, Kosygin persuaded Ayub and Shastri against the odds to reach an accord. But the declaration they signed there did not resolve the Kashmir dispute, nor did it establish any new mechanism for its settlement. It merely restored the status quo ante bellum along the Kashmir cease-fire line and the international India-Pakistan border. The shopworn, ultimately meaningless phrases of the declaration could not disguise this outcome. Washington publicly welcomed the agreement, which Johnson termed constructive. Prime Minister Shastri had died of a heart attack hours after signing the agreement, and Johnson had Vice President Hubert Humphrey pass word to Kosygin when the two met in New Delhi at Shastri's funeral that he was gratified by the outcome of the Soviet effort.[58] Formally congratulating Kosygin on his role a few days later, the president said he was sure the Soviet leader shared his view that the agreement left many difficult problems between India and Pakistan unresolved.[59] Johnson later told Humphrey that Ayub had reached an accommodation with India in good part to maintain his credibility with the United States.[60] American diplomats told their NATO allies in an upbeat confidential briefing that if the progress toward a more durable peace sparked by Tashkent could be sustained, this would far outweigh whatever gains the Soviets had made there.[61]

This acquiescent American attitude toward Soviet involvement vividly highlighted how sharply Washington's assessment of the importance of South Asia had changed between 1962 and 1965. For years, successive U.S. administrations had sought to limit Moscow's influence in the region. Containing Communism had in fact been the principal rationale for Washington's security alliance with Pakistan and its large-scale economic assistance programs there and in India. But by January 1966 the Johnson administration was more than willing to pass the seemingly poisoned South Asian chalice to the Soviet Union. The prospect of Moscow acting as a countervailing force to Beijing in the region played some role in bringing about this remarkable American accommodation. But the basic reason for it was that Washington, frustrated by the war and the events of the two years leading up to it, had concluded that efforts to bring about a reconciliation between India and Pakistan would not work and were not worth the trouble given the limited value for American interests in strong political and security engage-ments with either country.

Washington's increasing preoccupation with Vietnam reinforced the view that India and Pakistan, with their apparently intractable internecine strife over Kashmir and other lesser disputes, no longer deserved the attention given them in the 1950s and early 1960s. The United States continued to assist the South Asian countries to promote economic development and meet humanitarian challenges. But its assessment of the political value of India and Pakistan in helping it achieve its broader cold war objectives was sharply downgraded.

This reappraisal applied in particular to the Kashmir issue. Almost a quarter-century would pass before the outbreak of a widespread insurgency in the Valley, soon abetted by Pakistan, again prompted the United States to pay serious attention to the impact that rival claims to the state had for wider American interests.

6

Off the Radar Screen—
And Back Again

The postwar quiet in India-Pakistan relations and in Kashmir itself reduced even further the attention U.S. policymakers gave to the state during the rest of the 1960s. As the Tashkent agreement stipulated, the two countries withdrew their forces from areas they had seized during the fighting and cut back their military presence along the cease-fire line. Although wholesale rigging again accompanied the elections held in Indian Kashmir in early 1967, they passed peacefully. By December 1967 the Indian government felt secure enough about the situation on the ground in Kashmir to release Sheikh Abdullah from detention, though he was later forced to leave the state and the Plebiscite Front party he had recently organized was banned. But as I observed during visits I made there in those years, the political calm that fell over Indian-held Kashmir did not mean that the Muslims of the Valley had become reconciled to their tie to New Delhi.

Meanwhile, India and Pakistan slowly and grudgingly restored the links they had ruptured during the war. To American policymakers, it seemed that neither had any enthusiasm for this "Tashkent process" or any serious interest in more far-reaching efforts to develop better bilateral relations. In any event, both governments were obliged to focus on the growing economic and political problems they faced at home. In Pakistan the failure of Ayub Khan's regime to wrest the Valley from the Indians, the growing demand of East Pakistanis for a fairer share of national power and wealth, and a spreading awareness that the Ayub regime's vaunted economic achievements had mainly benefited wealthy Pakistanis all weakened the sick and aging field marshal and put him on the political defensive. In India Jawaharlal Nehru's daughter, Indira Gandhi, faced serious problems on a variety of political, economic, and social fronts as she sought to consolidate her power following the Congress Party leadership's consensus decision to make her Shastri's successor as prime minister. Preoccupied by these daunting domestic matters, neither New Delhi nor Islamabad seemed interested in changing the postwar status quo either through negotiations or armed conflict.

The United States for its part urged both governments to maintain and implement what it hopefully called "the spirit of Tashkent." To Washington this meant their seeking to achieve progress in resolving lesser problems while at least undertaking to discuss the Kashmir issue. The Johnson administration welcomed the meetings that the Indian and Pakistani foreign ministers held in 1966. But it was not inclined to use its reduced leverage in the two countries to try to influence their discussions. After the trauma of the 1965 war, there would be no replay of Kennedy's 1962–63 intervention.

Dramatic developments in Pakistan in 1969 set the stage for further India-Pakistan conflict. A collapse of political and popular support for his government in both wings of the country led President Ayub to give way to a martial law regime headed by General Agha Mohammad Yahya Khan, the army chief of staff. Unlike other military leaders who have taken power in Pakistan in more recent coups, Yahya not only promised early free and fair elections but actually held them.

The result of this 1970 balloting was a disaster for the unity of the country. The landslide victory in East Pakistan of a party dedicated to maximum autonomy for the province within a weak confederation sparked an unprecedented crisis that Yahya's military government and the newly elected political leadership in the two wings of the country could not resolve. The army's crackdown in March 1971 on pro-autonomy forces led to virtual civil war in East Pakistan, a massive flight of Hindu refugees to India, the growing involvement of the Gandhi government, and, in December 1971, a full-scale India-Pakistan war that the much larger Indian forces quickly won. The outcome was the dismemberment of united Pakistan, the creation of independent Bangladesh, and international acceptance of India as the dominant power in South Asia. Pakistan, which had lost more than half its population, would no longer be in a position to challenge the victorious Indians on Kashmir or other bilateral disputes. Or so it seemed.

The administration of Richard M. Nixon, which took office in January 1969, abandoned Washington's reluctance to become politically involved in India-Pakistan confrontations and pursued policies during 1971 that famously "tilted" toward Islamabad. Nixon and his national security adviser, Henry A. Kissinger, viewed the crisis in a global cold war context. Their interest in enlisting Communist China in a new international framework designed to counter Soviet power significantly influenced the way they dealt with it. They paid only limited attention to the crisis's South Asian origin and scope. Following India's victory, Nixon and Kissinger lost much of the interest they had so suddenly taken in subcontinental developments. The outcome of the war reinforced Washington's earlier desire to extricate itself politically from the region.

The 1971 war was the only conflict between India and Pakistan not sparked by their competing claims on Kashmir. Although the security situation in the Valley had begun to deteriorate in 1970, Kashmir played only a marginal role in the war. The United States, the international community, and the two antagonists focused on developments in East Pakistan.

But some American policymakers also worried about what might happen in the Kashmir region during the fighting. Their concerns deepened when in the opening days of the war, the Pakistan Army launched an offensive into Indian-held Kashmir at the same place it had unrolled Operation Grand Slam six years earlier. The attack led U.S. Army chief of staff William Westmoreland and other senior officials to conclude that Pakistan was trying to seize Kashmir as compensation for the eventual loss of its eastern wing.[1] Whatever Pakistan's motives, the attack soon fizzled out. Kashmir was subsequently never more than a minor theater of military operations. The Valley remained quiet throughout the war.

A few days after Westmoreland had worried about a chimerical Kashmir-for-East Pakistan swap, Henry Kissinger waded in. The national security adviser was greatly upset by a CIA report that Prime Minister Gandhi had told her cabinet colleagues she would not accept a UN call for a cease-fire until India had "liberated" the "southern part of Azad Kashmir." This presumably meant all of the Pakistan-administered part of the state other than the remote areas in the far north.[2] The State Department asked L. K. Jha, the Indian ambassador to the United States, to provide New Delhi's assurance that India had no intention of taking any Pakistan-held territory, including any part of Azad Kashmir. Jha said that India had never planned to annex territory in West Pakistan. He was less certain about Azad Kashmir and said he would have to query his government.[3]

Indian foreign minister Swaran Singh later told George H. W. Bush, the American permanent representative to the United Nations, that India would not provide an unequivocal commitment to desist from taking any Azad Kashmir territory. The Indians were prepared to say only that they had no "major ambitions" there. They informed the future president that even in peacetime they had talked with the Pakistanis about minor rectifications of the cease-fire line. Considering their long-standing claim that all of the old princely state was an integral part of India, this was probably the farthest they could go in easing U.S. concerns. After the fighting ended, the international India-Pakistan border was restored but the two armies stayed where they were in Kashmir. The new line between them, renamed the Line of Control, was only slightly different from the 1949–71 cease-fire line.[4]

The Simla agreement, which Gandhi and Pakistan president Zulfikar Ali Bhutto signed in July 1972, effectively removed the Kashmir issue from the international stage for almost two decades. In effect a peace treaty ending the 1971 war, the agreement spelled out a process for resuming normal bilateral relations. Its clauses on Kashmir prescribed a new approach, but did not formally resolve the dispute.

The two countries agreed to settle their differences, including Kashmir, by peaceful means through bilateral negotiations. They declared that the principles and purposes of the UN Charter would govern future relations, a gratuitous provision designed to soothe Pakistani opinion. They also undertook to respect the new dividing line in Kashmir without prejudice to their existing claims. The agreement did not mention a plebiscite or refer to the UN resolutions calling for one.

There was an important policy reason for this. India wanted to remove the United Nations as an actor in the Kashmir dispute. The maps were drawn up and the treaty worked out without a UN presence. Even the renaming of the dividing line reflected this Indian determination to flout the international organization. The old 1949 cease-fire line was devised with UN help; the new 1972 Line of Control was not. Some observers have maintained that in an eleventh-hour one-on-one meeting with Gandhi, Bhutto secretly agreed to make the status quo a permanent settlement. What is important is that the two countries put the Kashmir issue into cold storage. It remained there until the outbreak of an insurrection in the Indian-held portion of the state at the end of the 1980s.

The United States hailed the Simla agreement, which the State Department termed an important step toward establishing a durable peace in South Asia.[5] Less publicly, American policymakers recognized that the agreement gave them an unassailable, thoroughly respectable rationale for remaining on the sidelines, where Washington's consistently unhappy experience in dealing with the Kashmir issue had persuaded them was the best place to be. Aware that it could do little if anything to help resolve the dispute, the United States was cheerfully prepared to let the Indians and Pakistanis deal with the issue themselves. If they chose to disregard the problem and allow the status quo to become a de facto settlement—as seemed likely throughout the 1970s and 1980s—that would be fine with Washington.[6]

Successive American administrations followed this satisfying hands-off approach. They confined their activity to gently encouraging the two sides from time to time to move forward toward a settlement. When the Indians and Pakistanis failed to make progress, they saw no reason for concern. They were reassured by the continuing quiet on the ground in Kashmir and by the apparent acceptance of the status quo by the Muslims of the Valley and the Pakistan government and people.

Important political developments in Kashmir reinforced U.S. determination to remain uninvolved. Recognizing the post-1971 India-Pakistan power balance, Sheikh Abdullah came to terms with the Indian government. With Indira Gandhi's support he became state chief minister in 1974, two decades after he had been dismissed from that position and imprisoned with her father's connivance. The state's political future seemed settled and was no longer a matter for diplomatic concern or media attention. Few if any suspected that this situation would prove deceptive and that the Kashmir issue would return to the international stage in a more dangerous way than ever before.

Internal developments in the mid- and late-1980s radically changed Kashmir's political and security landscape, however. Sheikh Abdullah died in office in 1982, five years after winning a vote of confidence in the state's first arguably free and fair election. His son and successor, Farooq Abdullah, a medical doctor, did not have the political acumen, the leadership ability, or the iconic stature of the Lion of Kashmir. Soon afterward, the Indian government resumed the unscrupulous political manipulation that had long been the hallmark of New Delhi's dealings with the state.

The shameless rigging of the 1987 state elections to assure the victory of a coalition New Delhi favored accelerated the deterioration of the political situation. It also intensified the Valley Muslims' sense of alienation from India. This feeling was especially strong among younger people, many of them angered and frustrated by the sham that democratic rule had again so evidently become in the state. Law and order in the Valley worsened in a series of violent developments—riots, strikes, unauthorized demonstrations, destruction of property, and assassination of government officials and supporters. Many of the militants who engaged in these acts called for Kashmir's separation from India, either as an independent state or to join Pakistan.

Kashmiri dissidents were also influenced by international developments. The Soviet withdrawal from Afghanistan in 1989 inspired them to believe that bold action could also end Indian control over Kashmir. Later, this sense that things were changing—or could be changed—was reinforced by the breakup of the Soviet Union and Yugoslavia and the emergence of independent republics in Muslim Central Asia. Some dissidents were convinced that Islam was on the march and that Kashmir should and could play an important part in that historic movement.

The central and state governments handled the rapidly deteriorating situation in Kashmir ineptly and haphazardly. The gathering crisis reached its point of no return in December 1989, when militants kidnapped Rubaiya, the twenty-three-year-old daughter of Mufti Mohammed Sayeed, the home minister in the newly installed Indian coalition government led by Prime Minister V. P. Singh. As home minister, the mufti was the cabinet member responsible for India's internal security. A Kashmiri from the Valley, he was the first Muslim ever appointed to that powerful post.

The Jammu and Kashmir Liberation Front (JKLF), a separatist group that advocated independence for Kashmir, took responsibility for the kidnapping.

The JKLF demanded that the authorities release five jailed militants in return for its freeing the minister's daughter. During the five tense days of negotiations that culminated in the five-for-one exchange, Washington strongly urged Pakistan to intervene with Rubaiya's captors to secure her release. The Pakistanis assured the Americans that they had already done so.

The kidnapping and its denouement sparked a vast popular upheaval. In Srinagar and other Valley cities and towns, thousands marched in defiance of curfews and police cordons to demand *azadi*—literally independence—for Kashmir. As violence surged in January 1990, government authority in the Valley virtually collapsed. Hundreds of Kashmiri civilians were killed. New Delhi ordered in the army to reinforce police and paramilitary units, dismissed the badly shaken Kashmir state government, and placed the state under central control.

Washington had paid limited attention to the situation in Kashmir as it worsened in 1988 and 1989. American South Asia policymakers had other, more pressing issues on their plates. The U.S.-supported effort to force the Soviets out of Afghanistan had reached its crucial endgame phase. The ongoing Indian and Pakistani nuclear programs continued to attract Washington's serious attention. Administration efforts to supply a second tranche of F-16 aircraft to Pakistan ran into problems on Capitol Hill. In Sri Lanka Tamil insurgents battled against an Indian peacekeeping force, and a second civil war broke out pitting government forces against radical elements within the Sinhalese majority community. Highly publicized disturbances in the Indian Punjab triggered by Sikh demands for independence seemed considerably more dangerous to U.S. interests and had greater resonance in domestic American politics than did the much fainter rumblings in Kashmir. Political instability in both India and Pakistan and the evident frailty of their new and inexperienced coalition governments also raised concern.

Few in the U.S. government expected the growing violence in Kashmir to spin out of control, as it did at the turn of the decade. Like other observers, they were stunned by the speed with which public order dissolved in the Valley. William Clark, the career diplomat who assumed charge of Embassy New Delhi in December 1989 just before the Rubaiya Sayeed kidnapping, recalled that his Indian contacts told him when he first arrived that the situation in the Punjab was much more worrisome.[7] It was not that the embassy did not know that trouble was brewing in the Valley. Walter Andersen, an officer in the political section of Embassy New Delhi whose beat included Kashmir, remembers that in reports he prepared following visits there in 1988 and 1989, he had mentioned the rising disaffection, the lack of a coherent government response, and the dangers that lay ahead.[8] But the embassy's awareness of the problem did not lead it to anticipate the blowup. As R. Grant Smith, an "old India hand" who was deputy chief of mission from 1988 to 1991, put it, "We didn't expect the Kashmiris to do anything about it." So he and his colleagues were astonished when they saw TV clips of the huge demonstrations in the Valley.[9] Traveling in the subcontinent on official (non-Kashmir-related) business in January 1990 with Under Secretary of State for Political Affairs Robert Kimmitt, Teresita Schaffer, the deputy assistant secretary of state for South Asia, also recollects being surprised by the magnitude of the uprising. She phoned the State Department from Embassy New Delhi to make certain that her colleagues there were giving the matter their full attention. (They assured her that they were.)[10]

American officials who dealt with South Asia continued to pay careful heed to Kashmir during the early 1990s, as they would later. But it is important to recognize that dangerous and troubling as the Kashmir issue was, it very rarely got top billing on Washington's South Asia agenda in those years. Both the George H. W. Bush and first Clinton administrations gave higher priority to efforts to dissuade India and Pakistan from developing nuclear weapons. Pakistan's nuclear activities obliged the Bush administration to cut off U.S. economic and security assistance to Islamabad in October 1990, and the fallout from that congressionally mandated decision became a major focus of Washington's relations with Islamabad for years afterward. The effort to influence Pakistan and other regional states to support U.S.-led efforts to force Iraq to withdraw from Kuwait following Saddam Hussein's seizure of the emirate in August 1990 was another agenda item that in late 1990 and early 1991 loomed larger for Washington than did Kashmir and India-Pakistan relations more generally. The volatile political situation in Afghanistan also ranked high on America's South Asian list of policy priorities both in Bush's last years and after Clinton entered the White House in January 1993.

Washington nonetheless soon recognized that the uprising in the Valley posed problems for the United States that went well beyond those sparked by the Kashmir-related crises so troubling to American administrations in the pre-Simla era. Most critical was the danger that a combination of draconian Indian measures to suppress the rebellion and Pakistani cross-border efforts to abet it would prompt a confrontation that could escalate into a South Asian nuclear war. India had not conducted another nuclear test after its 1974 "peaceful nuclear explosion" and Pakistan had never undertaken one. But it was widely believed in Washington that both countries had the know-how and the access to critical components to develop nuclear weapons quickly if they chose to.

Well before the outbreak of the massive uprising, Indian and Pakistani officials began blaming one another for the violence in Kashmir. As the security situation in the Valley deteriorated, their mutual allegations became increasingly charged. India accused Pakistan of directly inciting subversion, violence, and terrorism and claimed that the Pakistanis were providing the militants with money, training, and arms. Pakistan denied these charges and insisted that the Indians were trying to turn it into a scapegoat for troubles of their own making. It called on India to accept a plebiscite to determine the future of the state as called for in UN resolutions. This evident flouting of the bilateral approach spelled out in the Simla agreement brought angry retorts from New Delhi.

Washington concluded that Pakistan had not triggered the Kashmir upheaval. In its view, the massive disturbances had been primarily a spontaneous outbreak. Both American ambassadors on the scene, Clark in New Delhi and Robert Oakley, the influential and well-informed senior Foreign Service officer at the helm in Islamabad, concurred. So did other foreign diplomats in South Asia. When Indian foreign secretary S. K. Singh came to Washington in January 1990, even he acknowledged to State Department officials that the insurgency was basically home grown. (The Indians soon discarded this talking point.)

But if the Pakistanis were not significantly involved in fomenting the outbreak, Pakistan government organizations, especially the Inter-Services Intelligence Directorate, could not long resist the temptation to fish in troubled Kashmiri waters. The intelligence service, widely known as ISI, had a decade of experience equipping, training, and providing logistical support to the Afghan mujahedin. It made use of its expertise and contacts among these jihadists to ratchet up the difficulties the Indians faced in Kashmir. Moreover, as Dennis Kux points out, "Quite apart from providing a means to support self-determination for Kashmir . . . helping the insurgency was also regarded as a fit way to pay India back for its support of the East Pakistan independence movement and the dismemberment of Pakistan in 1971."[11]

Pakistan government efforts in Kashmir were supplemented by the activity of the small Jamaat-i-Islami party and other Muslim extremist organizations that Islamabad readily sanctioned and probably helped arrange. Pakistan's deliberate introduction of Islamic militancy into the Kashmir equation was at the expense of traditional secular militant organizations, most notably the Jammu and Kashmir Liberation Front. The Pakistan-sponsored insurgents rejected the concept that self-determination might lead to an independent Kashmir. Their goal was the state's integration with Pakistan. Pro-Pakistan militants assassinated some of the leaders of the JKLF and likeminded organizations, and membership in these groups sharply declined. Ambassador Oakley recalls that Pakistani policymakers, flush with the victory in Afghanistan, told him that the combination of Islamic zeal and Afghan nationalism had defeated the powerful Soviet Union, and the same should be true when Islam was systematically injected into Kashmir.[12] Moreover, with the departure of Soviet troops from Afghanistan, militants who had been fighting there became available to stir up trouble for the Indians. These factors would have momentous, highly perilous consequences.

Pakistani public opinion, especially in the Punjab, strongly sympathized with the Kashmiri insurgents. Although most Pakistanis had long been willing to accept the post-Simla status quo, reports of the rising of their fellow Muslims and the harsh Indian countermeasures that followed soon made Kashmir a highly emotional issue for them once again.

Whatever the extent of Pakistani backing for the Kashmiri militants before and during the mass uprising, a crisis in India-Pakistan relations soon developed. In their careful study of these events, P. R. Chari, Pervaiz Iqbal Cheema, and Stephen Philip Cohen conclude that Pakistan's support—and, specifically, Pakistani transfer to Kashmir of militants who had been fighting against Communists in Afghanistan—was at the heart of the crisis. The three coauthors found that "it was the suspicion that India would move militarily against the training camps organized [by the Pakistanis] for the militants [in Azad Kashmir] that raised the possibility of Pakistan military escalation, which could have led on to a nuclear response "[13] The presence in both New Delhi and Islamabad of weak, inexperienced, and insecure governments fearful of being branded insufficiently resolute by powerful rivals and outraged publics heightened the danger of a confrontation. As would become even more evident following the Indian and Pakistani nuclear weapons tests in 1998, U.S. concern about another conflict and, closely linked with it, a fear that such a war could lead to a nuclear exchange, became the major drivers in determining Washington's post–cold war South Asia policy. U.S. interest in helping the two countries reach a Kashmir settlement, though obviously linked to the nuclear issue, was a secondary consideration.

The United States soon became involved in efforts to defuse the dangerous situation, which had been made worse by irresponsible talk of war by senior Indian and Pakistani leaders. These American initiatives grew more urgent when both countries began military deployments in early 1990 that the other side considered threatening. As the confrontation developed, Ambassadors Clark and Oakley worried that an exercise in mutual force escalation might develop similar to one that had roiled India-Pakistan relations three years earlier. At that time, India had conducted its largest-ever military maneuvers (Operation Brasstacks) close to the Pakistan border, and the Pakistanis, fearing that the maneuvers might be a cover for an attack, countered with a buildup of their forces. The two envoys, who enjoyed a mutual rapport often absent in relations between American ambassadors serving in India and Pakistan, urged the State Department to weigh in at the top levels of both governments. They also recommended that the United States appeal to the Soviet Union and China to make parallel representations to both governments. The department agreed. Moscow and Beijing subsequently brought their influence to bear, the Soviets in New Delhi, the Chinese in Islamabad, as did several Western European countries.

The two armed forces tended to overreact to one another's movements, and Washington's initial interventions were designed to reduce their largely unwarranted concerns. Fairly early in the crisis both the Indians and the Pakistanis recognized the usefulness for them of this U.S role, which included embassy defense attachés in both countries assessing army deployments and passing their intelligence on to the other side about what was *not* taking place. The attachés found little evidence of provocative military activity. With this information in hand, the United States was able to help damp down the unjustified mutual suspicions that had been fueled by the habitual tendency of the Indian and Pakistani intelligence services to engage in wild worse-case reporting.

However, both governments continued to find themselves under strong domestic political pressure to take tougher measures—Islamabad to support the Kashmiri "freedom fighters," New Delhi to deal more firmly with Pakistan-supported "terrorists" slipping into the Valley. Despite the success the two embassies achieved in reassuring their host governments about the limited nature of military deployments in border areas, some American policymakers and intelligence analysts continued to worry about the danger of escalation. (None reportedly believed that war was imminent, however.) In mid-April 1990, Under Secretary Kimmitt, who had become a key South Asia policymaker in the Bush administration, publicly called attention to "a growing risk of miscalculation which could spin dangerously out of control." He urged both sides to take "immediate steps to reduce the level of tension by lowering rhetoric and avoiding provocative troop deployments, and instead to devote their energies to addressing this issue through dialogue and negotiations."[14]

The following month Washington announced that it was sending a special envoy, Deputy National Security Adviser Robert Gates, an experienced intelligence officer, to India and Pakistan. Mentioning President Bush's deep concern about the escalating crisis, which he said the president had discussed with Indian and Pakistani leaders, a White House spokesman declared that a presidential envoy could make a more realistic and accurate appraisal of the situation. A senior U.S. official told the media that Gates's mission "was designed to address the immediate possibility of miscalculation and inadvertent escalation . . ., not the long-term problems besetting the India-Pakistan relationship."[15] This approach, which Gates and his colleagues followed when they visited Islamabad and New Delhi May 19–21, made good sense. As Washington surely recognized, the Indians would once again have rejected a more far-reaching American role.[16]

Gates's visit to Islamabad came at a difficult time in U.S.-Pakistan relations. The Soviet withdrawal from Afghanistan had dramatically lessened

Washington's stake in Pakistan as a "frontline state." Islamabad's nuclear ambitions had consequently returned to the top of the Bush administration's agenda. The Pakistanis feared that the United States would again abandon them, as it had in their view in the mid-1960s. (Four months after the mission, the administration, no longer able to certify that Pakistan did not possess a nuclear explosive device, cut off military and economic assistance as mandated by legislation enacted in 1986, known as the Pressler Amendment.)

Meeting with President Ghulam Ishaq Khan and General Mirza Aslam Beg, the chief of army staff, Gates urged the two leaders to refrain from supporting the Kashmiri insurgents, avoid military deployments the Indians could regard as threatening, and tone down incendiary rhetoric. He offered them U.S. intelligence support to verify a confidence-building regime to be established by India and Pakistan that involved both countries limiting deployment in border areas. He also warned Ghulam Ishaq and Beg that Pakistan could not win a war against India and should not expect U.S. support if one broke out. Gates and his colleagues were not impressed by the Pakistani leaders' insistence that they were not aiding the Kashmir insurgents.[17]

When Gates went on to New Delhi, U.S.-Indian relations had been improving for five years and were on the cusp of the impressive further gains that the end of the cold war and the disintegration of the Soviet Union helped make possible. As a result, the special envoy received a warmer reception from the Indians than they would have given earlier to an American emissary perceived to be "interfering" in South Asian matters. Uncharacteristically for the visit of a senior U.S. official to both countries, it was also friendlier than the grudging welcome Gates and his colleagues had received in Pakistan. This was one of the first significant signs that the Indians were beginning to see the United States as an asset on Kashmir and was part of the larger shift in bilateral relations that would become more apparent later in the decade.

In his meetings with Prime Minister V. P. Singh, Foreign Minister I. K. Gujral, and other senior officials, Gates stressed, as he had to the Pakistanis, the importance of avoiding provocative actions. He also urged the Indians to stop their own meddling in Pakistan's Sindh province and improve their human rights record in Kashmir. And he reiterated the offer of American intelligence support he had made in Islamabad.

Following the Gates mission, the Indian and Pakistan governments adopted a number of confidence-building measures that effectively defused the crisis. (They did not accept a role for U.S. intelligence, however.) Whether they would have undertaken these steps absent Gates's visit and the earlier efforts initiated by Embassies New Delhi and Islamabad remains uncertain. But at a minimum, the U.S. actions helped move the two governments to reduce tensions in a context that avoided either losing face. Ambassador Clark probably had it right when he said that "at the end of the day, I think you could say that both Delhi and Islamabad used Bob Gates and his mission as an excuse . . . to back off positions they had been taking."[18] Ambassador Oakley and Indians and Pakistanis close to the event share this view that the crisis had peaked before Gates reached South Asia. As Chari, Cheema, and Cohen conclude in their study, "The Gates mission . . . certainly could not have hurt, and might indeed have helped the impulse of peace in South Asia."[19]

The mission proved to be the first in a series of skillful and timely U.S. diplomatic interventions over the next fifteen years that were designed to head off or end conflicts ignited by Kashmir-related developments. Like Gates, the senior officials who undertook these later efforts did not offer fresh formulas for a Kashmiri settlement. As he had, they limited themselves to calls on India and Pakistan to take steps that would lessen tensions and eventually lead to a resolution (or effective management) of the problem without direct international involvement.

Washington was also concerned about the worsening human rights situation in the Valley. American policymakers gave the issue high priority and were tenacious in pursuing it. Fostering international respect for human rights had been a major U.S. foreign policy goal since the Carter administration (1977–81) and enjoyed wide congressional and public support. The State Department had begun publishing an annual report assessing the status of human rights in all countries that received U.S. military or economic aid. Recognizing that their human rights record could significantly influence levels of American assistance, foreign governments took these reports seriously.

The State Department assessments issued in the early 1990s were forthright in discussing the dismal human rights situation in Kashmir. They cited many credible allegations that Indian human rights groups had made of abuses by security forces. These included torture of detainees, mass shooting of demonstrators, large-scale arrests, gang rapes, detentions without trial, and extrajudicial killing of prisoners. The reports noted with disapproval the Indian government's refusal to permit visits to Kashmir by international human rights groups such as Amnesty International and the Red Cross. While they focused on human rights violations by government security forces, the annual reports also called attention to abusive behavior by militants such as the killing, kidnapping, and harassing of government officials and political opponents.

The 1991 assessment found that the legal system in Kashmir barely functioned and that no terrorist detainees had been tried for their alleged crimes. Subsequent reports were often even more critical of India's human rights record. The 1993 report, for example, stated that "extrajudicial executions in areas facing separatist insurgency were generally tolerated by state authorities, who claimed the breakdown of judicial systems left security forces no alternative for dealing with accused terrorists." It declared that the newly enacted broad legal protection given all military and civilian officers in Kashmir contributed to the security forces' sense of impunity. "There is no evidence," the report concluded, "that any member of the security forces has been punished for an incident of custodial death or custodial torture in Jammu & Kashmir."[20]

(Only later did the reports also call attention to a tragic development that had historic implications for the state—the forced flight of almost all of its Hindu Pandits, a small but influential upper caste group numbering about five percent of the Valley population. The Pandits had for centuries been an integral part of the life and culture of Kashmir. They were relocated in squalid, makeshift camps in Jammu and Delhi following their mass exodus. Few of the displaced community ever returned to the Valley despite professions by Kashmir state authorities that they would be welcomed back.)

State Department and other U.S. officials regularly testified about the human rights situation at congressional hearings called to review regional policy and consider aid legislation. They also appeared as witnesses in Kashmir-focused meetings that the U.S. House human rights caucus convoked. Like the drafters of the human rights reports, these officials were forthright in discussing egregious activities by government forces. They also gave India credit for actions it took to improve the situation. In the early years of the insurgency, they found these actions few and far between.

American diplomats made démarches on the Indian government "regularly but not often" on human rights issues, but they were not a major item on Embassy New Delhi's agenda. Not surprisingly, the Indians did not welcome these calls.[21] The embassy also maintained contact with Indian human rights organizations, and officials in Washington made a practice of quoting these groups' findings in congressional testimony and other statements. This approach made it easier to deflect criticism in India that Washington was infringing on Indian sovereignty when it called New Delhi's attention to human rights abuses and urged it to allow international human rights organizations access to Kashmir.

While American officials also called attention in congressional hearings to human rights violations by the insurgents, they judged these less glaring than the abuses government forces perpetrated. Some officials noted how the abuses the two sides practiced interacted with one another. Testifying in March and November 1990 before the House Subcommittee on Asian and Pacific Affairs chaired by Stephen J. Solarz, a New York Democrat well disposed to India, Assistant Secretary of State John H. Kelly described the "sadly familiar cycle of violence—militant/popular actions leading to police reaction leading to further radicalization of militants." In Kelly's view, "The Kashmiri militants have exacerbated the situation through tactics we find repugnant. But the Indian authorities have a special responsibility not to depart from due process of law and to maintain law and order in a humane manner."[22]

But while the Bush administration faulted the Indian government's human rights failings in Kashmir, it resisted calls by some legislators to cut off American economic aid and military training for India because of them. Recalling these legislative efforts, a senior State Department official complained in a 2007 interview, "Wherever I looked, another proposal came forward that would penalize India and make life difficult for us."[23] The Pakistan Embassy in Washington was active in promoting anti-Indian sentiment and employed experienced and well-connected lobbyists to support its efforts.

The demands for an assistance cutoff were voiced most sharply and persistently by Representative Dan Burton. Long an outspoken critic of India, the Indiana Republican introduced lurid evidence of Indian wrongdoing in

Kashmir as he confronted government officials in hearings that became highly tendentious.[24] A feature of these sessions was testimony by witnesses in support of an independent Kashmir (and an independent "Khalistan" to be carved out of Indian Punjab for the Sikhs). Burton and those who shared his negative view of India may have been genuinely shocked by what was happening in Kashmir, as were others on Capitol Hill who spoke out at the hearings. But as the same State Department official put it, "The congressmen were really waving the bloody shirt. It was a way to bash India by those who had long-time problems with such things as its earlier closeness to the Soviet Union and its socialistic economic policies." Despite the administration's opposition, Burton gained increasing backing for his aid cutoff initiative and ultimately won majority support for it in the House. The Senate never concurred, however.[25]

The issue of terrorism conducted by separatist groups with the connivance of Pakistani authorities was another serious concern. The administration repeatedly urged Islamabad to stop this support. Nicholas Platt, a career diplomat who was ambassador to Pakistan in 1991 and 1992, has said that it was at the top of his agenda along with the nuclear issue. John Monjo, another experienced Foreign Service officer who succeeded Platt and remained in Islamabad until 1995, recalled that his embassy regularly expressed its concern to Pakistan officials and urged them to make sure that the government itself was not involved in supporting terrorists. He noted that the embassy's Pakistani interlocutors invariably replied that Islamabad limited its activity to political and moral support of the insurgents. So any military assistance to insurgent forces had only private sources. This has long been one of Pakistan's principal talking points in replying to charges about its role in Kashmir.[26] It had at least a veneer of plausibility: ISI had increasingly farmed out these activities to private groups.

In early 1990 the State Department revoked the visa of Amanullah Khan, the chairman of the Jammu and Kashmir Liberation Front, which it had designated a terrorist organization. In the course of the next few years, the department put other militant groups on its terrorist list. Some members of Congress and others wanted it to go farther and place Pakistan on the list of countries that sponsored terrorism. This designation would have triggered severe sanctions. The department stopped short of taking this step on the ground—dubious at best—that Islamabad was making an effort to address the issue. Instead, it put Islamabad on the terrorism "watch list." But the director of central intelligence, James Woolsey, publicly warned that Pakistan "stood on the brink."[27]

Aside from contending that Pakistan was seriously endeavoring to turn things around, American opponents of labeling Pakistan a terrorist state echoed Islamabad in maintaining that there was insufficient evidence of its *direct* involvement in terrorist acts. Moreover, adding Pakistan to the list would further reduce the already limited leverage Washington had in Islamabad after Pakistani nuclear ambitions had triggered drastic American sanctions. And listing Pakistan was wrong, they said, because Pakistan was only doing in Kashmir what the United States had recently done in Afghanistan to help the mujahedin forces oust the Soviets. This was a familiar Pakistani complaint.

Testifying before congressional committees, administration witnesses sometimes found that they were grilled as much about Pakistan's support for terrorism in Kashmir as they were about India's human rights record there. Not surprisingly, pro-Indian members of Congress chided them more about their failure to force Pakistan to stop abetting terrorism in Kashmir, while those unfriendly to India mostly berated them for not doing enough to get New Delhi to improve its sorry performance.

The confrontation on the listing of Pakistan continued from one congressional session to another. Despite strenuous efforts, those who favored the action ultimately failed to win their case with either the Bush or Clinton White House.

Terrorism in Kashmir hit home for Americans when a group of foreign tourists including John Childs of Connecticut and Donald Hutchings of Washington State were kidnapped on July 4, 1995, while trekking in the Pahlgam district of the state. Childs, a chemical engineer and avid jogger, escaped after a few days. Tricked by his feigned dysentery, his captors allowed him to go outside frequently, setting the stage for his getaway. Hutchings, a psychologist, remained in captivity along with two Britons, a West German, and a Norwegian. The Norwegian was found beheaded a few weeks after the kidnapping. While there had been earlier abductions of Westerners, they had always been released unharmed.

A group called Al-Faran claimed responsibility for the kidnappings. Al-Faran was reportedly a spin-off of Harakat-al-Ansar, a prominent Pakistan-based terrorist gang that the State Department later placed on its list of terrorist organizations. The kidnappers demanded the release of twenty-one militants, most of them Harakat-al-Ansar members. By then, five and a half years after the abduction of Rubaiya Sayeed when it first made headlines, the practice of demanding the freeing of insurgents for the release of hostages was not uncommon. The militants seemed to believe that as an added dividend the kidnappings would attract international attention to the Kashmir issue, a long-standing separatist goal. This they did, but not in a way helpful to the militants' cause.

Ambassador to India Frank Wisner, an outstanding career diplomat with a well-deserved reputation for unremitting energy, threw his embassy into the effort to secure the release of Hutchings and the other hostages. Embassy counselor Alan Eastham recalls that the political section he headed worked almost full-time on the matter in an intense effort that was unlike anything in his Foreign Service experience. Along with the British, German, and Norwegian diplomatic missions, the embassy maintained a continuous presence in Kashmir, rotating officers to Srinagar from July 1995 to early spring 1996. Wisner and the chiefs of the other three missions made a joint visit to the Valley. The Federal Bureau of Investigation joined in the effort, sending agents to India on four-week assignments. American officials worked closely with the Indian government, which sent thousands of troops to carry out search-and-rescue operations. Washington also made strong appeals through diplomatic channels to Pakistan, Saudi Arabia, and other Muslim countries sympathetic to the insurgency. The U.S. Army's crack Delta Force and elite British and West German counterterrorism groups mounted secret missions. Bill Richardson, then a U.S. representative from New Mexico, also sought to play a role, as he had in other humanitarian missions.[28]

John Burns, the New Delhi bureau chief of the *New York Times,* reported two years after the abduction that some Indians believed that the Research and Analysis Wing (RAW), the Indian intelligence organization, was involved in the hostage-taking operation. In this view, the kidnappings were designed to discredit Pakistan for allegedly helping the militants. Some Pakistanis and prominent dissidents in the Valley shared these suspicions, which came naturally in a region of the world where conspiracy-theorizing is commonplace.

But Burns quoted American officials as saying that "if RAW ever contemplated a covert action program that involved kidnapping an American, they would have realized that it was a virtual certainty that we would have discovered it and that would have killed it dead."[29]

Hutchings and the others were never found. The most plausible theory is that their captors killed them in December 1995, but this has never been conclusively proven. Alan Eastham is convinced that they were killed as a result of an "encounter" at that time between Indian security forces and a group of militants, in which the Indians killed a senior Al-Faran commander who was the group's channel of communication with Harakat-al-Ansar in Pakistan. "When he died," Eastham told me, "the kids who were holding the prisoners, weary from marching up and down the hill every day and bored after five months, simply did what seventeen-year-olds do about a serious problem and inconvenience when they have no leadership—they got rid of the problem. . . . Unfortunately, it took us most of that winter to figure that out."[30]

The insurgency led Washington to develop its position on key elements of the Kashmir dispute in greater detail. Since the signing of the Simla agreement, American officials had avoided commenting on such basic issues as the continuing validity of the UNCIP resolutions of 1948 and 1949. They confined themselves to warm support for the pact's call for a peaceful, bilateral settlement of the dispute. As one longtime State Department South Asia hand put it at the time, "The public face of U.S. policy was 'Simla, Simla, Simla.'"[31]

A few months after the insurgency broke out, the State Department added "taking into account the wishes of the Kashmiri people" to its formulaic call on India and Pakistan to resolve the issue of the state's future peacefully and bilaterally. Deputy Assistant Secretary Teresita Schaffer, the most senior department official working full time on South Asia policy in those years, recalls that she initiated this change because she believed that the popular uprising in the Valley had significantly altered the situation. The Kashmiris had become actors, and "it seemed that events had moved beyond the point when Kashmir could be disposed of without taking into account the wishes of the people who had taken up the insurgency."[32] The department did not offer any suggestions about how these wishes should be ascertained, however.

Schaffer remembers that she consulted with the State Department's Office of the Historian and was told that the department had not publicly discussed the U.S. position on the UNCIP resolutions since well before the 1965 India-Pakistan war. Based on this finding, she concluded that the United States should continue to avoid talking about the plebiscite called for in the resolutions. When asked if these resolutions had become invalid, U.S. officials would say no. But if asked if the United States supported holding a plebiscite, the answer would be that this was not a practical way to solve the problem.

When Assistant Secretary John Kelly testified before the House Subcommittee on Asian and Pacific Affairs in March 1990, chairman Solarz quizzed him closely on the administration's position on the plebiscite. In their often testy exchange, Kelly told Solarz that the United States believed that Kashmir is "disputed territory." He said that the Bush administration had called on the Indian government to seek a political dialogue with responsible elements that would help satisfy the Kashmiris' legitimate political and economic needs. Reiterating U.S. support for the Simla formula, Kelly declared that whether or not there should be a plebiscite was a matter that India and Pakistan should determine between themselves. The United States was no longer urging that a plebiscite be held and would accept whatever the rival claimants agreed to. He was not asked to offer the administration's view of the validity of the UNCIP resolutions, nor, understandably, did he volunteer it. When Representative Solarz tried to get him to say what the administration's stand would be if the Indians and Pakistanis agreed to include Kashmiri independence as a third plebiscite option, Kelly replied, "We haven't spoken to that position."[33]

Three years later, in 1993, a few months after the Clinton administration took office, John Malott, the interim head of the State Department's newly created Bureau of South Asian Affairs, expanded on Kelly's comments in testimony before the same House subcommittee, by then chaired by Gary Ackerman, another New York Democrat. Addressing the knotty plebiscite issue, Malott asserted that Kelly's 1990 remarks were still cited in South Asia as a major change in U.S. policy. Indians and Pakistanis had concluded that the U.S. government no longer believed that a plebiscite was necessary. The correct position, he said, was that the United States was "neither accepting nor rejecting a plebiscite." Seeking to justify this ambiguous stance, Malott said that it was not useful "to take one part of this rather complex Kashmir equation and pull it out and then say, 'Does the administration support or not support this one specific point?'" He recalled that for years the plebiscite issue "had been put on the back shelf" and implied that it had been wise policy to keep it there.

Malott also offered the Ackerman subcommittee some sage advice: "If there is one thing I have learned, it is that [the Kashmir problem] is a zero sum situation, and anything we say will immediately produce a reaction either from India or Pakistan, or from those Kashmiris who are seeking independence. In such a situation, the most valuable role we can sometimes play is to remain silent on . . . these issues."[34] Many U.S. officials who have dealt with South Asia would agree.

The subcommittee went some way beyond Malott's position. Representative Ackerman and his colleagues said they were inclined to believe that the UNCIP resolutions calling for a plebiscite had been "overtaken by history." They found that while a plebiscite might remain the most desirable means for allowing the Kashmiris to express their own views, which they thought would be to favor independence, they held that "it is almost impossible to imagine a situation where both Delhi and Islamabad would agree to such a vote."[35]

Malott's private view at the time, which he said in a 2007 interview was shared by most of his South Asia bureau colleagues, was that the dispute should be resolved by accepting the territorial status quo in the state.[36] But he recalled that he and others talked about the issue of an eventual settlement only informally "at lunch table discussions." They spent much more time on other, more immediate aspects of the Kashmir problem such as promoting the reduction of tensions along the Line of Control and urging the demilitarization of the Siachen Glacier, a forbidding area in the northern part of the state that Indian troops had occupied in 1984.

John Malott's warning that comments by administration officials on the equities of the Kashmir issue could cause them trouble was underscored by the experience of Robin Raphel, who took charge of the South Asia bureau as assistant secretary in the summer of 1993. Like Malott a career Foreign Service officer, Raphel had served earlier in Islamabad and then in New Delhi where she was political counselor, a third-tier embassy position. Her relatively low rank and what they alleged were her pro-Pakistan sympathies led some senior Indian government officials to regret her appointment to such an important job—and to make no secret of their appraisal.[37] In Raphel's view, which many who dealt with U.S.-Indian relations at the time share, this personal bias against her heightened the uproar in India over comments she made about U.S. Kashmir policy to Washington-based South Asian correspondents just before her initial visit to the region in her new job.[38] More fundamentally, however, the outcry reflected Indian sensitivity to influential outsiders' publicly questioning Kashmir's accession to the Indian Union in 1947. Indians regarded such expressions as a tacit endorsement of Pakistan's claim that the accession was flawed.

Answering what appears to have been a loaded question, Raphel told the correspondents on an unattributed basis that the United States viewed "the whole of Kashmir as disputed territory, the status of which needs to be resolved."[39] As noted, State Department officials John Kelly and John Malott had taken similar positions in on-the-record congressional testimony. Raphel went on to say that this stance "means that we do not recognize the instrument of accession as meaning that Kashmir is forever an integral part of India." This, too, was long-standing policy dating back to the confidential memorandum assistant secretaries John Hickerson and George McGhee drafted in the Truman administration (see chapter 1). But neither Kelly nor Malott had mentioned it in their testimony, and Malott avoided it when he reaffirmed in a widely reported speech in New Delhi, a few months before Raphel's controversial comments, that the United States held that both Indian- and Pakistani-occupied Kashmir were disputed territory.

When Raphel said it, however, the statement struck a particularly raw Indian nerve. Given Indian sensitivity on the accession issue, Raphel should have dealt with the correspondents' queries without calling attention to the U.S. position. She could have avoided any outcry by simply stating that the United States welcomed the terms of the Simla agreement and looked to India and Pakistan to resolve the dispute, taking into account the wishes of the Kashmiri people, Washington's standard mantra. As one American South Asia specialist put it, "To go beyond this [position] publicly has always been like walking across a minefield and getting nothing in return for the heroism."[40] Some of Raphel's senior colleagues in the State Department and Embassy New Delhi were surprised and troubled by her remarks and wondered why she had ventured into this sensitive area when there had been no reason to do so.

Although Michael McCurry, the State Department spokesman, quickly (and correctly) told the media that "there is nothing that was said [by Raphel] indicating a change in U.S. policy on Kashmir," the Indian government and media reacted sharply to her comments. Her name became almost instantly a household word to those Indians who followed foreign policy issues. The Indian press reported that the ministry of external affairs had called in the American chargé d'affaires and told him that New Delhi considered the statement unfair and interpreted it as a significant shift in U.S. policy that tilted it toward Pakistan.[41]

Some commentators angrily denounced Raphel's comments and forecast that they would have dire consequences. The *Hindustan Times's* Washington correspondent excitedly declared that "the gloves finally came off and the Clinton administration today bared its talons." In his view, Raphel was pushing the Pakistani line "to the limit." Other papers predicted that her remarks would encourage dissident elements in Kashmir, where government forces were besieging militant separatists who had seized the Hazratbal shrine, the Valley's most revered Muslim holy place. There was even speculation that Washington had "turned nasty on Kashmir" in order to pressure India to sign the Nuclear Non-Proliferation Treaty.[42]

Indian commentators also found a suspicious connection between Raphel's remarks and President Clinton's passing reference to Kashmir in a speech he had made at the UN General Assembly a few weeks earlier. Discussing serious threats to peace in the world, the president had noted that "bloody ethnic, religious, and civil wars rage from Angola to the Caucasus to Kashmir," a seemingly unexceptionable point that troubled some Indians more than it should have. J. N. Dixit, who was Indian foreign secretary at the time, recalled later that "the reference [to Kashmir] led to speculation in the Ministry of External Affairs and in the Indian press that Robin Raphel was up to her usual tricks, and had slipped [it into] Clinton's speech."[43] Perhaps with greater reason, Indians were again upset when a few months later Clinton told the newly appointed Pakistan ambassador to the United States that "we share Pakistan's concerns about human rights violations in Kashmir."[44]

The furor over Raphel's remarks took some time to die down. Even now some Indians remember her—unfairly—as an American diplomat who was hostile to India's interests. In her remaining years as assistant secretary before she became ambassador to Tunisia in 1997, she continued to point out that her statements reflected U.S. policy, not her personal views. She reiterated in congressional testimony that Clinton's was only the latest in a line of American administrations dating back to 1947 that held that all of Kashmir was in dispute. But she was careful not to discuss how the dispute arose. Instead, she very sensibly sought to persuade India (and Pakistan) to focus on the present and future, not dwell on the past.

In a speech at the Asia Society in February 1994, Raphel spoke eloquently to this point. The United States, she said, would like to see India and Pakistan "escape the tortured history of the conflict and deal with the problem based on the situation in Kashmir today." But she keenly recognized the limits that constrained U.S. policy in the conflict and understood, as Malott had, that "any approach on our part seems doomed to be interpreted by one side or the other as a tilt."[45]

Reference by U.S. officials to the accession and the continuing validity of the UNCIP resolutions, especially their plebiscite provisions, continues to be dangerous to this day. Anything that they say on the subject publicly, or even privately, is scrutinized, parsed, and analyzed for its hidden "real" meaning. Further complicating the matter is the tendency in discussions of Kashmir for interlocutors to ask leading questions intended to elicit support for a position or to catch the American official out. But U.S. diplomats have also found that they can raise the hackles of Indians, Pakistanis, and Kashmiris simply by using what one or another of these groups considers politically incorrect terms in talking about Kashmir.

Among these potential pitfalls is the seemingly innocuous matter of the nomenclature used to describe various parts of the state. For the Indians, the whole state is *Jammu and Kashmir.* The part held by the Pakistanis, in their view illegally, is *Pakistan Occupied Kashmir,* or POK. The Pakistanis call the southern part of the state that they control *Azad (free) Kashmir.* This is short for the Azad Government of Jammu and Kashmir and does not include the region that Pakistan rules directly in the high Himalayas, the *Northern Areas.* For the Pakistanis, the area of the state New Delhi controls is *Held-Kashmir,* known in Urdu by the evocative term *Maqbooza Kashmir.* American officials have concluded that the best way to approach this nomenclature problem in any official statements is to refer simply to the Indian and the Pakistani "sides" of Kashmir. In ordinary conversation, diplomats assigned to the two embassies often use the locally preferred term, which is less awkward.

Then there is the dilemma of what to call the problem. For the Pakistanis it is a *dispute.* Indeed, it is more than that. It is the *core dispute* between the two countries. The Indians for their part do not accept *dispute,* let alone *core dispute.* That would suggest that there is in fact a dispute over the future of the state, which they claim has long since been settled: all of the state is an integral part of the Indian Union. American diplomats are advised to refer to the Kashmir *issue,* a more neutral—and safer—designation.

However annoyed the Indians were by Raphel's remarks, President Clinton's statements, publicly expressed American dissatisfaction with India's human rights record, and other evidence they interpreted as U.S. bias in favor of Pakistan on the Kashmir issue, they had no cause for complaint about the role Washington believed it should play in efforts to find a Kashmir settlement. American officials consistently stressed that the United States would be willing to become involved in these efforts only if both India and Pakistan agreed. Clinton made this clear at a joint press conference when Prime Minister Benazir Bhutto visited the White House in April 1995. Answering a newsman's question, the president declared that "a mediator can only mediate if those who are being mediated want it."[46]

Karl F. (Rick) Inderfurth, who had worked with Secretary of State Madeleine Albright when she was permanent U.S. representative to the United Nations during the first Clinton administration, had succeeded Raphel as assistant secretary for South Asia. He was proud to be the first North Carolinian since Frank Graham to play a major role in Kashmir matters. Expanding on the president's statement in testimony before a House subcommittee in 1997, Inderfurth declared, "We do not see ourselves as mediators. . . . We would be willing to offer direct assistance, if asked by both parties, but we have not received that request from both parties. We're going to watch and see where our influence or support could be useful. . . . But South Asia's problems must be settled by South Asia's people."[47] Washington took the same position regarding its possible intervention in other bilateral India-Pakistan disputes, such as demilitarizing the Siachen Glacier.

It urged the Indians and the Pakistanis to focus on reducing tensions through practical, incremental measures.

Washington recognized that this "only-if-requested" policy gave New Delhi the power to veto any unwanted intervention on its part to help bring about a negotiated settlement. American policymakers did not doubt that as the stronger, status quo power, India would exercise that veto.

Although the United States chose not to play an active role in helping to resolve the Kashmir problem, American officials followed developments in the state carefully. Embassy New Delhi officers regularly visited the Indian-held part of the state, even establishing contact with insurgents.[48] By 1993 tough and unremitting Indian measures had successfully weakened the popular mass movement calling for separation. But as Victoria Scofield has written, "Although the militancy had decreased in and around Srinagar militants continued to operate throughout the countryside and were still capable of mounting serious attacks on the security forces."[49]

I and others who visited the Valley in the mid-1990s reported that it seemed like an occupied country. I recall that perhaps the most prominent (and depressing) aspect of the Srinagar scene was the sight of security forces hunkered down in heavily sandbagged bunkers keeping close watch on a sullen local population. These Kashmiri civilians, who had undergone years of trauma, found themselves trapped in the continuing political and military cross fire between the government and the insurgents and between competing militant groups. The human rights situation, an ongoing source of American concern, showed no real signs of improvement as the decade of the 1990s wore on.

Pakistan used the human rights issue in its revived effort to involve the international community in the Kashmir problem. In what was the clearest and, for the Indians, the most provocative evidence yet of Islamabad's flouting the bilateral approach it had agreed to at Simla, Prime Minister Benazir Bhutto submitted a draft resolution to the United Nations Commission for Human Rights in March 1994 expressing "grave concern at the gross and consistent violations of the human rights of the people of Jammu and Kashmir" and calling for the dispatch of a UN fact-finding mission to the state. India angrily opposed the resolution, which was cosponsored by two other

Muslim countries. Prime Minister P. V. Narasimha Rao alleged that Pakistan's initiative was "based only on the strategy of interfering in the internal affairs of another state for ulterior reasons." The Pakistanis withdrew their draft at the urging of China, Iran, and several other Muslim countries. But they had the satisfaction of bringing Kashmir to world attention in a very well publicized way. The United States and other Western countries made it clear during the debate that they would abstain if the resolution were brought to a vote.

As it resisted outside involvement in the dispute, India tried to initiate a political process in Kashmir designed to normalize the situation through state elections that would restore representative government and end the long period of direct rule from New Delhi. Separatist politicians, organized loosely in the All Parties Hurriyet Conference, firmly resisted this effort and refused to participate in any election held within the framework of the Indian constitution. They repeatedly pointed out to American diplomats and others that to do so would mean their accepting New Delhi's contention that Kashmir was an integral part of India. Nor did they trust the Indians to hold free and fair elections, hardly surprising given their experiences in 1987 and earlier. The separatists boycotted elections held under heavy security in 1996 for the state's six representatives in the Indian parliament, the first balloting in Kashmir since 1989. As repeatedly happened over the next ten years, New Delhi claimed a large spontaneous voter turnout while the separatists maintained that many Kashmiris had been forced to the polls at gunpoint.

At the national level, the 1996 elections led to the establishment of a United Front coalition government. The new prime minister, H. D. Deve Gowda, called Kashmir state elections a few months later. Boycotted by the separatists and widely disparaged by them and others as rigged, the vote brought back to power Farooq Abdullah and his National Conference, which ran on a platform of maximum autonomy. For the first time since New Delhi imposed its direct rule of the state in January 1990, Kashmir enjoyed at least a semblance of representative political government.

Washington saw the elections as a positive step. They will not resolve the dispute, a senior official said in Capitol Hill testimony, but "they do provide an opportunity to begin a real dialogue between the Indian Government and the Kashmiri people. . . ." The United States hopes, she added, that "India and the Kashmiris will take full advantage of that opportunity."[50]

There was general agreement in the mid-1990s among American South Asia specialists in the government and outside that the Clinton administration had it right in making the curbing of Indian and Pakistani nuclear ambitions the highest priority among its regional goals. But some argued that in focusing so single-mindedly on the nuclear issue it had wrongly neglected other attractive, more positive political and economic opportunities in its dealings with New Delhi and Islamabad. Proponents of a more active U.S. policy on Kashmir were among these critics. Outside the government they were spearheaded by the Kashmir Study Group (KSG), which was organized in July 1996 under the leadership of Farooq Kathwari, a highly successful Kashmiri-American businessman who had come to the United States in 1965 and had useful high-level contacts in the American establishment as well as in India and Pakistan.[51]

Kathwari was the first American of Kashmiri background to become actively involved in efforts to find a feasible basis for a settlement. Other Kashmiri-Americans have essentially been lobbyists for particular causes. The most active among these have been Ghulam Nabi Fai of the Kashmiri American Council, a pro-Pakistan group,[52] and Vijay Sazawal, whose Indo-American Kashmir Forum represents the interests of the displaced Kashmiri Pandit community, thousands of whom have come to the United States.[53] The (non-Kashmiri) Indian-American diaspora and, to a lesser extent, Americans of Pakistani background have also been involved in efforts to persuade the executive branch, Congress, the media, and other influential Americans to adopt attitudes sympathetic to the positions they favor on the issue.

The Kashmir Study Group includes senior retired U.S. diplomats, South Asia academic specialists, lawyers and business people, and a few members of Congress. The prominent standing of its members has prompted Indian, Pakistani, and American policymakers to give the group's ideas serious attention.

The KSG issued its first set of proposals in 2000.[54] These recommended that portions of the former princely state be reconstituted as a "sovereign" entity, but one without an "international personality." India, Pakistan, and appropriate international bodies would guarantee its sovereignty. Its legislature would deal with all matters other than defense and foreign affairs. India and Pakistan would be responsible for the entity's defense and it would have open borders with them. The Line of Control would remain in place until India and Pakistan decided to alter it in their mutual interest.

Acting mostly on suggestions from people in the region, the group refined its ideas and, in 2005, came up with a second set of proposals.[55] These explored the concept of creating five self-governing entities in the Kashmir region: the three India administers—Kashmir, Jammu, and Ladakh—and the two governed by Pakistan—Azad Kashmir and the Northern Areas. Each set of entities would be represented in higher-tier bodies, one on the Indian side, one on the Pakistani. These would coordinate issues of general interest to them, such as internal trade and transportation. Additionally, an all-Kashmir body, including representatives of the five entities plus India and Pakistan would coordinate areas of broader concern such as regional trade, tourism, the environment, and water resources. As in the earlier version, the Line of Control would remain in place. India and Pakistan would demilitarize the entities on their sides of the line. Some of these ideas figured in proposals put forward by Pakistan President Pervez Musharraf soon afterward (see chapter 7).

Well before the KSG was organized and issued its first set of proposals, the reigniting of the Kashmir problem had stimulated other Americans to look for useful ways to move it toward resolution. Selig Harrison, the doyen of Washington's South Asia–watching community, advocated a settlement that integrated most of Jammu and Ladakh with India and gave special autonomous status to the remaining, predominantly Muslim part of Indian Kashmir as well as to Azad Kashmir. The Line of Control would become a porous border and Kashmiri travelers would not require visas to cross it. Indian and Pakistani armed forces would be withdrawn but could be reintroduced under special conditions. Ross Munro of the Foreign Policy Research Institute argued for the creation of an autonomous, demilitarized, secular Kashmir Economic Zone comprising portions of the state on both sides of the Line of Control, possibly including Ladakh and the Northern Areas, but excluding Jammu, which would become a separate Indian state. James C. Clad, who has been a journalist, academic, and diplomat, suggested a repartitioning of the state that would give India more territory in the Jammu area and Pakistan more land in the north. His proposal, too, called for open borders between the two parts of Kashmir, steady withdrawal of Indian and Pakistani forces from the state, and autonomy in matters other than defense and foreign affairs.[56] Hurst Hannum, a legal authority who teaches at Tufts University, has written valuable studies of the concept of divided or partial sovereignty and how these could be applied to Kashmir.[57] Joseph E. Schwartzberg, a professor of geography and South Asian studies at the University of Minnesota, urged regional referendums in which Kashmiris would choose between integrating their areas fully with either India or Pakistan or becoming part of a Kashmir Autonomous Region. The new border would be open and demilitarized and the autonomous region would function as a free trade zone. Schwartzberg and others also proposed the conversion of the disputed Siachen Glacier area into an international peace park recognized as a UNESCO world natural heritage site.

More recently, other American specialists have weighed in with ideas for dealing with Kashmir. Ambassador Teresita Schaffer, by then director of the South Asia program at the Center for Strategic and International Studies, published a study called *Kashmir: The Economics of Peace Building* in 2005. A joint effort with the Kashmir Study Group, her paper catalogued several dozen economic measures that could help build peace constituencies within Kashmir. These included steps that either side could take on its own as well as arrangements that would integrate both sides of Kashmir through cooperative or coordinated action.[58] The same year Michael Krepon of the Stimson Center and Ashley Tellis of the Carnegie Endowment for International Peace proposed a series of measures that they argued should be implemented in advance of a settlement. These included a cessation of firing and infiltration of armed men across the Line of Control, resumption of trade across the line, major improvements in India's human rights performance, and the return of the Pandits to their homes. Professor Robert Wirsing, who has written extensively on Kashmir, concluded in 2003 that it was currently impossible to resolve the dispute because of India-Pakistan hostility. He called for a UN-led international peacekeeping force on the Line of Control. Wirsing suggested hopefully, and unrealistically, that economic and political incentives could persuade India and Pakistan to agree to this. In 2005 Jon P. Dorschner, then an instructor at the U.S. Military Academy, proposed that Indian-administered Kashmir become autonomous within the Indian Union. Azad Kashmir would receive similar status within Pakistan, and Kashmiris would travel freely between the two sides. Indian and Pakistani armed forces would eventually be withdrawn from the whole state.[59]

This list is certainly not exhaustive Many think tanks and foreign policy groups such as the United States Institute of Peace, the Center for Strategic and International Studies, and the Council on Foreign Relations have produced papers on India-Pakistan relations that include helpful ideas on the Kashmir issue.

American nongovernmental organizations also have sponsored track-two dialogues that bring together influential private individuals. The Neemrana Process, the Balusa Group, the Shanghai Process, and the Stimson Center Dialogues along with the Kashmir Study Group have been the most prominent of these. Neemrana, organized in 1991 and financed by the U.S. government and the Ford Foundation, brought together prominent Indians and Pakistanis, mostly retired military and civilian officials, under an American chair. However, by the late 1990s the process began to run out of steam as it became increasingly obvious that the participants were failing to influence their governments to accept ideas they had themselves rejected when they were in power. The Balusa Group was cofounded in 1995 by Shirin Tahir-Kheli, a Pakistani-American academic who has held senior government positions in Republican administrations, and her brother, Toufiq Siddiqi, an environmental and energy expert. Like Neemrana, Balusa convoked meetings of influential Indians and Pakistanis. It also has published a number of valuable studies, including a seminal monograph on the costs of the India-Pakistan confrontation written by Mahmud Durrani, a retired Pakistan Army general who became Islamabad's ambassador to the United States during the Musharraf government and later served as national security adviser under the successor regime.

The Shanghai Process, initiated in 1994, includes Chinese and American participants as well as Indians and Pakistanis. It, too, has discussed and produced papers on a wide range of India-Pakistan issues including Kashmir. The Stimson Center Dialogues date back to 1991, when the center began training Indian, Pakistani, and Chinese officials, military officers, and journalists on issues of regional confidence building and arms control. Aside from efforts to facilitate movement on the Kashmir issue, its South Asian program promotes stabilizing and reducing the danger of nuclear weapons and encouraging regional stability and India-Pakistan normalization. The center's study on the dangerous confrontation between India and Pakistan in 2001 and 2002 is particularly valuable for an understanding of the role the United States has played as an indispensable manager in a major Kashmir-related crisis (see chapter 7).[60]

Congressmen have also been involved in these unofficial efforts, at least nominally. In 2002 members of the House of Representatives organized a Kashmir Forum designed, they said, "to educate their colleagues about the troubled territory and seek avenues for peace."[61] The forum, which was probably inspired by G. N. Fai's Kashmir-American Council, has not played a significant role on Capitol Hill, however.

With South Asia now more salient to U.S. global interests than ever before, there will no doubt be further efforts by private American organizations and individuals to develop useful ideas on India-Pakistan relations in general and on Kashmir in particular. The government will do well to maintain contact with them as it develops new policy directions in the region.

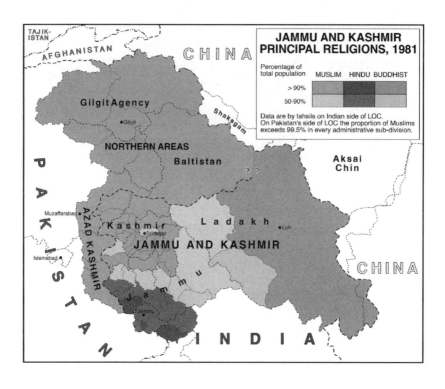

JAMMU AND KASHMIR PRINCIPAL RELIGIONS, 1981

Percentage of total population: MUSLIM HINDU BUDDHIST

> 90%

50-90%

Data are by tahsils on Indian side of LOC.
On Pakistan's side of LOC the proportion of Muslims exceeds 99.5% in every administrative sub-division.

TAJIK-ISTAN

AFGHANISTAN

CHINA

Gilgit Agency

•Gilgit

Shaksgam

NORTHERN AREAS

Baltistan

Aksai Chin

P A K I S T A N

Muzaffarabad•

AZAD KASHMIR

Kashmir

•Srinagar

L a d a k h

•Leh

JAMMU AND KASHMIR

Islamabad▲

CHINA

J a m m u

•Jammu

I N D I A

7

"The Most Dangerous
Place in the World"

Two major events in the last years of the 1990s further heightened Washington's apprehensions about the danger the Kashmir dispute posed for American interests in South Asia and beyond. These were the Indian and Pakistani nuclear weapons tests in May 1998 and the armed conflict that followed Pakistan's seizure of territory on the Indian side of the Line of Control in the remote Kargil area of Kashmir a year later. Many U.S. policy-makers and commentators became more convinced than ever that Kashmir was a flash point that could ignite a nuclear war. Some observers called South Asia the most dangerous place in the world. President Clinton shared these concerns.[1]

On May 11, 1998, the newly installed Indian coalition government headed by Atal Bihari Vajpayee, the leader of the Bharatiya Janata Party, surprised Washington intelligence analysts and policymakers by testing five nuclear weapons in the Rajasthan desert not far from the Pakistan border. The Clinton administration reacted sharply to the tests, which represented the failure of three decades of effort by successive American administrations to head off the nuclearization of South Asia.

The administration immediately mounted a campaign to persuade Pakistan not to follow suit. The president, who made five phone calls over the next two weeks to Prime Minister Muhammad Nawaz Sharif, took the lead in a major international jawboning effort designed to spell out the advantages that would accrue to Pakistan if it did not test and the serious consequences it would face if it did. The carrots included a presidential invitation to Sharif to make an official visit to the United States—an honor that Pakistani heads of government have always prized. The administration enlisted leaders of other countries that enjoyed influence in Islamabad in this campaign. To supplement these endeavors, the Washington bureaucracy quickly assembled a generous package of economic and military assistance that it hoped would make nontesting an attractive option, not least to Pakistan's politically powerful armed forces. Although Americans in government and outside who were familiar with Pakistan recognized that the odds were heavily against success, they agreed that the effort was worth making.

Pursuing its dual strategy, the administration sent a high-level team headed by Deputy Secretary of State Strobe Talbott to Islamabad to make a determined pitch to Sharif and other influential members of the Pakistan power structure including the chief of army staff, General Jehangir Karamat. The watchwords Talbott used with the Pakistanis were "restraint and maturity." The deputy secretary recognized that the poor state of Pakistan's economy offered him a potentially useful bargaining chip. As he points out in his fascinating play-by-play account of his efforts, Pakistan "could literally cash in by showing restraint" as aid donors withheld funds from New Delhi and shifted them to Islamabad.[2]

But the argument that by not testing, the Pakistanis would gain the moral high ground and receive a large bundle of economic and military aid in the bargain could not overcome their fear that India would use its nuclear arsenal to solve the Kashmir problem once and for all by forcing Pakistan to give up its claims. These fears could be allayed only if Pakistan, too, possessed nuclear weapons. The Pakistanis' conviction that the United States had failed to fulfill its promises of support against Indian aggression in the past heightened their determination to test.[3] Finally, and perhaps most importantly, naked domestic political considerations doomed Talbott's efforts. Given the always highly charged nature of India-Pakistan relations, no prime minister of Pakistan, even one in the strong position that Sharif then enjoyed, could have agreed to refrain from testing and expect that the armed forces, the political leadership, and an anxious public would allow him to remain in power.

Could the administration have successfully played the Kashmir card to change the odds? Kashmir came up repeatedly in Talbott's conversations. But

Washington recognized that there was nothing that it could do to bring about a settlement that would satisfy Pakistani interests. Bruce Riedel, the special assistant to the president and senior National Security Council director for the Near East and South Asia who accompanied Talbott to Pakistan, recalls:

> The one area Sharif hinted that would make a difference was Kashmir. If the United States and the international community committed itself to a major effort at peace making in Kashmir then he might have the cover to not test. . . . [But] Clinton saw this as a trap. While he was personally very interested in trying his hand at resolving Kashmir in order to defuse tensions in the subcontinent, he knew that a high visibility mediation effort was a non-starter for India and would be refused, leaving him exposed and ineffective.[4]

Basically, Washington lacked the power to compel India to make major territorial and political commitments on Kashmir, and these were absolute requirements for a settlement of the dispute that would justify not testing in the minds of Pakistan's leaders.

Soon after Talbott headed back to the United States, the Pakistanis set off six nuclear explosions in the remote mountains of Baluchistan. The news was rapturously welcomed throughout the country.

Following the Indian tests, Washington took the lead in rallying international support to punish New Delhi, imposing sanctions and other measures that could damage Indian economic and security interests. Other nations joined in the harsh U.S. criticism of India's action. After Pakistan tested, the administration launched a diplomatic campaign in international forums, including the five permanent members of the Security Council and the group of eight (G-8) major industrialized countries, that was designed to induce India and Pakistan to accept specific measures to head off a nuclear arms race in the subcontinent and to bolster the badly shaken regional and global nonproliferation regime. These measures were included in a UN Security Council resolution.[5]

Washington added an article to the resolution urging India and Pakistan to resume their dialogue and encouraging them to "find mutually acceptable solutions that address the root causes" of the tensions between them, "including Kashmir." A widely shared perception that the tests significantly raised the danger of another India-Pakistan confrontation, this time possibly sparking a nuclear war, prompted this addition. It was quickly accepted by other council members. The world community was convinced that only an improvement in the two countries' bilateral relations could reduce this peril. Islamabad welcomed this vivid evidence of renewed international interest—especially Washington's—in a Kashmir settlement. To no one's surprise, the "encouragement" went down badly in India.

But the Indians *were* willing to engage in an extended dialogue with the United States that dealt with the two countries' immediate security and nonproliferation agendas as well as longer-term bilateral issues and their concepts of their roles in the world. Deputy Secretary Talbott led the American team; Jaswant Singh, a prominent figure in India's ruling Bharatiya Janata Party, headed the Indian side. Though they did not produce an agreement on nonproliferation, the discussions were widely hailed as the most useful sustained exchange of views on security issues Washington and New Delhi had conducted during their often troubled half-century relationship.[6]

Talbott made a similar effort to hold a dialogue with the Pakistanis. Islamabad's delegation to the first session with him and his team was led by Sahabzada Yaqub Khan, a highly respected former foreign minister and ambassador to the United States. Civil servants who were less well connected, influential, and personable soon replaced Yaqub, however, and subsequent meetings proved much less productive than those Talbott and his team had with the Indians.[7]

For a time, it seemed that New Delhi and Islamabad had heeded the world community's admonitions. Traveling to Pakistan on one of the public buses recently put into cross-border service, Vajpayee met with Sharif in Lahore in February 1999. In a cordial atmosphere, the two prime ministers pledged to take immediate steps to reduce the risk of nuclear war and seek solutions to their bilateral problems, including Kashmir. They recognized that resolving the issue was "essential" and declared that they would "intensify their efforts" to reach a settlement. Although they did not make much progress at the meeting on the issues, their agreement to conduct a government-to-government dialogue under "the Lahore process" led at least more sanguine observers to hope that there was a serious prospect for better bilateral ties. In Washington President Clinton declared that "South Asia—and, indeed, the entire world—will benefit if India and Pakistan promptly turn these commitments into concrete progress." The president promised that his administration "will continue our own efforts to work with India and Pakistan to promote progress in the region."[8]

These hopes were soon dashed when, in mid-May 1999, the Indians became aware that Pakistan had surreptitiously seized commanding heights on the Indian side of the Line of Control that overlooked Kargil, a small town on the strategically vital highway linking the Kashmir Valley to the Ladakh region of the state bordering China. A northern spur of the road also provides India's only access to the disputed Siachen Glacier. The Pakistanis had moved forward during the forbidding winter months, when the Indian Army had redeployed its troops from the heights to lower, warmer ground. Such seasonal withdrawals had been the long-standing practice of both forces, though the stand-down had been regularly violated by both sides. The Pakistani advance caught the Indians unaware—Pakistani troops had moved into the high ground months before Indian reconnaissance discovered them.

Once Pakistan's move was discovered, it was obvious that the infiltration had begun well before Vajpayee and Nawaz Sharif held their amicable and apparently successful conference in Lahore. Understandably, the Indians felt they had been double-crossed. Although Vajpayee's government had lost a parliamentary vote of confidence a few weeks earlier and was carrying on in a caretaker capacity pending fresh elections, it reacted vigorously. Indian troops along the Line of Control were reinforced, and the prime minister declared that New Delhi would take all steps necessary to flush out the infiltrators, believed at that point to number around seven hundred. These measures included heavy artillery fire, which the Pakistanis reciprocated, as well as strikes by Indian Air Force jets. Two of these planes were quickly lost, at least one to Pakistani fire. By publicizing specific evidence identifying some of the intruders as Pakistan Army regulars, the Indians sought to refute Pakistan's specious claim that it had given no military or financial support to the infiltrators. According to the Pakistanis, they were indigenous Kashmiris battling "Indian occupiers." In fact, the Pakistan army had infiltrated regular troops and deceptively maintained that the mujahedin had crossed the Line of Control on their own.

India rejected Pakistan's calls to stop the air raids and agree to neutral monitors or UN observers on the Line of Control. Then, after some hesitation,

Vajpayee accepted Nawaz Sharif's offer to send the Pakistan foreign minister to New Delhi for talks to deal with the crisis. He warned, however, that India's determination to drive out the intruders from its side of the Line of Control was nonnegotiable. The Indian prime minister also made it clear that he would reject out of hand any attempt by Pakistan to discuss the broader Kashmir issue during the talks. When the discussions did take place, they quickly went nowhere.[9]

From the outset of the Kargil crisis, Washington worried that the fighting could spin out of control and lead to a fourth India-Pakistan war. Rick Inderfurth, assistant secretary of state for the region, told the *New York Times* on May 29: "Clearly, the ingredients are there for miscalculation. Our hope is that both sides will take steps to move this in a peaceful direction." According to Inderfurth, the fighting would end only after the infiltrators left. "They have to depart and they will depart, either voluntarily or because the Indians will take them out."[10]

Driven by these apprehensions, the United States acted vigorously on the diplomatic front to defuse the crisis. American diplomats in India and Pakistan were instructed to express Washington's strong concern. The officials urged their Indian and Pakistani interlocutors to show restraint and prevent the fighting from spreading.

At the State Department, Inderfurth and Under Secretary for Political Affairs Thomas R. Pickering, a gifted and forceful former ambassador to India, made clear to Pakistan ambassador Riaz Khokhar that Pakistan must withdraw its forces immediately. The American officials held that Pakistan was to blame. They dismissed Khokhar's claim that the infiltrators were Kashmiri separatist freedom fighters acting on their own. (Even some Pakistani officials privately admitted that the claim was unfounded: William B. Milam, the career diplomat who was U.S. ambassador in Islamabad at the time, recalls that in conversations with him his contacts in the Pakistan army disavowed the official government line.) State Department officials also called in Indian ambassador Naresh Chandra to tell him the same thing. They remained in close touch with both envoys throughout the crisis to ensure that the two received identical renditions of U.S. positions and diplomatic activities.[11]

If Washington's blunt stance on the nature of the infiltration and its call for prompt Pakistani withdrawal was a rude shock to Khokhar and his bosses at home, it came as a pleasant surprise to the Indians. Most Indians had for years accepted as received wisdom that in India-Pakistan disputes, especially those involving Kashmir, the United States would invariably tilt toward Pakistan. Some of them had seen this preference as part of a broader U.S. effort to weaken India. Pickering is right in finding that Washington's handling of the Kargil crisis contributed importantly to the heightening of Indian trust in the United States.[12]

Secretary of State Madeleine Albright reinforced her officers' message in phone calls to the Pakistan prime minister and the Indian foreign minister. When Pakistan refused to comply, Riedel, the action officer for Kargil on the NSC staff, publicly called on it to respect the Line of Control.[13] The United States also actively engaged its partners in the G-8 and other countries, including China, to forge a common position.

Deputy Secretary of State Talbott has written that the greatest danger Washington feared at that point was that the Indians would launch a counteroffensive across the Line of Control, a move that could have had disastrous results, including a possible nuclear conflict. In Islamabad Ambassador Milam was less worried about the consequences of an Indian move across the line, which the Pakistanis were confident they could stop, than he was about an offensive across the international border into Pakistan proper. The Pakistanis' positions there were more vulnerable, and they would have viewed such a move as an even greater provocation than an attack into their portion of Kashmir.[14]

In his highly regarded account of his diplomatic efforts in South Asia, Talbott offers a doomsday scenario of the way the crisis might have developed:

> It was conceivable that while mobilizing for all-out war, Pakistan might seek support from China and various Arab states, while India would perhaps turn to its newer partner Israel. The result could be an international free-for-all in which all the wrong outsiders would be looking for ways to score points against one another rather than concerting their energies to pull the combatants back from the brink of what could easily become a nuclear cataclysm.[15]

American diplomats worked hard to head off such dire developments. The Pakistanis' deceptive insistence that their armed forces were not involved in Kargil made realistic dialogue with Islamabad difficult. U.S. efforts were also hampered at first by New Delhi's claim that it had the situation under control and did not require help from outsiders. The Indians soon abandoned this position and welcomed the intervention of the United States and other foreign powers. This was a departure from their historic aversion to a Western role in Kashmir-related matters.

During most of Pakistan's troubled history, its military leaders have played the dominant role in forging national security policy. This has been the case whether or not the military formally held the reins of government. When civilian governments try to get out in front, as Nawaz Sharif did in undertaking his Lahore initiative, the army has the power and the audacity to undercut them. But as the operation faltered and Pakistani forces were pushed back, it was not clear to American policymakers whether it was Prime Minister Sharif or Chief of Army Staff General Pervez Musharraf who was calling the shots in determining Kargil policy.

The prime minister seemed to be in a powerful political position. After winning a lopsided parliamentary majority in Pakistan's 1995 elections, he had felt strong enough to fire the chief of army staff, the soft-spoken and level-headed General Karamat. Karamat had offended Sharif by calling publicly for the establishment of a mixed civilian-military national security council that would function as a powerful supercabinet. The prime minister had chosen Musharraf to replace Karamat, apparently in the mistaken expectation that Musharraf would be more subservient. Karamat's dismissal incensed many senior military officers and intensified their unhappiness with the prime minister. More important, the selection of Musharraf placed at the head of the powerful Pakistan military a brash, headstrong commando officer who had little regard for the policy of better relations with India that Sharif initiated at Lahore or for democratic institutions.

Musharraf was widely recognized as the mastermind—the Indians would say evil genius—behind the Kargil offensive. The general proudly acknowledged this role later, though in highly misleading form, when as president of Pakistan he wrote his autobiography, *In the Line of Fire.*[16] The most plausible explanation of Sharif's role is that despite the stake he seemingly had in the Lahore peace process, he went along with the Kargil operation, believing that Pakistan could deny authorship. But what the prime minister knew and when he knew it remain the subject of much self-interested and self-exculpatory debate in political and military circles in Pakistan.

As fighting intensified along a widening front and Indian forces took heavy casualties in their literally uphill battle to clear the heights in June and July 1999, Washington stepped up its diplomatic offensive. Clinton sent personal messages to Vajpayee and Sharif and followed these with phone calls to the two prime ministers. Talking to Sharif, the president bluntly asserted that the United States regarded Pakistan as the aggressor and rejected his continuing contention that the intruders were Kashmiri separatists. General Anthony Zinni, the head of U.S. Central Command who had accompanied Talbott on his unsuccessful mission a year earlier, returned to Islamabad to underscore this message. Zinni told Sharif and Musharraf that India might cross the Line of Control or escalate the conflict elsewhere if Pakistan did not withdraw its forces. The tough and articulate Marine Corps general reiterated American goals, which were shared by others in the G-8. Aside from a pullback to Pakistan's side of the Line of Control, these included reestablishment of the line, an end to the fighting, and the resumption of the Lahore process. Ambassador Milam, who participated in both of Zinni's main meetings with the Pakistanis, recalls that in the long session with Musharraf it seemed clear from the chief of staff's body language that although he was the author of the Kargil strategy he now wished to withdraw.[17]

By late June Nawaz Sharif recognized that Kargil had become a fiasco for Pakistan. He had been rebuffed by the Chinese when he flew to Beijing to seek their support. Back-channel efforts to arrange for him to stop in New Delhi on his way back to Pakistan from China to work out a deal with Vajpayee had collapsed. Washington continued to insist that Pakistan withdraw behind the Line of Control and threatened to hold up an International Monetary Fund loan that Islamabad sorely needed. The Indians relentlessly continued their costly advance up the heights. Although they still refrained from crossing the Line of Control, their artillery began to shell Pakistani positions on the Pakistan side.

In desperation Sharif appealed to Clinton to develop a plan that would stop the fighting and lead to an American-brokered Kashmir settlement. As it had when it tried to provoke an uprising in the Valley in 1965, Pakistan had seen the Kargil operation as a way to return the Kashmir issue to the international stage. The Pakistanis evidently believed, as they always had, that an intervention by Washington would favor them, although by 1999 that assumption was no longer valid. At the very least, to their way of thinking, an announced willingness on America's part to become involved would provide Sharif cover for a failed operation. But Clinton said he would intervene only if Pakistan agreed to withdraw behind the Line of Control.

Anxious to find a way out, Sharif asked to see the president face-to-face to plead his case. Clinton firmly (and wisely) stuck to his guns: he would become involved only if the Pakistanis withdrew. At the same time, the president reassured Prime Minister Vajpayee that he was resolute on this point. He also told Vajpayee that the United States continued to support the Lahore process of direct India-Pakistan talks, not third-party intervention, as the way to resolve the Kashmir issue.

Sharif became even more desperate. As Riedel recounts: "On the third [of July] Sharif . . . told the President he was ready to come immediately to Washington to seek our help. The President repeated his caution—come only if you are ready to withdraw, I can't help if you are not ready to pull back. He urged Sharif to consider carefully the wisdom of a trip to Washington under these constraints. Sharif said he was coming and would be there on the 4th."[18]

Riedel and Talbott provide almost identical detailed insider accounts of the dramatic Fourth of July meeting between Clinton and the self-invited Sharif at Blair House, the VIP presidential guest quarters across Pennsylvania Avenue from the White House. They make several main points:

—Clinton was absolutely firm in rejecting Sharif's reiteration of the longtime Pakistani plea that the United States intervene directly and press India to commit to resolve the larger Kashmir issue within a specific time frame. The president sternly insisted that the Pakistan army and its Kashmir-insurgency allies withdraw completely and promptly behind the Line of Control. Only then could the United States help Pakistan. Such a full withdrawal without preconditions would give Washington leverage with India.

—The president was prepared to support a resumption of the Lahore process and asserted that the United States would work hard to help advance that bilateral India-Pakistan dialogue. When Sharif compared the efforts the United States had undertaken to bring about a Mideast settlement with its much less activist approach on Kashmir, the president made the obvious retort that all the parties to the Arab-Israeli dispute wanted America to have a role. That was not the case in South Asia. He warned Sharif in strong language of the danger of accidental nuclear war if India concluded that it had to cross the Line of Control because of Pakistan's actions. Clinton's fears on this score had been heightened by reports he had received just before the meeting that the Pakistani military was preparing nuclear-armed missiles for possible use in a war against India. It became evident to the American side that Sharif did not know everything his armed forces were doing and did not have complete control over their activities.

—Sharif, for his part, was obviously very worried about the consequences the Kargil operation could have for his own political standing. He had brought his wife and children to Washington with him. This led some Americans to conclude that he feared he could not safely return to Pakistan if he came away from Blair House empty-handed. As the meeting went on and his arguments were rejected, the prime minister became increasingly distressed, eventually telling the president that he desperately wanted to find a solution that would offer some cover. Unless he had something to point to, he claimed, fundamentalists, or the army egged on by fundamentalists, would overthrow him.

At the conclusion of the conference, Sharif accepted an American draft press statement that said that he had "agreed to take concrete and immediate steps for the restoration of the Line of Control." The draft statement called for a cease-fire, but only after the Pakistanis had withdrawn. The prime minister swallowed these terms but asked for one addition, a sentence that would say "the President would take personal interest to encourage an expeditious resumption and intensification of the bilateral [India-Pakistan] efforts once the sanctity of the Line of Control had been restored." Clinton agreed and the conference ended.

President Clinton had won a major diplomatic victory, forging an agreement with Pakistan acceptable to India that headed off a possible catastrophe for both countries and the rest of the world. Sharif got little in return for his capitulation to Clinton's demands. There would be no American-brokered resolution of the Kashmir issue. Nor would the president's vague promise to take a personal interest in India-Pakistan bilateral efforts save Sharif from angry accusations in Pakistan, not least from the military, that by agreeing to withdraw behind the Line of Control he had sold out the country. The finger-pointing was not all one way, however. Sharif for his part blamed the military for what had gone wrong.

After the Pakistani armed forces had pulled back, Clinton invited Sharif to send a trusted colleague to Washington to discuss how he could best follow up the personal commitment he had made to the prime minister at Blair House to encourage the Lahore process. According to Ambassador Milam, the Americans had in mind a quiet, unpublicized back-channel session in which the Pakistan side would be represented by someone who was not in the public limelight. They got something quite different. After some delay, the prime minister dispatched his brother and close political confidant Shahbaz Sharif, the chief minister of the Punjab, hardly a behind-the-scenes figure.

According to Riedel and Inderfurth, his principal interlocutors, all Shahbaz wanted to discuss was how his politically beleaguered brother could hang on to power, not ways to move forward on the Kashmir issue. As Riedel recalls, he "all but said they knew a military coup was coming."[19] On Kashmir, Shahbaz tacitly acknowledged that back-channel discussions were going on with India and that these focused on a division of the state. (The exchanges were foundering, as the talks in 1963 had, because the territorial claims of the two sides conflicted wildly.) Walter Andersen, a senior official in the State Department's Bureau of Intelligence and Research, acted as notetaker at the meeting Riedel and Inderfurth had with Shahbaz in his suite at the Willard Hotel in downtown Washington. According to Andersen, Shahbaz asserted that Islamabad could not have realistic discussions with New Delhi on Kashmir unless the United States pressed the Indians. But he cautioned that anything Washington did would have to be subtle.[20]

Soon afterward, as speculation mounted in Pakistan about a coming coup, a senior U.S. official stated in an interview to a news service that Washington would strongly oppose any attempt to overthrow the Nawaz Sharif government. "We hope," the unidentified official declared, "that there will be no return to the days of interrupted democracy in Pakistan."[21]

This highly unusual public warning failed to prevent Nawaz Sharif's overthrow by the military on October 12. Ironically, Nawaz actually provided the immediate trigger for the coup. In a clumsy maneuver designed to strengthen his position, he replaced Musharraf as chief of staff with a more trusted general while Musharraf was airborne, returning from a conference in Sri Lanka. When Karachi airport was ordered to deny permission for his plane to land, the army took matters into its own hands and moved swiftly to remove Sharif from power. Some well-informed Pakistanis maintain that Sharif's action merely provided a pretext for the army to carry out carefully prepared plans for his ouster. But the important point is that the military had long since become fed up with the prime minister over Kargil and what they considered the threat his rule posed for their institutional and personal interests. The coup won widespread public support in Pakistan. Although Washington had limited respect for Nawaz, official U.S. reaction was negative, and the Clinton administration called for the prompt restoration of democratic government.

Washington's actions during the Kargil crisis reflected the importance the nuclearization of South Asia had in shaping its approach to the Kashmir issue. The Indian and Pakistani tests strengthened the primacy the Clinton administration and other concerned foreign governments gave to preserving stability in the subcontinent. This explains the joint statement's reference to the "sanctity" of the Line of Control, a newly coined term.[22]

The nuclear tests further lessened the importance the administration attached to the equities of the Kashmir issue that had informed American handling of it from 1948 on. For the United States and other members of the international community, the use of violence to change the status quo had become an unacceptable option in nuclear-armed South Asia.

This major shift in emphasis became even more evident when Clinton briefly visited Islamabad in March 2000, less than a year after Kargil. "There is no military solution to Kashmir," he warned his Pakistani television audience. "International sympathy, support, and intervention cannot be won by provoking a bigger bloodier conflict.... This era does not reward people who struggle in vain to redraw borders in blood."[23]

The net effect of the Indian and Pakistani nuclear tests and the Kargil conflict was to eliminate any possibility of changing the status quo in Kashmir by military means. Since there was no possibility of India giving up more than insignificant slivers of land in negotiations (and that only in a swap for similarly limited Pakistani-held areas), the territorial contours of a Kashmir settlement had become effectively set. The overwhelming international consensus—which included China—in favor of forcing Pakistan to leave Kargil demonstrated that a sea change had taken place in the world community's position. Clinton's words on Pakistan television underscored the same point. After the tests and Kargil, any effort to settle the Kashmir issue would have to focus on redefining the political relationship among India, Pakistan, and the Kashmiris and on expanding the movement of people and goods across the Line of Control, not on redrawing the map (see chapter 9).

Nearly ten years later, Pakistanis still seem to be coming to grips with this change in world attitudes. Most continue to press for an international role in the mistaken belief that this will promote Pakistan's interests. Nor have the Indians much changed their long-standing attitude. They still look askance at any role for outsiders on Kashmir. They do not seem to recognize that such an intervention could be to their advantage, as it proved to be in Kargil. In Kashmir itself, dissident leaders, especially those who favor independence, have also persisted in calling for outside, read American, intervention. This position is even more unrealistic than the attitudes that persist in Pakistan and India. At no time since the British briefly promoted the internationalization of the Valley in the failed 1962–63 negotiations has any major government or significant political lobby called for a separate status for Kashmir.

During its final year, the Clinton administration focused its South Asia policy on efforts to induce India and Pakistan to take measures that would reduce the danger their nuclear programs posed to the nonproliferation regime. The immediate objective was to help bring about a resumption of the shattered India-Pakistan dialogue that Vajpayee and Sharif had begun at Lahore. The administration encouraged the two sides to develop some positive thinking and movement on Kashmir and continued to affirm that it was prepared to play a role if the two claimants wished it to.

Clinton reasserted this position with typical flair at a press conference in February 2000, a month before he left on the first trip to South Asia an American president had made since Jimmy Carter's 1978 visit to India. Asked whether Washington would be willing to help mediate the dispute if India and Pakistan requested American assistance, the president declared: "Absolutely, I would. Why? For the same reason we've been involved in Northern Ireland and the Mideast. Because, number one and most importantly, it is a hugely important area of the world. If the tensions between India and Pakistan . . . could be resolved . . . the Indian subcontinent might very well be the great success story of the next fifty years." But Clinton cautioned, "If they don't want us, it won't do any good. We'd be just out there talking into the air. And I'm not for that."[24]

The president struck the same note during his visit to the subcontinent. He told the Indian parliament, "I have not come to South Asia to mediate the dispute over Kashmir. Only India and Pakistan can work out the problems between them. . . . But if outsiders cannot resolve the problem, I hope you will create the opportunity to do it yourself, calling on the support of others who can help where possible. . . ." He repeated this message in Pakistan a few days later.[25]

Clinton's prescription in both countries was that they respect the Line of Control, show restraint, reject violence, and restore their dialogue. In diplomatic shorthand, this formulation came to be known as "the Four Rs." The president rebuffed efforts to draw him out on the specifics of a settlement or how one could be brought about. When ABC news anchor Peter Jennings asked him in New Delhi if he favored a referendum to determine Kashmir's future as provided in the 1948 UN resolution, the president carefully replied: "Well, there's been a lot of changes since 1948, including what happened in 1971 and a number of things since. . . . What I support is . . . some process by which Kashmiris' legitimate grievances are addressed, and I support respecting the Line of Control. . . . And I think the Pakistanis and the Indians have to have some way of talking to their own Kashmiris about it that recognizes there's not a military solution."[26]

For its remaining months in office the Clinton administration continued to urge the contestants to practice the Four Rs that the president had prescribed to them during his South Asian visit. The administration persuaded the two sides to reduce shelling across the Line of Control, a practice that could easily escalate and was a great hardship to Kashmiris living close to the line.[27] As the end of his term neared, Clinton was satisfied that his call for restraint seemed to have had some resonance in New Delhi and Islamabad. In his last statement on the Kashmir issue as president, he welcomed Prime Minister Vajpayee's assertion that India would continue the cease-fire within Kashmir that it had recently initiated. He also hailed Islamabad's announcement that it would withdraw part of its forces deployed along the Line of Control and exercise maximum restraint there. "They raise the hope of the world community that peace is possible in Kashmir," the outgoing president declared on December 20, 2000, exactly a month before he turned the White House over to George W. Bush.[28]

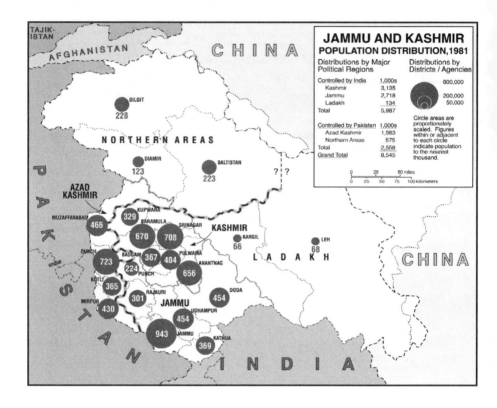

JAMMU AND KASHMIR
POPULATION DISTRIBUTION, 1981

Distributions by Major
Political Regions

Distributions by
Districts / Agencies

Controlled by India   1,000s
  Kashmir   3,135
  Jammu   2,718
  Ladakh   134
Total   5,987

Controlled by Pakistan 1,000s
  Azad Kashmir   1,983
  Northern Areas   575
Total   2,558
Grand Total   8,545

800,000
200,000
50,000

Circle areas are
proportionately
scaled. Figures
within or adjacent
to each circle
indicate population
to the nearest
thousand.

0   25   50 miles
0 25 50 75 100 kilometers

8

Focus on Crisis Management

In its first months in office, the George W. Bush administration followed Clinton's pattern in developing better relations with India. This seemed to be one area of Bush foreign policy that demonstrated continuity in contrast to the more typical tendency of the new Republican White House to disparage any strategy that was associated with its predecessor. The administration actively sought new ways to build on the progress that Clinton had made in his visit to India. New Delhi welcomed this heightened U.S. interest, and over the course of the Bush presidency the two countries found many promising new areas for cooperation. U.S.-India relations reached levels never considered possible in the 1990s, let alone during the cold war era.

Washington's ties with Islamabad remained poor during Bush's first months in power. The administration was unhappy with the authoritarian regime General Pervez Musharraf had established following the 1999 coup and badgered him to set out a timetable for fresh elections and a return to democracy. It was also highly displeased with Islamabad's continuing support for the Taliban regime in Afghanistan that the Pakistanis had helped come to power in the mid-1990s.

And it was troubled by developments in Kashmir. Despite Clinton's hopeful end-of-term statement praising the two sides for demonstrating restraint in the disputed state, elements based in Pakistan continued to cross the Line of Control and engage in violent activity on the Indian side. Although the

169

Indians had scant regard for the Musharraf regime and its leader, the two governments had made an effort to move forward on the Kashmir issue when Musharraf and Vajpayee met in Agra in July 2001. Despite some early hopeful signs, the meeting ignominiously broke down amid mutual charges of bad faith and greatly different appraisals by the two sides of what had gone wrong. The Indians emerged convinced that Musharraf was not someone they could do business with on Kashmir or anything else. The Pakistanis felt betrayed. In their view Vajpayee, under pressure from hard-liners in his government, had reneged on a promising joint statement he and Musharraf had worked out for characterizing the Kashmir dispute and charting ways to deal with it.[1]

The terrorist attacks of September 11, 2001, profoundly changed U.S. relations with Pakistan. Washington swiftly put maximum pressure on Islamabad to break with the Taliban regime and cooperate with American efforts to root out Al Qaeda from its bases in Afghanistan. It signaled Musharraf that if he did not agree to cooperate with the United States in this newly launched global war on terrorism, Pakistan could become a target for American retaliation. Musharraf had little choice and quickly agreed to the U-turn in Pakistan's policy in Afghanistan that Washington demanded. Many Pakistanis, including some senior army officers, faulted this decision. Musharraf shelved a number of key generals who apparently shared such misgivings.

India welcomed what it regarded as America's valuable if belated entry into a war against terrorism it had been fighting in Kashmir and elsewhere for years. Immediately after 9/11, the Indian government announced its unqualified support for America's antiterrorist campaign and offered to make its airfields and intelligence facilities available to U.S. forces for their anticipated offensive against Al Qaeda and its Taliban backers in Afghanistan. But, as Indian analyst Arun Swamy points out, "Indian hopes that the aftermath of September 11 would result in a closer relationship with Washington and help to isolate Pakistan foundered on the simple fact of geography. Pakistan bordered on Afghanistan; India did not."[2] Musharraf alleged that the Vajpayee government's swift decision to support the American antiterrorist effort was designed to win Washington's backing for India's position on Kashmir. He prominently played this India card in his efforts to persuade the Pakistani public to support his decision to throw in Pakistan's lot with the United States.[3]

Despite Bush administration reassurances, New Delhi worried that the military supply agreement the United States made with Pakistan to reward it for its assistance against Al Qaeda and the Taliban would work against Indian interests, especially if Washington provided weapons that Pakistan could turn against India, which New Delhi feared would happen. Inevitably, many Indians saw the resumption of close U.S.-Pakistan political and security cooperation in the context of the "zero-sum" approach that Indians and Pakistanis had long used in weighing America's policies in South Asia: U.S. policies that support Pakistan will harm India, and vice versa. The revived relationship evoked bad memories of the 1950s and 1980s, when Pakistan had also been a "frontline state" in the struggle against Washington's enemy. Then the threat was from international Communism, now it came from global terrorism.

Defense Secretary Donald Rumsfeld visited New Delhi briefly in November 2001 to reassure the Indians that the new U.S. support for Pakistan would not come at India's expense (and to remind them that they had a long-term interest in remaining in America's good books). The Vajpayee government eventually accepted the Bush administration's repeated assertion that it wanted to have strong ties simultaneously with both New Delhi and Islamabad. It resolved to live with a major buildup of American military assistance to Pakistan. But there were probably few takers in India for the American argument that better ties between Washington and Islamabad would benefit Indian interests. Although murmuring continued in India, the U.S.-Pakistan reengagement proved to have little if any adverse impact on Washington's burgeoning relations with New Delhi.

While Musharraf jettisoned the Taliban under irresistible American pressure, he sought at the same time to preserve his policy of support for the Kashmir struggle. Indian security forces had resumed offensive action in the state in the spring of 2001 after the insurgents ignored the cease-fire New Delhi had unilaterally declared the previous November. For Musharraf, the political price of abandoning both Pakistan's long-standing close ties with the Taliban and its backing of the Kashmiris of even longer standing would have been very great. He evidently believed that the United States would not try to force him to pay it and would allow him to "compartmentalize" Kashmir from Afghanistan.

The issue quickly became a major bone of contention between Washington and New Delhi. India insisted that the war on terror was indivisible. In its view, America's willingness to relink with Pakistan despite the Musharraf government's continuing backing for the Kashmir insurgency was inconsistent with the stated purpose of the renewed Washington-Islamabad relationship—combating global terrorism. For New Delhi, any definition of terrorism that ignored or downplayed what the Pakistanis were doing in Kashmir was inadequate and hypocritical. If India was to be America's ally in the war on terrorism, Washington needed to pressure the Pakistanis to end their support for the Kashmir insurgency. At the same time, the Indians saw in the greatly enhanced American concern about the dangers of terrorism an opportunity to win more understanding in Washington for the problem they confronted in Kashmir and support for their efforts to deal with it.

There were sharp differences of view among American policymakers. President Bush himself used rhetoric identical to India's in discussing the indivisibility of the war on terrorism. But the approach was different at the State Department, where Secretary Colin Powell and his tough-talking deputy, Richard Armitage, took the lead in dealing with Pakistan. Though it used the same rhetoric the president favored, the department adopted a more equivocal attitude. Powell and Armitage were willing to cut Pakistan some slack on Kashmir. They believed that the United States should get what it could from Pakistan. But the importance of keeping Islamabad engaged against the Taliban and Al Qaeda was central to their approach.

Powell and Armitage had heated discussions on this issue with Robert Blackwill, the American ambassador to India. A strong-willed, outspoken man, Blackwill had left the Foreign Service to teach at Harvard, then become a senior adviser to Bush during his campaign for the presidency. He was ably supported in New Delhi by Ashley Tellis, an outstanding academic authority on India whom Blackwill recruited as his special assistant. Blackwill saw the post-9/11 situation as the most promising opportunity in years to persuade Pakistan to make a break with terrorism and embark on a new course.[4] But in the opinion of senior figures at the State Department and the National Security Council, the war on Al Qaeda was going well, the Pakistanis were delivering the goods in Afghanistan, and the insurgency in Kashmir did not pose an immediate threat to U.S. interests. Moreover, at least some Washington policymakers suspected that Embassy New Delhi was engaged in special pleading on behalf of the Indians. They knew that more than any other recent American envoy to India Blackwill was determined to do everything he could to bring about a massive improvement in U.S.-India relations. The ambassador's difficult personality and management style did not help his cause.

The problem of Pakistani support for the insurgency in Kashmir and its connection with the global war on terrorism was brutally underscored when a suicide attack on the state assembly building in Srinagar on October 1, 2001, killed more than forty civilians. The Indians blamed the attack on terrorists based in Pakistan.[5] Vajpayee wrote to Bush warning that the patience of the Indian people with Pakistani support for militancy in Kashmir was wearing thin. He hinted that India would be forced to take matters into its own hands if Washington could not convince Islamabad to rein in groups based on the Pakistan side of the Line of Control.[6] Reflecting concern among U.S. policymakers that the situation could lead to war, President Bush called on the two countries to "stand down" in Kashmir.

As tensions mounted, Secretary Powell tried hard in his mid-October visit to India and Pakistan to persuade the two sides to show restraint, that familiar word in America's South Asian diplomatic lexicon. For Washington, crisis management now became the name of the game it sought to play in dealing with the Kashmir issue. Faced with immediate problems in India-Pakistan relations that had major implications for U.S. efforts in Afghanistan, American policymakers had no time in either sense of that phrase for the broader issue of a Kashmir settlement.

Powell was criticized in India and Pakistan for saying different things in each country during his visit. In Islamabad the secretary stated publicly that resolving the Kashmir conflict was "central" to improved India-Pakistan ties. Another example of the linguistic pitfalls American diplomats face when discussing Kashmir, his use of "central" caused problems for Powell in New Delhi, where Indians interpreted it to mean that blame for the violence was evenly shared. (Generations of American diplomats who have similarly used "incorrect" terminology with South Asian audiences when discussing Kashmir can sympathize with the secretary.) He backpedaled from this formulation in New Delhi the next day. There his public statements focused on the dangers of "cross-border terrorism," Indian shorthand for terrorism carried out in Kashmir by groups based in Pakistan. He told his Indian audience that "the United States and India are united against terrorism and that includes terrorism that has been directed against India." A senior official traveling with Powell told the *New York Times* that the secretary had conveyed to the Indians a pledge from President Musharraf "to take steps to control or reduce extremism."[7]

The situation seriously worsened on December 13 when terrorists attacked the Indian Parliament in New Delhi. Twelve died in the assault, including five terrorists. The repercussions would have been much worse had the terrorists succeeded in entering the parliament building and holding ministers and MPs hostage, as they had apparently planned. Many in Washington, fearing that New Delhi's "red line" had been crossed, concluded that an Indian attack on Pakistan was now likely. India claimed that two Pakistan-based groups, Lashkar-e-Taiba and Jaish-e-Mohammed, were responsible, although the intelligence trail linking the groups to the attack was not that clear. Both organizations the Indians accused were heavily involved in the Kashmir insurgency. Pakistan maintained that there was insufficient evidence and refused to take action against them.[8]

Demanding that Pakistan cease cross-border terrorism immediately, India suspended transit links to Pakistan and withdrew its high commissioner and half its diplomatic staff from Islamabad. More important, and more dangerously, it deployed large forces to the India-Pakistan border and the Line of Control. Reacting to New Delhi's "coercive diplomacy," as the massive troop movements were quickly and accurately labeled, Pakistan redeployed its own troops and put them on high alert. Within a few weeks a million men were eyeball to eyeball in combat mode.

As Polly Nayak and Michael Krepon observe in their detailed and carefully researched study of U.S. efforts to manage the crisis, for many American policymakers "the December 13 attack and the subsequent Indian and Pakistani deployments were serious and unwelcome diversions from the war on terror."[9] Washington recognized the great impact the attack had on the Indian government and public. But it framed its public reaction in an even-handed manner, to Indian dismay. The administration took into account the obvious similarity between the attack and the events of 9/11, yet it also understood Pakistan's important role in the war against terrorism. An India-Pakistan war or even the sizable redeployment of Pakistani forces from the Afghan frontier to the Line of Control and the India-Pakistan border would seriously damage U.S. counterterrorism efforts. As the authors of another well-regarded study of the problem aptly put it: "American policy was torn between two logics . . . the logic of the American-Indian entente, which presupposed that India was a rising power of considerable strategic potential and that the U.S.-India relationship was the new cornerstone of American policy toward South Asia, . . . and the logic of the revived relationship with Pakistan."[10] President Bush stated that the attack had been designed to strike at India's democracy as well as to undermine Pakistan, harm the rapidly improving U.S.-Pakistan relationship, and destabilize the global coalition against terrorism.

Bush phoned Musharraf and Vajpayee the day after the attack and again later in December to urge restraint, a message that did not go over well with the Indian prime minister. The president called on Musharraf to take decisive action against terrorist organizations and reported approvingly that the Pakistani leader had said he would do so. He offered Musharraf full U.S. support, including the expertise of the Federal Bureau of Investigation for these promised efforts. The State Department placed on its terrorist list the two organizations reportedly involved. It also froze their assets in the United States.

The administration warmly welcomed Musharraf's January 12, 2002, speech, in which he announced his decision to ban five terrorist organizations and take other actions against terrorists. In this address, Musharraf pledged that Pakistani soil would not be used for terrorist or subversive activity inside or outside the country. At the same time, he restated his government's support for the Kashmiri cause and the people of Kashmir. Washington, which had provided detailed advice to Musharraf on the contents of the speech, urged the skeptical Indians to allow him time to deal with the terrorist problem. Some observers believe that one of the purposes India had in mobilizing its forces was to lead the Americans to exercise just this kind of pressure on Pakistan. The Indians said they would wait and see what happened when the snows melted in the Kashmiri mountains in April and May, the season when cross-border activities heighten.

Meanwhile, Indian and Pakistani troops continued to confront one another. Wendy Chamberlin, a career diplomat who had succeeded William

Milam as American ambassador in Islamabad in September 2001, believes that by not responding more positively to Musharraf's speech, the Indians lost an opportunity to move the confrontation forward toward a settlement through bilateral talks. She holds that the Pakistanis, concerned about the buildup, would have been prepared to engage on Kashmir "had the Indians shown a little leg."[11] A senior American diplomat then serving in New Delhi maintains that the Indians, suspicious of Musharraf as the perpetrator of the Kargil operation and uncertain of his agenda, were not ready to give him the benefit of the doubt.[12]

A few days after Musharraf delivered his speech, Secretary Powell briefly visited South Asia on yet another crisis management operation. The *New York Times* likened him to a doctor on an extended diplomatic house call. Powell's message to India and Pakistan was to cool the situation and, when tensions eased, reopen the border and resume their broken dialogue. "We need a campaign against terrorism," he said, "not a campaign with these two countries fighting one another." The secretary reiterated America's unwillingness to play a mediator's role. But it wanted to be helpful in getting the dialogue started.[13] He could not win concrete agreement from either side to ease their military standoff along the border, however.

In mid-May, the confrontation perilously escalated when terrorists attacked an Indian army base in Kashmir, killing many military dependents and arousing deep anger among the Indian military and public. Infiltration of armed men across the Line of Control rose again as the weather improved, leading Indians to question even more sharply Musharraf's sincerity when he promised that he would not allow terrorists to operate out of Pakistani territory.

Many American officials in Washington, New Delhi, and Islamabad now believed that war was imminent. In New Delhi, Ambassador Blackwill and the embassy's Emergency Action Committee recommended to the State Department that dependents and nonessential embassy personnel leave as soon as possible. The department's reply was ambiguous. Its discussion of the issue suggested that it agreed with the embassy, but it called only for a voluntary departure. Blackwill chose to interpret the message to mean mandatory departure and ordered the evacuation of nonessential staff and dependents. Soon afterward, the department urged nonofficial Americans to leave India and advised U.S. citizens not to travel to the region. A number of other countries followed the American example.[14]

The well-publicized decision to thin out the American presence caught the Indians by surprise and had a salutary impact on the way they viewed the confrontation. According to one senior State Department official close to these events, many Indians unfamiliar with the situation on the ground had considered previous expressions of American concern overblown.[15] The decision brought home to them how strongly the U.S. government feared an outbreak of war. In this view, the American exodus led the Indian government to take the situation more seriously and helped prompt New Delhi to look for a way out of the crisis. The thin-out also brought home to the influential Indian business community the cost of the confrontation and may have led some with important commercial connections with the United States to press their government to moderate its position. Some observers have ironically called the episode "American coercive diplomacy."

Personal intervention by senior U.S. officials to defuse the situation now kicked into high gear. Soon after the embassy thin-out was announced, Deputy Secretary Armitage came to South Asia to engage in a brief exercise in shuttle diplomacy.[16] In Islamabad and New Delhi, he offered senior officials suggestions about various methods of preventing infiltration across the Line of Control. These included creating a monitoring force and sharing U.S. national intelligence with both sides. He got a pledge from Musharraf to stop cross-border activities permanently. The president told him, Armitage reported, that he was "quite keen . . . on entering into a dialogue [with India] on the whole question of Kashmir."[17] Armitage made Musharraf's pledge public when he reached New Delhi, reportedly at the request of Indian government officials.

The deputy secretary's visit helped prompt the two sides to begin to back away from the confrontation. Ambassador Nancy Powell, a career diplomat with long service in South Asia who had replaced Wendy Chamberlin in Islamabad just before Armitage reached Pakistan, believes that the Indians saw the deputy secretary's mission as a handy way to disengage from a situation that to them was becoming less and less productive. In her view, which some other American South Asia specialists share, the morale of the Indian forces on the battlefront and aboard the naval ships off Karachi was falling, hot weather had set in, training programs had been delayed, much money had been spent, and New Delhi was looking for a way out. (The Pakistanis faced similar problems, Ambassador Powell and other commentators note.) If this reading is correct, then Armitage and other U.S. senior officials who came to the subcontinent in the spring and summer of 2002 played somewhat the same role that the Gates mission had a dozen years earlier when it helped defuse the crisis that followed the outbreak of the Kashmir insurrection. As Gates had, they did so with admirable skill and in their case with great patience and perseverance.[18]

Following up the Armitage mission, Bush again phoned Vajpayee and Musharraf, and Rumsfeld and Powell went to South Asia once more on separate visits in June and July. Armitage returned in August for another shuttle bout. Powell phoned Musharraf repeatedly, sometimes adopting a general-to-general mode in these conversations. (Armitage's military background was also useful in the exercise.) Meanwhile Washington also worked with other countries that could bring their influence to bear in New Delhi and Islamabad. It encouraged visits by their representatives to the region, in part at least on the assumption or in the hope that neither India nor Pakistan would attack while foreign dignitaries were physically present in the region.[19]

In their discussions, American officials continued to lean hard on the Pakistanis to stop infiltration and honor the commitment that Musharraf had made to Armitage and in public. They and their Pakistani counterparts disagreed on the number of infiltrators and the Pakistan government's role in their activities. Not surprisingly, the Indians came to their own, more drastic conclusions. But in making their démarches, American diplomats were careful not to jeopardize the important help Islamabad was providing Washington in rounding up Al Qaeda and Taliban elements who had fled to Pakistan from Afghanistan. They were in effect playing a delicate balancing act, trying to convince the Indians that the United States was making a serious effort to get the Pakistanis to stop infiltration while delivering that message to Islamabad in a way that would not impede Pakistan's support for U.S. objectives in Afghanistan. Despite these American initiatives and others by the British and Russians, it was not until October 2002 that India fully redeployed its troops from their forward positions, the Pakistanis reciprocated, and the dangerous confrontation finally ended.

Elections were held for the state assembly of Indian Kashmir in the fall of 2002. To the surprise of almost all observers, a coalition of the Indian National Congress and the newly organized, locally based People's Democratic Party swept the National Conference from power and formed a government led by PDP leader Mufti Mohammed Sayeed, the veteran Valley politician. Mufti Sayeed had been home minister in the central Indian government when his daughter's abduction sparked the outbreak of the insurgency thirteen years earlier.[20] All the contesting parties favored Kashmir's association with India, though they differed on the nature of center-state relations. The PDP projected itself as a secular party supporting self-rule and sought to stake out a middle-ground position between the other pro-India parties and the separatist Hurriyet (which once again boycotted the elections). Although some complained about irregularities, the contest was generally considered free and fair.[21] The new government offered a "healing touch" to the dissidents.

When he visited South Asia a couple of months before the Kashmir polling, Secretary Powell told a New Delhi press conference that "an inclusive election meeting these [acceptable] standards [for fairness] can serve as a first step toward peace and reconciliation." He called on India to foster Kashmiri confidence in the election process by freeing political prisoners and permitting independent observers to monitor the contest at least on an informal basis. This would give greater credibility to the results. The secretary gave an ambiguous reply to a question about Hurriyet participation: "Groups that have demonstrated responsible action and wish to participate in the free and open election process should be allowed to do so."[22] Powell said much the same thing about the state elections at a second press conference later in the day in Islamabad, though he must have known that most Pakistanis believed that India could not be trusted to hold a free and fair election in Kashmir and that outsiders were foolish to believe otherwise. The Pakistanis could be pleased, however, with Secretary Powell's much publicized statement to the media that "Kashmir is on the international agenda," even though it exaggerated the importance the world community gave to the issue at that point. Not surprisingly, the statement was loudly criticized in India.[23]

The State Department welcomed "the successful conclusion of the elections" when the results were announced on October 10. Using Secretary

Powell's language, the department spokesman expressed the hope that the election would be "the first step in a broader process that will bring peace to the region." He pointedly commended "the courage of candidates and voters who chose to participate despite violence and intimidation." As Washington saw it, or said it did, "The Kashmiri people have shown that they want to pursue the path of peace."[24]

Washington's considerable interest in the elections and their outcome reflected the greater importance it now attached to reconciliation between India and the Kashmiris living under Indian rule as a key element in a settlement of the dispute. This interest reflected the conclusion many American policymakers and analysts had long drawn about the nature of a Kashmir settlement. In this view, a resolution needed to involve the division of the state along the Line of Control, or a boundary very close to it. Though they might not like it, and would opt for independence if they could, the Muslims of the Kashmiri Valley were fated to remain permanently under New Delhi's control.

Under those circumstances, an arrangement that helped reconcile Kashmiris to their Indian ties would be an important part of any peace settlement. Better governance of Kashmir, a substantial degree of autonomy for the state, and the induction of the more moderate dissident groups into the mainstream of Indian politics would all help. A meaningful "New Delhi–Srinagar dialogue" was needed to achieve these goals

In New Delhi and on their visits to Kashmir, American diplomats promoted this New Delhi–Srinagar dialogue while avoiding any public judgment about what its outcome should be. They maintained a broad range of contacts with central and state government officials, mainstream and dissident political leaders, and other influential people in Kashmir, as well as with people in India proper who were knowledgeable about Kashmir developments. Indian officials for their part did not object to Embassy New Delhi contacts with Kashmiris. They may have judged that sessions between American officials and the more moderate among the dissidents could be helpful. It seems reasonable to conclude that they knew from their own sources what was being said.

During his July 2002 travels, Secretary Powell reasserted that the Kashmir issue had to be resolved by the two parties. This would presumably take into account the wishes of the Kashmiri people, as the formal American position continued to state. The United States, Powell said, could facilitate the start of a dialogue. But it was up to India and Pakistan to work out an agenda and action plan to resolve the problem. He said at a New Delhi press conference: "To the extent that at that time, if they wish to share ideas with us, we would be more than happy to respond to any ideas that might come from either side in the course of their discussion and dialogue."[25]

An unanticipated warming in India-Pakistan relations that began in the spring of 2003 gave Washington an opportunity to play the helpful if modest role that Powell had proposed. In a speech in Srinagar in mid-April, Prime Minister Vajpayee offered a "hand of friendship" to Pakistan. Although the Indians continued to insist that no talks were possible until the Pakistanis had ceased supporting terrorism in Kashmir, Islamabad welcomed what it read as an invitation to resume the bilateral dialogue. Washington hailed Vajpayee's "bold offer" and the "positive response" he made to Mir Zafrullah Khan Jamali, the prime minister of Pakistan, when Jamali phoned him a few days later.[26] Soon afterward the two governments announced that they had agreed to take steps to upgrade diplomatic relations and restore transportation links. The *New York Times* lauded these promising developments in a hopeful editorial, "Spring Thaw in the Subcontinent."[27]

Vajpayee's Srinagar speech and the India-Pakistan agreement to begin normalizing relations came shortly before Armitage began a scheduled visit to the two countries. On the eve of the trip, Secretary Powell affirmed that his deputy "will encourage [the] process of reaching out and the United States will be ready to assist both sides as they move forward."[28] Armitage was widely expected to press Islamabad to curb infiltration into Kashmir and urge New Delhi to resume the interrupted dialogue. Commenting on the timing of the Vajpayee statement, which came just before Armitage's arrival in South Asia, the *Times* New Delhi correspondent speculated: "Rather than try to placate Armitage . . . Vajpayee has managed to preempt him."[29]

If that was the Indian prime minister's goal, he seems to have achieved it. Visiting New Delhi, Armitage praised Vajpayee's new peace initiative as a "far-reaching act of statesmanship." He was careful to note that the prime minister had taken these steps to defuse tensions on his own; it was not the work of American diplomats. The press reported that American embassy officers had gone out of their way to play down any U.S. government involvement in possible talks, and Armitage stated that he was not an interlocutor. Washington evidently recognized that it was in America's best interest not to be seen to be pushing Vajpayee too hard, and given the prime minister's initiative there was no need to pressure him. The deputy secretary sensibly understood that it would be a long road to a final settlement. "I just hope we've begun the process," he stated as he was leaving New Delhi.[30]

Armitage told the Indians, as he had told the Pakistanis in Islamabad a couple of days earlier, that he was "cautiously optimistic" about future prospects. He declared publicly that he had not come to bring pressure on either country on the Kashmir issue but hoped to encourage a bilateral dialogue.

This approach reflected Washington's recognition that it was in no position to engage in an arm-twisting exercise. As noted it continued to need Pakistani support in the war on terrorism. At the same time it wished to avoid measures that would disrupt the unprecedented warming of its relations with India that sprang in important measure from its growing appreciation of India as a key geostrategic factor in Asia.[31] During the visit President Musharraf told Armitage that infiltration across the Line of Control had stopped and that any militants' camps found in Azad Kashmir would be "gone tomorrow."[32] The deputy secretary had of course received similar assurances before. But it was true that although crossings continued, the number of infiltrators had fallen since the two men had last met in the summer of 2002.

It took months before transportation links and normal diplomatic relations were restored. Meanwhile the Indians publicly drew a distinction between resuming those ties and conducting a dialogue. They continued to insist that the Pakistanis cease their support of the Kashmiri insurgents before talks could take place. The momentum toward normalization of ties quickened in late November when Pakistan announced a unilateral cease-fire along the Line of Control and said it was prepared to start bus service between Srinagar and Muzaffarabad, the capital of Azad Kashmir.[33] This would be the first legal transit link across the Line of Control available to Kashmiris in a half-century. New Delhi promptly welcomed the cease-fire initiative. But it cautioned that "cross-border terrorism had to stop to allow the cease-fire to hold."[34] Secretary Powell phoned the two foreign ministers to commend them for the cease-fire, which came into effect at midnight November 25–26.[35]

The cease-fire set the stage for a major diplomatic breakthrough a few weeks later. Meeting at the annual summit session of the South Asia Association for Regional Cooperation in Islamabad in early January 2004, Musharraf and Vajpayee hammered out an agreement that Secretary Powell rightly termed historic. Musharraf reassured Vajpayee that "he will not permit any territory under Pakistan's control to support terrorism in any manner." The two leaders agreed to commence a sustained dialogue covering many divisive matters and expressed confidence that this process would lead to "a permanent settlement of all bilateral issues, including Jammu and Kashmir, to the satisfaction of both sides."[36]

The mention of Kashmir as a subject of this dialogue represented a concession by New Delhi. It was widely seen as a quid pro quo for Musharraf's antiterrorism commitment, the first time the president had offered such an assurance directly to an Indian leader and not through an American intermediary. Including the commitment in the context of a peace process gave it greater credibility, at least to more optimistic observers.

American commentators found many reasons for the breakthrough. Many cited the seventy-nine-year-old Vajpayee's apparent interest in leaving behind a legacy that included peace with Pakistan and his likely calculation that improved India-Pakistan relations would help his Bharatiya Janata Party–led coalition win upcoming parliamentary elections. Some speculated that two near-miss attempts on his life had led Musharraf to conclude that he could no longer compartmentalize the activities of terrorists in Kashmir from those operating in Pakistan. Observers also called attention to Musharraf's increasing preoccupation with problems along Pakistan's border with Afghanistan; India's desire to burnish its international image as a responsible, mature, rising power; and the room for maneuver made possible by the political strength that Vajpayee and Musharraf enjoyed or seemed to enjoy. They also noted the gradual improvement in the mood of the publics in each country toward one another and an apparent newfound appreciation in India that Musharraf might well be its last, best chance for a settlement with Pakistan—an idea that the Pakistan president himself promoted.[37]

Persistent American efforts to persuade the two sides to resume their dialogue also seem to have played a useful role. Eight months of secret back-channel negotiations between Indian and Pakistani emissaries preceded the breakthrough. Both governments briefed the local American embassies from time to time on the progress of the negotiations. American officials welcomed the talks and encouraged the two sides to push forward. But neither the State Department nor the embassies tried to inject substantive ideas of their own into the back-channel process, nor did the two sides bounce any off their American interlocutors. In Islamabad, Nancy Powell thought this was just as well. In her view it would have been a mistake to insert any concepts that could have been disparaged as "made in America." Generally the Pakistanis were more forthcoming in keeping American officials informed of developments and how they assessed future prospects. This was to be expected given their greater interest in drawing the international community—especially the United States—into the Kashmir issue. The Pakistanis appear to have been more optimistic in their comments than later events justified.[38]

The extent of American assistance became a subject of public dispute later in 2004. Speaking to the editors of *USA Today* that October, Secretary Powell recalled a phone conversation he had with President Musharraf, apparently soon after Prime Minister Vajpayee had delivered his "hand of friendship" speech. "Do you think if my prime minister . . . were to call the Indian prime minister he would take the call?" Powell said Musharraf had asked him. The secretary recalled taking prompt action. "We [then] set it up, the call was made. We also arranged for the call to be 'How are you?' 'Fine. How are you?' 'Fine,' just to begin the dialogue. And now," Powell told the editors, "the dialogue has paid off with the return of diplomatic relations, and the ministers are meeting and talking about . . . cross-border infiltration and Kashmir. . . . I think that's been a success of the [Bush] administration."[39]

Jaswant Singh, who had been Indian foreign minister at the time of the Powell-Musharraf conversation, quickly took strong exception to the secretary's account. By then no longer in office following the BJP's defeat in parliamentary elections, Singh termed it "entirely incorrect." The reason Vajpayee offered the hand of friendship to the Pakistanis, Singh maintained, was the successful conclusion of assembly elections in Kashmir, not a nudge from the Americans. Washington wisely chose to ignore Singh's allegations.[40]

Whatever its role may have been, Washington was publicly ecstatic about the agreement. In an interview with Pakistan TV, Armitage congratulated Vajpayee and Musharraf for their statesmanship and said he had a great deal more confidence now that the Kashmir issue "will be resolved peacefully and to the mutual satisfaction of both India and Pakistan and most importantly the people of Kashmir."[41] His boss, Colin Powell, personally phoned the two leaders and later pledged at a press conference that "in the months ahead, we will lend our good offices to our Indian and Pakistani friends to whatever purpose these good offices could be used to keep the process moving forward."[42]

The unexpected defeat of the Vajpayee government in elections in early 2004 brought to power a Congress Party–led coalition headed by Prime Minister Manmohan Singh. The new government accepted the agreement Vajpayee had reached with Musharraf a few months earlier. But progress in the formal talks that agreement called for was disappointing during the remaining four years of Musharraf's government. Officials of the two countries met regularly to discuss issues on their comprehensive dialogue agenda, including Kashmir. Additionally, Musharraf and Singh conferred on the margins of multilateral meetings they both attended. The two leaders held a more substantial bilateral session in April 2005, when Musharraf paid an amicable three-day visit to New Delhi, his first travel to India since the failed Agra summit four years earlier. In a joint statement, they declared that the peace process was irreversible and reaffirmed their commitment to resolve the Kashmir issue.

The sessions between senior Indian and Pakistani officials were friendly by past standards. They continued despite several terrorist acts that Indian officials blamed on elements operating out of Pakistan. One of the most egregious of these, the bombing of commuter trains in Mumbai in July 2006, prompted India to suspend the talks for a few months. (After Musharraf had fallen from power, the talks were again broken off when even more serious terrorist attacks took place in the city in November 2008.) With few exceptions, the two sides sought to put relatively positive spins on the outcome of their meetings. But no significant progress was made even on the "easy" issues that seemed most conducive to resolution, such as their competing claims to a small area at the western end of their long boundary (Sir

Creek). There was no movement in the formal talks toward resolving the Kashmir dispute, which Pakistani representatives continued to characterize over Indian objection as the "central" or "core" issue between them.

By contrast New Delhi and Islamabad developed impressive confidence-building measures. People-to-people contact substantially increased. Bilateral trade expanded, and because it still remained far below potential, the two sides agreed to develop it further. In Kashmir itself, the 2003 cease-fire along the Line of Control held and infiltration decreased. But extensive violence and human rights violations continued within the Indian-held portion of the state.

In April 2005 the two governments overcame differences over passengers' documentation and launched a bus service between the two sides of Kashmir with great fanfare and expressions of satisfaction, in which Washington conspicuously joined.[43] This move was followed by other measures similarly designed to "soften" borders both in Kashmir and along the frontier between India and Pakistan. New Delhi's attitude toward the more moderate Kashmiri separatists eased. Representatives of the All Parties Hurriyet Conference were allowed to accept Musharraf's invitation to travel to Pakistan and, for the first time, to Azad Kashmir. Hurriyet representatives also had an inconclusive meeting with Manmohan Singh, the first session Kashmiri separatist leaders held with an Indian prime minister. The Pakistan government encouraged this exchange. Musharraf stated publicly that it could be the first step in the trilateral dialogue the Kashmiri separatists have long called for.

India also offered to provide emergency assistance when a devastating earthquake struck northern Pakistan and Pakistani-held parts of Kashmir in October 2005. (The earthquake also damaged Indian Kashmir, but much less severely.) But the limits Pakistan set on what it would permit India to do and the shamefully long time the two sides took to open border crossing points to help the victims undercut the good feeling the gesture created. "It is plain," David Rohde wrote in the *New York Times*, "that even as landslides washed away the very hills that India and Pakistan fought over so bitterly, their 58-year-legacy of mistrust and bitterness continues."[44]

In October 2004 President Musharraf launched an initiative on Kashmir outside the established dialogue. Typically, he did not staff it out in advance with Foreign Ministry or national security officials. Offering his ideas initially as "food for thought," Musharraf declared that a solution could be found only if the two governments agreed to move beyond their stated positions. He said he was prepared to abandon Islamabad's long-standing demand for a plebiscite (unacceptable to India) if New Delhi did not insist that the Line of Control remain the de facto border (unacceptable to Pakistan). He was inconsistent in explaining the different parts of his proposal, which drew on the Kashmir Study Group's recommendations, and never provided a precise idea of what he had in mind. He said he recognized that the Kashmir problem was "complex" and would require time and great effort for a solution, unusual positions for a Pakistani leader to take publicly.

Musharraf proposed that Kashmir be divided into seven "self-governing" regions on the basis of local culture and demographic composition. These regions should be gradually demilitarized, and India and Pakistan should then discuss under whose control they should be placed. He mentioned joint control, UN administration, and independence as well as assignment to India and Pakistan as options. Borders should be softened to the point that they became "irrelevant." The president also stated, remarkably, that there could be no solution to the Kashmir problem on religious lines, although his proposal to designate seven regions seemed to do just that.[45]

New Delhi gave Musharraf's initiative a frosty reception. The Indians at first dismissed it as a trial balloon that was not serious enough to merit a formal response. They complained that the president had unveiled his proposals in the media before approaching New Delhi through diplomatic channels. They later became less negative and said they were willing to look at various options and "listen out" Musharraf's proposals. But they were never prepared to consider them carefully as a feasible way to move toward a settlement.

Prime Minister Singh, for his part, repeatedly declared that he would not agree to any redrawing of the border or "another partition" along communal lines. Otherwise, he said, he was open to fresh ideas. Like Musharraf, Singh declared that he hoped that borders would eventually become irrelevant. His government stated that the disarmament Musharraf had called for was possible only if Pakistan substantially reduced cross-border infiltration.[46] It did not address the issue of greater autonomy for its part of Kashmir.

Aware that Pakistanis suspected that India was stonewalling, Singh publicly offered Islamabad a treaty of peace, security, and friendship in March 2006. (Pakistan declined the offer for the same reason it had rebuffed Indian interest in a no-war treaty decades earlier: such a treaty would not bring about a Kashmir settlement nor establish a mechanism to reach one.) At the same time, the prime minister declared, more constructively, that he envisaged a situation "where the two parts of Jammu and Kashmir can, with the active encouragement of the governments of India and Pakistan, work out cooperative, consultative mechanisms so as to maximize the gains of cooperation in solving problems of social and economic development of the region." He spoke favorably of an arrangement that would allow people to move and trade across the Line of Control.[47]

In his discussions with American officials, Musharraf argued that he represented the best, perhaps the last, chance for Pakistan's agreeing to terms for a Kashmir settlement. Some of these officials privately concurred that the president did offer a "window of opportunity" for progress. But the Bush administration avoided developing a formal position on his proposals. In public statements, officials said encouragingly that the proposals had prompted fresh thinking and debate, which they welcomed.[48]

President Bush discussed Kashmir with Musharraf when he visited Pakistan and India in March 2006. But Bush, too, appears only to have said once again that his administration wished to be helpful. An Indian scholar wrote succinctly and accurately: "During his trip to South Asia, President Bush has done his best to whistle past the diplomatic graveyard of Kashmir, issuing only bland encouragement to the leaders of India and Pakistan to resolve the status of the disputed territory."[49] Like many of his post-Kennedy White House predecessors, the president stressed that it was up to the leaders of the two contending governments to take the initiative. He did not mention Musharraf's recent proposals.

When Musharraf paid a return visit to Washington that September, Bush went somewhat farther. Telling a joint news conference that he was "impressed" by the Pakistan president's will "to get something done in Kashmir," Bush said once again that the "Kashmir issue will be solved when [the] two leaders decide to solve it. And we want to help. The United States can't force nations to reach an agreement just because we want there to be an agreement. Lasting agreements occur when leaders of nations say, let's get the past behind and let's move forward."

Intriguingly, Bush reported to the media an exchange with Musharraf about an American role. "I asked the President, just like I would ask the Prime Minister of India, what would you like the United States to do to facilitate an agreement? Would you like us to get out of the way? Would you like us not to show up? Would you like us actively involved? How can we help you, if you so desire, achieve peace?"[50]

Unfortunately neither Bush nor Musharraf provided the Pakistan president's reply, and the media had no opportunity to press them on the matter. In any event, U.S. diplomatic activity on the Kashmir issue following the Bush-Musharraf White House meeting remained limited to muted cheering from the sidelines.[51]

In December 2006 Musharraf offered another set of proposals that went even further than his 2004 initiative had in making concessions on Kashmir. This four-point initiative, which he typically made public in an interview with an Indian TV channel, stated that the existing border, that is, the Line of Control, would remain the same but that people would be allowed to move freely across it. Areas on each side of the line would have "self-governance or autonomy," though not independence. There would be a phased withdrawal of troops, and a tripartite India-Pakistan-Kashmir mechanism would be established for "joint supervision" of the state. Musharraf said that his government would be willing to withdraw the dispute from the UN Security Council if talks showed tangible progress. Some of these proposals expanded on points he made in an interview in October 2006 with the highly regarded Indian analyst A. G. Noorani. In that interview, he implicitly accepted the permanence of the Line of Control.[52] He also spelled out his ideas in his autobiography, *In the Line of Fire,* published in 2006.[53] In his TV interview, the president did not define what he meant by self-governance or joint supervision. Nor did he explain what a reduction of forces would involve or suggest a timetable for it. And his office later clarified that his offer was not unilateral but contingent on India's attitude.[54]

Despite its uncertainties, Musharraf bold initiative offered a fresh basis for negotiations. New Delhi's public reaction to it was cool at first. But Prime Minister Singh said later that his government was seriously considering the proposal. India's more positive attitude to the initiative suggested that while the two sides were not making progress in their formal dialogue, the areas of disagreement between them were shrinking. As Amitabh Mattoo, the vice chancellor of Jammu University and a seasoned student of the Kashmir issue put it, the new flexibility in Pakistan's Kashmir policy helped give considerable space to back-channel negotiators "to work with and arrive at, hopefully, reconciliation between [the two countries'] positions."[55]

These unpublicized but acknowledged back-channel talks between designated representatives of the two governments began in 2004. According to two well-informed observers, one Pakistani, the other Indian, five elements of a likely solution emerged from these talks: no territorial change; open borders between the two sides in Kashmir; autonomy for them both; reduction of armed forces; and joint institutions or mechanisms that would operate throughout the state and deal with a range of noncontroversial matters.[56]

In public discussion tourism, forestry, and hydrology have been mentioned as possible subjects for these joint bodies. There has also been talk of setting up a joint legislative entity. So far those who favor such cooperative arrangements have not defined the powers and responsibilities of the proposed bodies.

Musharraf, increasingly distracted by domestic challenges that threatened his regime and by growing violence in Pakistan's western borderlands, made no further comments about the contours of a Kashmir settlement in 2007. But Manmohan Singh gave a lift to prospects for progress in a speech at Jammu University that July. Expressing his hope that Kashmir could one day become "a symbol of India-Pakistan cooperation rather than conflict," the prime minister reiterated his opposition to any change in borders, a point Musharraf had already accepted. The borders could become irrelevant, he said once again, as Musharraf had. He went on to declare: "The natural resources of the State could be used for the benefit of its people. They need no longer be points of contention or a source of conflict. We could, for example, use the land and water resources of the region jointly for the benefit of all the people living on both sides of the Line of Control."[57]

Washington applauded these developments in its bland and noncommittal fashion. Answering a question about Musharraf's December 2006 initiative, a State Department spokesman declared, "The United States had encouraged both sides to come together to resolve [the issue]. Whatever the solution is, certainly the people of the region need to have a voice in it . . . whenever the two sides choose to resolve it." But privately, a senior State Department official was more specific about what these recent developments signified. The two sides, he said in April 2007, had now accepted the main elements of a settlement. The question had become whether they would be willing and able to muster the political will to bring that resolution about.[58]

The defeat of Musharraf's "King's Party" (formally known as the Pakistan Muslim League-Quaid) by a coalition led by the Pakistan People's Party (PPP) in National Assembly elections in February 2008 ushered in a new, democratic phase in Pakistan's turbulent political history. Although he did not take public office until six months later, when he was elected president following Musharraf's forced resignation, PPP co-chairman Asif Ali Zardari was from the start the dominant political figure in postelection Pakistan. The widower of Benazir Bhutto, the former prime minister and PPP leader assassinated in December 2007, he had had no direct experience in dealing with the Kashmir issue.

Zardari adopted a constructive position on Kashmir. In an early postelection interview, he stated that the PPP would be willing to put aside the issue and focus on other matters in India-Pakistan relations just as India and China had done in dealing with their border dispute.[59] He welcomed the ongoing India-Pakistan peace process and affirmed that the long-standing back-channel discussions between the two sides would remain active.[60] In his maiden address to the UN General Assembly, he reaffirmed Pakistan's "complete commitment to the Kashmiri people in their just struggle for the restoration of their fundamental rights." But he made no mention in the speech of Pakistan's traditional stand on the Kashmiris' right to self-determination or the UNCIP resolutions.[61] He said a few days later in a New York press conference that his approach would be a continuation of the Musharraf regime's policy of holding direct talks with India. The UN should be involved "only when needed."[62] He aroused considerable ire in Pakistan and Kashmir (and appreciation in India) when he characterized as terrorists the militant Islamic groups operating in Indian Kashmir.

During this time, the Pakistan government proposed further confidence-building measures on Kashmir, and in October 2008 two routes between the

Indian and Pakistani parts of the state were opened to trade as well as passenger service. Earlier, Islamabad had adopted a moderate public posture when the Indian authorities cracked down harshly on peaceful demonstrations by massive crowds chanting pro-independence slogans in the Valley. These demonstrations, the largest popular outburst in the state since the early 1990s, were followed by counter protests in Jammu Province organized by Hindu nationalist elements.[63]

But Zardari's conciliatory statements and the actions of the government he dominates stopped well short of an endorsement of Musharraf's bold policy initiatives. Nor has the Manmohan Singh government offered any further ideas about terms of a settlement.

Facing critical parliamentary elections in May 2009, it was content to continue with the new Pakistan government the routinized bilateral dialogue it had had with the Musharraf regime and to keep the back-channel talks going. Like other governments in New Delhi, it saw no urgency in taking serious initiatives to resolve the Kashmir issue other than to press forward with confidence-building measures.

In late November 2008, as has happened so often in India-Pakistan relations, a new terrorist attack turned a moment of fragile promise into a fresh downturn. Ten gunmen, arriving from Pakistan by boat in the heart of Mumbai, held several high-profile tourist sites hostage for three days and killed more than 170 Indians and foreigners. The sophistication of the attack and information provided by the one surviving attacker led most observers to conclude that either current or former elements in Pakistan's intelligence services must have been involved. India made an early decision against a military response, but this episode effectively froze the dialogue on Kashmir.

While the India-Pakistan dialogue was active, Washington maintained its familiar approach. The Mumbai attacks sparked a crisis management effort, with Secretary of State Condoleezza Rice traveling to India and Pakistan to discourage any thought of military action. But fundamentally, in its final months in office, the lame-duck Bush administration was prepared to allow the Kashmir situation to drift as it focused its diminishing energies on what it perceived to be more pressing problems on its foreign policy agenda.

A Role for the United States

This account of the American experience in dealing with Kashmir underscores both the difficulty of resolving the problem and the risks to U.S. interests that stem from the parties' failure to reach a settlement. Kashmir remains one of the "frozen" disputes much written about in conflict resolution literature. These disputes hold back the contenders' potential for economic development and national security. They inhibit the growth of stable political institutions and robust civil societies in the contested areas. But as the record of the last sixty-one years demonstrates, neither the Indian nor the Pakistan government has perceived that the short-term damage to its own interests of the persisting impasse over Kashmir was severe enough to warrant the wrenching policy changes and concessions needed to bring about a mutually acceptable settlement. Many of the ideas for a solution of the issue that are talked about today have been bruited about for decades. None has provided the basis for a breakthrough.

During the Clinton and George W. Bush administrations, American policymakers and commentators generally agreed that Washington should be prepared to "facilitate" efforts by India, Pakistan, and the Kashmiris themselves to resolve the issue. But "facilitate" is a catch-all word defined in different ways at different times by different people. All that proponents of facilitation can agree on is that a facilitator's role is less intrusive than that of an arbitrator (who can impose decisions on the conflicting parties), a mediator (who suggests specific proposals to them), or even a moderator (who is expected only to create a congenial atmosphere for talks and, when appropriate, to develop a framework for discussion that can help the parties work out their disagreements by themselves).

In the Clinton and Bush years, the United States preferred a minimalist definition of facilitation. This has meant reminding the parties of the importance to their own interests of moving forward, encouraging them to do so, trying to be helpful in smoothing the *process* of bilateral efforts, but avoiding suggestions or judgments about the *content* of a settlement.

In pursuing this approach, U.S. diplomats have stayed well informed about Kashmir developments. They have stressed America's continuing interest in the issue to a wide range of Indian, Pakistani, and Kashmiri contacts. They have also kept in touch with American organizations and individuals concerned with Kashmir. They have sought and welcomed readouts about the progress of India-Pakistan back-channel talks. (These have come mainly from the Pakistanis, who are traditionally eager to draw Washington more meaningfully into the peace process.) But in both their private exchanges and their public statements, American officials have not gone beyond familiar, by now hackneyed, expressions of encouragement to the parties to move forward.

Washington's public position on its role has remained the same for years: If both India and Pakistan wish it to do so, the United States will be willing to offer its good offices to help them reach an agreement acceptable to both that takes into account the wishes of the Kashmiri people.

Some American South Asia specialists outside the government, including former diplomats such as myself, have from time to time urged Washington to take a more active approach. We have called on the Clinton and Bush administrations to go beyond offering to facilitate the process of India-Pakistan exchanges. We have urged Washington to develop substantive ideas (or adopt ours) that U.S. officials could informally suggest to the parties, especially when negotiations appear to be in the doldrums or moving in the wrong direction.

Most proponents of such an enhanced U.S. government role have recommended that Washington work quietly behind the scenes. In their view, which I share, this could help avoid the danger that suggestions made to the negotiating parties will be labeled and dismissed as "made in the U.S.A." Some commentators have contended that American ambassadors on the spot are best suited to play this unobtrusive role. They could act as conduits for ideas developed by policymakers back home, as well as their own.

Others who argue for a more interventionist American policy on Kashmir prefer a less diffident approach. Stephen Solarz, whose interest in South Asia continued after he left Congress in 1993, has for many years called on the government to publicly declare U.S. support for converting the Line of Control into a permanent boundary. Michael Krepon of the Stimson Center, a Washington think tank, has called for the appointment of a senior official to work with India and Pakistan as a kind of special negotiator, virtually a mediator. The idea has never gathered much traction. That was just as well since such an intrusive, high-profile approach would almost certainly be unacceptable to the Indians, as reaction to the report that President-elect Barack Obama was considering casting former president Bill Clinton in that role suggested. It would also probably spark unneeded turf problems in the U.S. foreign policy bureaucracy.

Obama said during the 2008 presidential campaign that he recognized that "working with Pakistan and India to try to resolve [the] Kashmir crisis in a serious way" would be among the critical tasks of his administration if he were elected. In one of the rare references to Kashmir any candidate for president has made in many years, he went on to tell Joe Klein of *Time* magazine:

> Kashmir in particular is an interesting situation [that] is obviously a potential tar pit diplomatically. But for us to devote serious diplomatic resources to get a special envoy in there, to figure out a plausible approach, and essentially make the argument to the Indians, you guys are on the brink of being an economic superpower, why do you want to keep on messing with this? To make the argument to the Pakistanis, look at India and what they are doing, why do you want to keep on being bogged down with this particular [issue] at a time when the biggest threat now is coming from the Afghan border? I think there is a moment when potentially we could get their attention. It won't be easy, but it's important.[1]

Obama's administration should follow up the interest in a more robust U.S. role in Kashmir he expressed on the campaign trail and seek out opportunities to play it. As it judges when, if at all, the time is ripe for meaningful intervention, it should keep a number of key considerations in mind.

Several developments in recent years argue for a more active American approach.

—The United States and India have dramatically strengthened their relations and developed a serious partnership. This may help New Delhi recognize, as it should have since the Kargil crisis, that greater U.S. involvement could actually benefit its interests. The improvement in U.S.-India relations has not come at the expense of American ties with Pakistan. These remain close, though they have been strained by disagreement and mutual mistrust over the handling of the resurgence of the Taliban and Al Qaeda along the Pakistan-Afghanistan frontier.

—India's ambition to play a major role on the international stage has intensified. In the past, the unresolved Kashmir issue detracted from India's image and lessened its prospects for major power status and the permanent seat on an expanded UN Security Council that Indians believe should go with it. (New Delhi is making a major bid for election to a nonpermanent seat in 2011.) Now that India's economic growth has made its gaining a place at the international high table a more achievable goal, it may see Kashmir as an obstacle to the recognition it seeks and be more prepared to rid itself of this albatross.

—A Kashmir settlement has become even more important to American interests in South Asia and beyond. Since India and Pakistan acquired the capacity to develop nuclear weapons in the 1990s, Washington has feared that another conflict between the two over Kashmir could escalate into a nuclear war. Following 9/11, the critical role of Pakistan in shaping the future of Afghanistan and otherwise contributing to the global war against terrorism has given the Kashmir issue a further major dimension. The traditional focus of the Pakistan armed forces on combating a perceived threat from India and the continued patronage that Pakistani intelligence agencies provide to Islamic extremists in Kashmir make it more difficult both politically and militarily for Islamabad to help the United States and its coalition partners combat these extremist forces in Afghanistan. These factors heighten Pakistan's own problems in contending with extremists in the Federally

Administered Tribal Areas along the Afghan border as well as in the settled areas further east. Pakistani support for armed Islamic insurgents in Kashmir also contributes significantly to tension with India and heightens Indian suspicions that Islamabad is responsible for perpetrating violence within India proper. And until a settlement is reached, there will be no dearth of "spoilers" eager for opportunities to inflame India-Pakistan relations.

—India's and Pakistan's positions on the terms of a settlement have grown closer. In public statements and, reportedly, in their back-channel exchanges, Pakistan and to a lesser degree India have floated ideas that go beyond their earlier standard positions. And although their formal dialogue to resolve the issue has made no meaningful progress, they were willing to continue it despite disappointments, particularly for the Pakistanis. This sharply contrasts with the long spells when New Delhi and Islamabad could find no basis for discussing Kashmir and other bilateral problems.

As Obama has said, it won't be easy.

Although President Asif Ali Zardari has highlighted his interest in improved India-Pakistan relations and has supported both the formal composite dialogue and parallel behind-the-scenes discussions on terms for a Kashmir settlement, as noted he has not endorsed former president Pervez Musharraf's initiatives or publicly called for any other steps that would involve major Pakistani concessions. His shaky regime has many more immediate political, economic, and security problems on its agenda and will not be eager to take on another daunting and potentially divisive issue until it becomes stronger and more confident. While Zardari has spoken of establishing a parliamentary committee to consider the Kashmir issue, there is no indication that he has begun to prepare the Pakistani people for the abandoning of important long-held positions that would be needed to bring about a settlement. Nor is it clear that the Pakistan Army under Musharraf's successor, General Ashfaq Pervez Kiyani, will be prepared to agree to such concessions. The army has always been a major player, sometimes *the* major player, in determining policy on Kashmir, whatever the political or constitutional complexion of the government.

Even if the new authorities in Islamabad accept Musharraf's position, or develop a similarly forthcoming approach, they will face formidable negotiating obstacles. When Musharraf effectively lost power early in 2008, important gaps still remained between the Indian and Pakistani positions.

India's informal response to Musharraf's call for greater self-governance for Kashmiris was to equate it with the powers all Indian states enjoy. This was difficult for Pakistanis to accept because in the absence of territorial change, all that remained for them to bargain for was a unique political status for Kashmir that gave them and the Kashmiris special standing. The Indian definition seemed to exclude any special status.

If the Pakistan political scene does not offer a promising backdrop for a settlement, neither does the political equation in India. There Manmohan Singh and his Congress-led coalition face major challenges as parliamentary elections loom. Like their counterparts in Islamabad, Singh and his colleagues cannot feel secure enough to take the political risk to their government that will go with a Kashmir settlement. They will not be willing to clinch and publicize a deal until they feel less threatened. Congress' principal rival for national power, the Bharatiya Janata Party, is again calling for the termination of Kashmir's special status within the Indian Union, a move that would seriously damage if not destroy prospects for a settlement. The possibility of forward movement might become more promising once the election has taken place and a new government headed by Singh or another non-BJP leader installed. But that is far from certain.

In Indian Kashmir, the unwillingness of the Hindu majority in Jammu and the Buddhist majority in Ladakh to accept political arrangements they fear would lead to their subjugation by the Muslims of the Valley still complicates any serious discussion of the autonomy issue between New Delhi and "its" Kashmiris. This New Delhi–Srinagar dialogue is a key element in bringing about a settlement. The secessionist All Parties Hurriyet Conference again boycotted the state election held in November and December 2008, and neither Sheikh Mohammed Abdullah's grandson Omar Abdullah, the head of the pro-India National Conference Party, who became chief minister in January 2009, nor any other political leader can credibly claim to speak for the Kashmiris. This leaves settlement efforts vulnerable to spoilers who favor continued conflict or have other political fish to fry. And on the disarmament of Kashmir, a major point in Musharraf's initiatives, the Indians have continued to link the reduction or redeployment of their armed forces in the state to the ending or sharp rollback of Pakistan-sponsored insurgent activities. Both countries tend to speak of disarmament as if it were a self-defining term, whereas in fact in would have to be spelled out in negotiations.

A final obstacle is the deterioration of India-Pakistan bilateral relations. These were rocked in 2008 by a series of events including the bombing of the Indian embassy in Afghanistan, the resumption of lengthy artillery clashes across the Line of Control, reports that infiltration across the line into Indian-held territory was increasing, and especially the murderous attacks in Mumbai. Growing violence attributed to Indian Muslims in other cities across India was also damaging. So were the widespread demonstrations in Kashmir. These unwelcome developments undercut the forthcoming public positions Zardari and his colleagues have taken. (They are, of course, another argument why a Kashmir settlement is important.)

Any settlement that Washington promotes should include several key elements similar to those reportedly under discussion in the India-Pakistan backchannel exchanges.

—The Line of Control, or something geographically close to it, will become the permanent border between Indian and Pakistani Kashmir.

—The border will be sufficiently porous to allow for the easy movement of people and goods across it.

—Kashmiris on both sides of the line will be granted a greater degree of self-government. There is a much greater call for this in Indian Kashmir than among residents of Azad Kashmir and the Northern Areas. But a settlement will be easier to sell in India if Pakistan-held areas are included in a Kashmir autonomy package.

—Joint institutions will be established on an all-Kashmir basis that will play a role in managing noncontroversial matters affecting Kashmiris on both sides of the line.

Quiet diplomacy is required.

If Washington does decide on making a stronger effort, American officials should work quietly. They should suggest useful building blocks to the parties to help them achieve a settlement along the lines sketched out here. They can helpfully act as a sounding board, advising each side of the likely acceptability to the other of proposals it is considering putting on the negotiating table. But Americans should not sit at the negotiating table—a bad idea and one that the Indians will not accept. Keeping to an informal, unobtrusive role, U.S. diplomats will want to discourage any public discussion of their activities. Although the Obama administration should not dispatch a highly publicized special envoy as President Kennedy did in 1962 when he assigned Averell Harriman to the task, a private visit by someone recognized to have the president's confidence should be considered despite the obvious danger of leaks. The task of acting as the Obama administration's point persons over the longer term should be given to the resident U.S. ambassadors backed by a carefully chosen team operating in the State Department.

It will be important in any event that the Indians and Pakistanis recognize that any such endeavor has the strong backing of President Obama. The president should avoid getting involved in the nitty-gritty of the effort, however. As Ambassador John Kenneth Galbraith put it during the failed 1962–63 negotiations, he should not freely issue presidential messages in the manner of Confederate currency and risk similar devaluation. Because negotiations may be protracted, Washington and its diplomats in the field should accept that they are in it for the long haul, stay patient, and repress the natural American preference for swift results.

Despite its improved relations with the United States, the Indians are likely to be more intransigent and more wary of an outsider's role than Pakistan is, at least at first. But the Pakistanis will also have misgivings, and these are likely to be heightened as the negotiations proceed and they become more aware of U.S. positions.

Washington needs to look for ways to persuade New Delhi to accept an agreement that does not meet all Indian demands and involves genuine and enforceable concessions on its part. (For example, Indian acceptance of a substantial degree of autonomy for Kashmir would need ironclad constitutional guarantees to be accepted by the Pakistanis.) An offer of strong and active U.S. support for a permanent Indian UN Security Council seat could be one approach worth weighing. Washington might also usefully consider providing support to some of the proposed mechanisms for joint management of certain issues in Kashmir by establishing with the World Bank and other potential donors a special fund for Kashmir reconstruction. It should also enlist other countries to brace its efforts while recognizing that it will have to bear the major international burden. Similarly, it will need to find creative ways to persuade the Pakistanis that a settlement that offers little or no change in the territorial status quo in Kashmir is worth their while. Pakistanis will perceive that they are getting the worst of the deal, and it will be important to find some way to sweeten that bitter pill.

As this list of obstacles to a settlement demonstrates, even under improved political circumstances a successful diplomatic initiative to resolve Kashmir is far from a sure bet; it can probably be more accurately termed a long shot at best. If any lesson is to be drawn from the events of the past six decades it is that the Kashmir issue is complex and difficult and needs to be addressed with due respect for its tortured history.

But the possibilities for a breakthrough, though limited, are likely to be higher than they were in 1962 when the Kennedy administration mistakenly concluded that the time was ripe for a settlement and tried to broker one in a very public way. Circumstances in India, Pakistan, and the United States, and the relations between them, have greatly changed since then. So have Washington's stakes in the issue. By undertaking the less intrusive role outlined above, and giving the Indians, Pakistanis, and Kashmiris the added push they need to get them across the elusive finish line they have never reached on their own, the Obama administration, supported by other governments, might—just might—help to bring to an acceptable conclusion a dangerous, seemingly intractable dispute that has undermined Indian and Pakistani interests, played havoc with the lives of the Kashmiri people, caused serious political problems for the United States and the international community, and made the state a potential tinderbox for nuclear war.

Chronology of America's Role in Kashmir

Truman Administration

1947

August. India and Pakistan become independent states as the British raj ends. A Hindu ruler in a state with a Muslim majority, the maharaja of Kashmir, Hari Singh, does not accede to either new dominion.

October. Facing an invasion of tribesmen from Pakistan and the revolt of some of his own subjects, the maharaja calls on India for help. The Indians are willing to provide military aid only if the maharaja accedes to India. He does so. Accepting the maharaja's accession, the Indian government pledges that once peace is restored and the invaders cleared out, the question of Kashmir's accession should be settled "by reference to the people."

1948

January. India takes the Kashmir issue to the United Nations Security Council under Chapter 6 of the UN charter. The U.S. delegation, headed by Ambassador Warren Austin, plays a leading role in trying to settle the conflict, cosponsoring with Britain a series of resolutions beginning with one establishing the United Nations Commission for India and Pakistan (UNCIP).

July. The five members of the UNCIP delegation, including American ambassador Jerome K. Huddle, make the first of their visits to India, Pakistan, and Kashmir to develop a basis for a settlement.

August. UNCIP adopts the first of two key resolutions that will over the years form the basis for UN consideration of the Kashmir issue. The resolution calls for a cease-fire, withdrawal of forces, and a two-option plebiscite to determine Kashmir's political future.

1949

January. A cease-fire takes effect in Kashmir. The UN Military Observers Group in India and Pakistan (UNMOGIP), which includes a large U.S. component, is organized to monitor it.

January. UNCIP adopts a second major resolution, which outlines the plebiscite process that is to begin with the UN secretary general's nominating a plebiscite administrator with sweeping powers.

March. U.S. Navy Fleet Admiral Chester W. Nimitz is chosen plebiscite administrator.

August. President Harry Truman writes to Prime Ministers Jawaharlal Nehru and Liaquat Ali Khan, calling on India and Pakistan to agree to arbitration of the Kashmir dispute. Nehru turns him down; Liaquat accepts.

September. Indians reject UN negotiator Sir Owen Dixon's Kashmir settlement proposal calling for the partition of the state with a plebiscite confined to the Kashmir Valley.

October. Nehru visits Washington, inconclusively discusses Kashmir with Truman and Secretary of State Dean Acheson.

1950

February. A seminal State Department memorandum spells out U.S. policy on Kashmir. It finds that Maharaja Hari Singh's signing of the instrument of accession to India did not settle the accession issue. The memo blames Indian intransigence for delaying a settlement.

September. U.S. ambassador to India Loy Henderson visits Kashmir, the first American envoy to do so.

1951

September. Frank Graham, an American, becomes UN special negotiator on Kashmir.

October. Chester Bowles succeeds Loy Henderson as U.S. ambassador to India. Washington disregards his call for a strongly pro-Indian U.S. posture.

Eisenhower Administration

1953

January. Dwight Eisenhower becomes president. He names John Foster Dulles secretary of state.

April. At Eisenhower's request, Paul Hoffman goes to India and Pakistan on a secret mission to find a basis for a Kashmir settlement. He fails.

April. Adlai Stevenson visits Kashmir and arouses unfounded Indian suspicions about his activities there.

May. Secretary Dulles travels to India and Pakistan as part of a lengthy trip to the Middle East and South Asia. He is impressed by the Pakistanis.

August. Kashmir prime minister Sheikh Abdullah is ousted and jailed. He is succeeded by Bakshi Ghulam Mohammed.

August. Nehru meets in New Delhi with Pakistan prime minister Mohammed Ali Bogra. They agree that the plebiscite should be carried out, but not by Admiral Nimitz.

September. Admiral Nimitz resigns as plebiscite administrator.

1954

January. Eisenhower decides to move forward with a military assistance package for Pakistan. It is signed in May and becomes one of the building blocks of the Baghdad Pact, later the Central Treaty Organization. Pakistan also joins the Southeast Asia Treaty Organization and becomes "America's most allied ally in Asia."

February. The Kashmir Constituent Assembly unanimously ratifies the state's accession to India.

March. Angered by the U.S.-Pakistan agreement, Nehru demands that U.S. military officers be forced to leave UNMOGIP. The last of them go in December.

1955

June. Soviet leaders Nikolai A. Bulganin and Nikita S. Khrushchev barnstorm through India. In Kashmir, they fully endorse India's position on the issue.

1956

December. Nehru visits the United States and has a series of amicable conversations with Eisenhower. U.S.-Indian relations subsequently improve.

1957

January. The UN Security Council takes up the Kashmir issue again but makes no progress toward a settlement.

March. Ellsworth Bunker becomes U.S. ambassador to India.

September. The UN Security Council returns to the Kashmir issue but is again unable to move forward toward a settlement.

1958

April. Eisenhower is personally involved in promoting his administration's proposal designed to help India and Pakistan find a solution to the linked problems of Kashmir, the division of the waters of the Indus River, and the South Asian arms race. Nehru rejects the U.S. proposal.

October. A military coup in Pakistan brings a martial law administration led by General Muhammad Ayub Khan to power.

1959

December. Eisenhower makes a historic journey to South Asia, where he is greeted with great warmth. His mild efforts to help improve India-Pakistan relations are unsuccessful.

1960

September. India and Pakistan sign the Indus waters treaty sponsored by the World Bank. Washington strongly supports the treaty.

Kennedy Administration

1961

January. John F. Kennedy succeeds Eisenhower in the White House.

May. Vice President Lyndon B. Johnson visits India and Pakistan. Ayub importunes him on Kashmir.

July. President Ayub comes to the United States on a state visit that is a triumph in public diplomacy. He again urges Washington to put pressure on the Indians to move a Kashmir settlement forward.

November. Prime Minister Nehru visits the United States, takes an uncompromising position on Kashmir.

1962

June. President Kennedy takes a personal role in winning UN Security Council approval for another Kashmir resolution called for by the Pakistanis. The Soviets veto it.

October-November. The Sino-Indian border war leads to the stunning defeat of the Indian army. Washington provides military supplies to the Indians at Nehru's request.

December. Following a unilateral Chinese cease-fire and withdrawal, Kennedy sends W. Averell Harriman to India and Pakistan to seek movement on the Kashmir issue.

December. Urged on by the United States and Britain, the Indians and the Pakistanis begin bilateral negotiations on Kashmir. Kennedy is deeply involved in the unsuccessful effort.

1963

May. The talks break down after six rounds.

Johnson Administration

1963

November. Vice President Johnson becomes president following Kennedy's assassination.

December. Demonstrations following the theft of a sacred relic from a Kashmiri shrine shake Indian rule in the state

1964

May. Nehru dies. Lal Bahadur Shastri becomes prime minister.

December. Washington protests the Shastri government's decision to integrate Kashmir further into the Indian Union, to no avail.

1965

June. Indian and Pakistani forces clash in the Rann of Kutch.

June. First reports of serious skirmishing along the cease-fire line in Kashmir.

August. The Pakistan army begins large-scale infiltration of armed personnel across the cease-fire line (Operation Gibraltar).

September. As Operation Gibraltar falters, the Pakistan army launches a major offensive into Indian-held Kashmir. The Indians counter with an attack into West Pakistan. A U.N.-sponsored truce is arranged later the same month. The United States cuts off military aid and suspends further economic assistance to India and Pakistan.

September-December. The Johnson administration takes a backseat role in efforts to bring about progress in Kashmir. It prefers that the United Nations take the lead.

December. President Ayub visits Washington. Johnson gives him no encouragement on Kashmir.

1966

January. Soviet Prime Minister Alexei Kosygin negotiates a Kashmir settlement between India and Pakistan at Tashkent in Soviet Central Asia. The accord merely restores the status quo ante bellum. The United States welcomes this Soviet success.

January. Shastri dies in Tashkent after the signing ceremony. Indira Gandhi replaces him as prime minister.

1966–69

For the balance of its tenure, the Johnson administration downgrades U.S. political interest in South Asia following the policy debacle of the India-Pakistan war.

Nixon Administration

1969

January. Richard Nixon succeeds Johnson in the White House.

1971

December. India and Pakistan go to war over East Bengal, the first conflict between the two countries not triggered by Kashmir.

December. Following the Pakistan army's surrender in East Bengal, National Security Adviser Henry A. Kissinger fears that the Indians will attack in the west and seize Pakistani Kashmir. His concerns prove unfounded.

1972

July. India and Pakistan sign the Simla agreement. They undertake to settle the Kashmir dispute peacefully and by bilateral means. The cease-fire line is replaced by a Line of Control. Washington applauds the settlement and makes it the basis for its Kashmir policy. For the next eighteen years Kashmir remains off the U.S. radar scope.

George H. W. Bush Administration

1989

December. A massive uprising shakes the Kashmir Valley. Demonstrators call for independence from India. The outbreak is homemade, but the Pakistanis soon begin fishing in these newly troubled waters.

1990

January. As India-Pakistan tensions rise because of the violence in Kashmir, the U.S. ambassadors in India and Pakistan try to reassure the two sides.

March. The State Department adds "taking into account the wishes of the Kashmiri people" to its formulaic call supporting the Simla pact's provision for a peaceful, bilateral settlement of the Kashmir dispute.

May. Deputy National Security Adviser Robert Gates leads a mission to India and Pakistan designed to calm the situation.

Clinton Administration

1993

January. Bill Clinton succeeds George H. W. Bush as president.

1995

May. Clinton affirms U.S. willingness to intervene on the Kashmir issue only if both India and Pakistan want it to. This has remained U.S. policy.

July. As trouble continues in Kashmir, two American travelers are kidnapped by Islamic extremists while trekking in the mountains of the state. One escapes; the other is never found and is presumed dead.

1996

July. The Kashmir Study Group is formed under the leadership of Farooq Kathwari.

1998

May. India conducts nuclear tests. Pakistanis raise the Kashmir issue repeatedly as the United States mounts efforts to persuade them not to follow suit. But Washington concludes there is nothing that it can do to bring about a Kashmir settlement satisfactory to Pakistan, which conducts tests later in the month.

June. Washington takes the lead in a diplomatic campaign designed to bolster the badly shaken nonproliferation regime and head off a South Asian arms race. Measures adopted by multilateral organizations include a U.S.-sparked call to India and Pakistan to find mutually acceptable solutions to the root causes of the tensions between them, including Kashmir.

1999

February. Indian prime minister Atal Bihari Vajpayee travels to Lahore, where he meets his Pakistani opposite number, Nawaz Sharif. They pledge to seek solutions to their bilateral problems, including Kashmir.

May. India becomes aware that Pakistan has surreptitiously seized areas on the Indian side of the Line of Control at Kargil. Washington calls on Pakistan to withdraw its forces. New Delhi is pleasantly surprised by this American demand.

July. Nawaz comes to Washington, where at a meeting at Blair House with President Clinton he agrees to take concrete and immediate steps for the restoration of the Line of Control. Clinton says he will take a personal interest in the India-Pakistan peace process once this has been done.

October. General Pervez Musharraf overthrows Nawaz Sharif in a military coup.

2000

March. Clinton visits India and Pakistan. In Islamabad, he tells the Pakistani people that there is no military solution to Kashmir.

George W. Bush Administration

2001

January. George W. Bush succeeds Bill Clinton as president.

September. Islamic terrorists based in Afghanistan attack the United States. Pakistan becomes a key ally in the subsequent global war on terrorism.

October. Terrorists attack the state assembly building in Indian Kashmir.

October. Visiting India and Pakistan, Secretary of State Colin Powell urges the two sides to show restraint.

December. Terrorists attack the Indian parliament in New Delhi. India claims they had Pakistani support. A war scare follows as both countries send massive forces to the Line of Control and the international border.

2002

January. Musharraf publicly pledges not to allow Pakistan-controlled territory to be used by terrorists.

June. Deputy Secretary of State Richard Armitage visits India and Pakistan to help calm tensions. He is followed by Powell and Secretary of Defense Donald Rumsfeld.

October. Washington welcomes what it calls the successful conclusion of state elections in Kashmir. Indian and Pakistani troops pull back from advanced positions.

2003

April. Vajpayee offers a hand of friendship to Pakistan. Washington hails the initiative.

May. Deputy Secretary Armitage visits India and Pakistan, reaffirms U.S. satisfaction with the warming of India-Pakistan relations that followed Vajpayee's initiative.

2004

January. Vajpayee and Musharraf agree to begin a comprehensive dialogue on divisive issues, including Kashmir. Powell terms it "historic."

October. Musharraf launches, outside the established dialogue, a bold initiative to settle the Kashmir dispute.

2006

October. Musharraf publicly offers another set of unorthodox proposals for a Kashmir settlement.

2007

March. Musharraf ousts the chief justice of Pakistan, ushering in a long bout of political turmoil that effectively makes any further progress on Kashmir impossible.

2008

February. Musharraf's party loses parliamentary elections.

March. A new coalition government led by the Pakistan People's Party takes power.

August. Musharraf is forced to resign. Asif Ali Zardari is elected president of Pakistan.

2009

January. Barack Obama succeeds George W. Bush as U.S. president.

Notes

I have relied extensively on two sources of original memoranda, telegrams, and other materials in documenting this work on Kashmir.

One source is the multivolume series called *Foreign Relations of the United States (FRUS)*, which archives State Department documents by year and geographic region. The series is compiled by the Office of the Historian in the Bureau of Public Affairs of the State Department. The latest volume available for South Asia covers the Bangladesh crisis of 1971.

The second source is the State Department Central Files (SDCF). These files are housed at the U.S. National Archives facility in College Park, Maryland.

Other abreviations used in these notes include:

NYT—*New York Times*

SCOR—Security Council Official Records, available through the United Nations in New York

UNCIP—UN Commission for India and Pakistan

USUN—United States delegation to the United Nations

Introduction

1. This section draws on the chapter "Kashmir: Fifty Years of Running in Place" that my wife, Teresita C. Schaffer, and I wrote in *Grasping the Nettle*, edited by Chester A. Crocker, Fen Osler Hampson, and Pamela R. Aall (Washington: United States Institute of Peace Press, 2005).

Chapter 1

1. See, for example, Department of State telegram 40 to Madras, July 16, 1947, *FRUS 1947*, III, p. 162, which told the consulate to rebuff overtures from representatives of the southwestern Indian state of Travancore, whose ruler was toying with the idea of independence. The Travancore officials were seeking to promote U.S. interest in acquiring strategic minerals from the state.

2. Victoria Schofield, *Kashmir in Conflict* (London: I. B. Tauris, 2000), ch. 3. Schofield's lengthy and well-researched account is the best available study of the events surrounding Kashmir's accession to India. The many earlier studies of Kashmir in 1947 include H. V. Hodson, *The Great Divide* (London: Hutchinson & Co., 1969); and Alastair Lamb, *Kashmir: A Disputed Legacy* (Hertingfordbury, Hertfordshire: Roxford Books, 1991). Lamb's account is sympathetic to the Pakistan case. For a good, brief, more recent study, see Alex von Tunzelmann, *Indian Summer* (New York: Henry Holt, 2007), ch. 17.

3. Department of State telegram 55 to New Delhi, December 3, 1947, *FRUS 1947*, III, p. 181. The message transmitted the instructions the department had sent to USUN. In these instructions, the department said that such a referendum should be carried out on the basis of universal suffrage. The existing rolls were weighted in favor of Hindus, and the department was concerned that India might try to use these as the basis of the vote. It also recognized the practical problems that conducting a referendum would pose, such as lack of electoral machinery, bad weather, and isolation.

4. Department of State telegram 814 to New Delhi, December 26, 1947, *FRUS 1947*, III, p. 184.

5. Ibid.

6. Under British rule, India had been a member of the League of Nations. It automatically became a UN member when the successor organization was established in 1945.

7. Lamb, *Kashmir: A Disputed Legacy,* p. 164.

8. U. K. High Commission New Delhi telegram, December 29, 1947, Oriental and India Office Collections, L/WS/1/1139, British Library, London.

9. U. K. Embassy Washington telegram, January 5, 1948, DO 142/490, British Archives, London.

10. Department of State telegram 817 to New Delhi, December 31, 1947, *FRUS 1947*, III, p. 193. The department sent the message the day after it had received the British request conveyed through the U.S. embassy in London. (Embassy London telegram 6608, December 30, 1947, *FRUS 1947*, III, p. 193.)

11. Embassy New Delhi telegram 10 to the State Department, January 4, 1948, *FRUS* 1948, V, p. 270.

12. Embassy Karachi telegram 3 to the State Department, January 2, 1948, *FRUS* 1948, V, p. 268.

13. Memorandum of discussion of South Asia, December 26, 1947, *FRUS 1947*, III, p. 175.

14. Department of State telegram 5 to USUN, January 6, 1948, *FRUS 1948*, V, p. 271.

15. For three recent examples of this analysis, see Prem Shankar Jha, *Kashmir 1947: Rival Versions of History* (Delhi: Oxford University Press, 1996); C. Dasgupta, *War and Diplomacy in Kashmir, 1947–48* (New Delhi: Sage, 2002); and Navnita Chadha Behera, *Demystifying Kashmir* (Brookings, 2006).

16. Embassy Karachi telegram 125 to the State Department, March 1, 1948, SDCF 1945–1949, 845F.00.

17. Memorandum of conversation, "India-Pakistan Dispute over Kashmir; Proposed Security Council Action," January 10, 1948, *FRUS 1948*, V, p. 276.

18. U.K. Embassy Washington telegram, January 13, 1948, DO 142/492, British Archives, London.

19. Department of State telegram 17 to USUN, January 14, 1948, *FRUS 1948*, V, p. 280.

20. Department of State telegram 79 to USUN, February 20, 1948, *FRUS* 1948, V, p. 300.

21. Memorandum of conversation, New York, February 27, 1948, Subject: "Exchange of Views with British Representatives with Respect to Kashmir." SDCF 1945–1949, 845F.00. Interestingly, the head of the American group was Dean Rusk, then director of the State Department's Office of United Nations Affairs, who served as secretary of state in 1965 during the second India-Pakistan War over Kashmir.

22. For excellent summaries of the two positions, see Sisir Gupta, *Kashmir, A Study in India-Pakistan Relations* (New Delhi: Indian Council of World Affairs, 1966), p. 148; and Josef Korbel, *Danger in Kashmir* (Princeton University Press, 1966), p. 10.

23. SCOR, 304th meeting, 1948. United Nations, New York.

24. Department of State telegram 101 to New Delhi, February 17, 1948, *FRUS 1948*, V, p. 299.

25. USUN telegram 105 to the State Department, January 28, 1948, *FRUS* 1948, V, p. 285. According to Austin, Abdullah said in effect that whether Kashmir went to Pakistan or India the other dominion would never accept the solution. He did not want his people torn by dissension between the two countries. It would be better, the

sheikh declared, if Kashmir were independent and could seek American and British aid for developing the country.

26. Department of State telegram 143 to New Delhi, March 4, 1948, *FRUS 1948*, V, p. 312. The department also opposed the nizam of Hyderabad's bid for separate status. (Department of State airgram 40 to New Delhi, March 29, 1948, *FRUS 1948*, V, p. 321.) The department had drafted the message in reply to an Embassy New Delhi telegram that reported that Canadian high commissioner John Kearney had suggested to the Indians that they and the Pakistanis agree to a Kashmir plebiscite for or against an independent status to be jointly guaranteed by the two dominions. If the Kashmiris rejected this option, they would be asked in a second vote to choose between the two. According to Kearney, Nehru favored this proposal. Kearney said that when he asked Nehru what the outcome of such a plebiscite would be, the prime minister replied that independence would win. (Embassy New Delhi telegram 178 to the State Department, March 4, 1948, *FRUS* 1948, V, p. 310.)

27. Embassy New Delhi telegram 150 to the State Department, February 21, 1948, *FRUS* 1948, V, p. 302.

28. U.K. New Delhi High Commission message, November 4, 1947, DO 142/494, British Archives, London. The British message said the information was based on information the high commission had learned unofficially from the Indian Civil Air Directorate.

29. Accounts of the Russell Haight story are in the *NYT,* January 29, 1948, and the *Times* of London, January 12, 1948, and in material in the British Archives, including a note dated December 8, 1947, that J. R. Symonds of the American Friends Service Committee wrote on the revolt in Poonch (DO 142/494).

30. Commonwealth Relations Office memorandum, May 29, 1948, DO 142/503, British Archives, London.

31. Korbel had been nominated by the Czechoslovak government headed by President Eduard Benes shortly before a coup brought the Communists to power in February 1948. Philip Noel-Baker, the British secretary of state for commonwealth affairs, has recalled that Korbel had not expected the new Communist government's foreign minister, Vlado Clementis, to allow the nomination to go forward to the United Nations. According to Noel-Baker, Korbel believed that Clementis decided to move ahead because he considered this a minor way to reduce the shock that the coup, the political emasculation of Benes, and the death under suspicious circumstances of former foreign minister Jan Masaryk had had on the country's relations with the outside world. Noel-Baker remembered Korbel telling him that aside from this perception of Czechoslovak national interests, Clementis's decision also reflected his friendship with Korbel. (Note by Philip Noel-Baker, April 29, 1949, and other Commonwealth Relations Office correspondence, DO 142/503, British Archives,

London.) Noel-Baker wrote his note in response to a State Department call for ammunition to resist demands by Czech refugee groups that Korbel be expelled from the United States because of his questionable political integrity, that is, his alleged sympathy for the Communist cause. The groups' demands were overruled.

32. The U.S. Embassy in Karachi had reported this Pakistani military presence to Washington two months earlier, on May 8, 1948, and had urged the prompt arrival of UNCIP to head off what it feared was the danger of an India-Pakistan war. The State Department decided not to share this information with the commission or the Indian government. The Indian Army chief of staff told the U.S. and British military attachés in New Delhi on June 9 that he had conclusive evidence that at least one Pakistani battalion was in Kashmir, and possibly more. Neither the British nor the Americans nor the Indians passed this report to the commission. (See Embassy Karachi telegram 265 to the State Department May 8, 1948, and the State Department's reply, telegram 180 to Karachi, May 12, *FRUS 1948,* V, pp. 340, 341.) Both messages were repeated to Embassy New Delhi. Embassy New Delhi telegram 464 to State Department, June 9, 1948, *FRUS 1948,* V, p. 345, relays the Indian information.

33. For an interesting description of the workings of the American delegation, see the oral history narrative prepared by American Foreign Service officer J. Wesley Adams in the Truman Presidential Library (pp. 25–52). Adams held the post of UN adviser on the four-officer U.S. UNCIP team that Huddle led.

34. For the text of the August 13, 1948, resolution, see *UN Security Council, 3rd yr., Supplement for November 1948* (New York: United Nations), pp. 32–34.

35. Korbel, *Danger in Kashmir,* p. 144.

36. The plebiscite administrator was to be appointed by the Kashmir state government, but this was considered a formality.

37. For a detailed account of the differences between U.S. and British approaches on the way to bring about a cease-fire, see Dasgupta, *War and Diplomacy in Kashmir,* pp. 191–99. Dasgupta found that London wanted to have the Security Council impose an unconditional and immediate cease-fire. Washington preferred to have UNCIP deal with the issue, in Dasgupta's opinion because the fact that it was represented on the commission had given the United States an active commitment to this approach. The American view prevailed. Dasgupta cites this episode as another example of the pro-Pakistan policy he alleges the Attlee government followed.

38. Acting secretary of state Robert Lovett's message to the prime ministers of India and Pakistan, January 4, 1949, *Department of State Bulletin,* January 23, 1949.

39. Secretary of State Acheson's statement, March 23, 1949, *Department of State Bulletin,* April 3, 1949. The names of several prominent U.S. military officers, diplomats, and politicians had come into play for the nomination. The Indians and Pakistanis had initially favored General Walter Bedell Smith, but he declined the offer.

40. See Embassy Karachi telegram 137 to the State Department, April 30, 1949 (*FRUS 1949*, VI, p. 1704), in which Hooker A. Doolittle, the chargé d'affaires, reported: "Embassy reluctantly records impression UNCIP status as objective arbitral body weakened due seeming readiness accept extraneous Indian government claims. . . . Only [U.S. delegation] still regarded as objective and as having more than superficial grasp Pakistan position." A few days earlier, the U.K. high commissioner had told Ambassador Henderson that in a recent conversation, G. S. Bajpai "had been quite critical of UNCIP because it showed weakness, vacillation, and hesitancy grapple firmly with problems facing it." (Embassy New Delhi telegram 449 to the State Department, April 20, 1949, *FRUS 1949*, VI, p. 1699).

41. Bajpai apparently did not mention to Henderson that Ambassador Grady had made a strong statement to him about Indian motives more than a year earlier, when American dissatisfaction with Indian attitudes was only beginning. Grady reported to the State Department at that time that he had told Bajpai: "There was a feeling in Washington and at [the United Nations] that the GOI [Government of India] was most anxious to hold [on] to Kashmir and that the plebiscite offer was eyewash to justify their making the accession to India stick because they know how difficult a proper plebiscite will be and how strong the presumptions are in favor of a verdict for the government controlling the country at the time of the plebiscite." (Embassy New Delhi telegram 178 to the State Department, February 7, 1948, *FRUS 1948*, V, p. 295). Bajpai contested this view. He said that Nehru had declared that while he was most anxious to keep Kashmir in the Indian Union, he wanted to have an honest plebiscite to ascertain people's desires.

42. Embassy New Delhi telegram 851 to the State Department, July 29, 1949, *FRUS 1949*, VI, p. 1726. State Department telegram 554 to New Delhi, August 5, 1949, *FRUS 1949*, VI, p. 1729.

43. Embassy New Delhi telegram 924 to the State Department, August 15, 1949, *FRUS 1949*, VI, p. 1732. For a pungent account of Henderson's view of Nehru, see H. W. Brands, *Inside the Cold War* (Oxford University Press, 1991), ch. 13, "The Most Charming Man He Ever Despised."

44. Washington and London carefully coordinated the Truman and Attlee messages (see U.K. High Commission New Delhi telegram, August 11, 1949, L/WS/1/1139, British Library, London).

45. The text of Truman's messages was sent to the two embassies in Department of State telegram 592 to Embassy New Delhi, 301 to Embassy Karachi, August 25, 1949, *FRUS 1949*, VI, p. 1733. The *New York Times* highlighted this anti-communist aspect of the president's appeal in a front-page story: "Truman Bids India, Pakistan End Kashmir Peril to Peace," on August 31, 1949.

46. Embassy Karachi telegram 379 to the State Department, September 8, 1949, *FRUS 1949,* VI, p. 1740, carries the text of Liaquat's message to Truman. Nehru's reply to the president is in New Delhi telegram 1043 to the State Department, also September 8, 1949, *FRUS 1949,* VI, p. 1736. Liaquat's message included a good deal of purple prose, which he no doubt thought would gratify the president. For example, "Had the proposal not hinged around the eminent personality of . . . Nimitz and had it not been so emphatically sponsored by the President of the United States, my government would have felt considerable hesitation in accepting it mainly on the score that the decision of any other arbitrator . . . might have been rendered to no effect by India's failure to implement it."

47. The memorandum of the October 13 Truman-Nehru discussion, prepared by Secretary of State Acheson, is in *FRUS 1949,* VI, p. 1750. See also S. Gopal, *Jawaharlal Nehru, A Biography,* vol. 2 (Harvard University Press, 1979), p. 60; and Dean Acheson, *Present at the Creation* (New York: W. W. Norton, 1969), p. 334.

48. For the text of the UNCIP report, see SCOR, 4th Year, Special Supplement, no. 7, p. 50. For the first time, the five UNCIP members could not reach unanimous agreement. The Czechoslovak representative, a committed Communist who had replaced Josef Korbel earlier in the year, submitted a minority report that castigated the United States and Britain and called for the reconstitution of UNCIP to include all members of the Security Council (including, of course, the Soviet Union). This minority report, which was largely ignored, marked the first time that the Kashmir dispute was seriously caught up in the cold war confrontation.

49. For the text of McNaughton's report, dated December 29, 1949, see SCOR, 4th Year, no. 54, pp. 4–8. McNaughton reported his subsequent negotiation efforts in a letter to his successor as Security Council president dated February 6, 1950 (UNSC General/S1453).

50. These included a proposal to hold regional plebiscites and the partition of the state according to the outcomes in each region. His formulas for the administration of the state during the plebiscite period included replacing the pro-Indian government of Sheikh Abdullah with a coalition regime, a government of impartial persons, and temporary UN administration. Dixon's report, dated September 15, 1950, is in Security Council Document S/1791, SCOR, 5th year, Supplement for September-December 1950.

51. The full text of the memorandum, dated February 6, 1950, is in *FRUS* 1950, V, pp. 1378–82.

52. McGhee reasserted this view in a 1991 interview with Dennis Kux. "We wanted to avert a full-scale war between India and Pakistan—this was always a threat. Our efforts failed—because of Nehru." Dennis Kux, *India and the United*

States: Estranged Democracies, 1941–1991 (Washington: National Defense University Press, 1993), p. 68.

53. The legal adviser's opinion was that "[E]xecution of an Instrument of Accession by the Maharajah in October, 1947, could not finally accomplish the accession of Kashmir to either Dominion, in view of the circumstances prevailing at that time; the question of the future of Kashmir remained to be settled in some orderly fashion under relatively stable conditions; this question is an important development in the dispute; and, in proceedings before the Security Council, neither party is entitled to assert that rights were finally determined by the Maharajah's execution of an instrument of Accession." The McGhee-Hickerson memorandum also noted the British position on the accession: "It is the view of the United Kingdom Attorney General and Foreign Office legal advisers that the Maharajah's execution of the Instrument of Accession to India was inconsistent with Kashmir's obligations to Pakistan, and for that reason perhaps invalid." The section of the memorandum on the accessions issue ("Legal aspects of Kashmir's contested accession to India") concludes that "because as a matter of law India is not entitled to assert that rights in Kashmir were finally determined by the Instrument of Accession executed in October, 1947, the Security Council should not permit this question to divert it from its basic task of bringing about a political solution of the Kashmir problem." *FRUS* 1950, V, pp. 1378–82.

54. Department of State telegram 664 to London, February 11, 1950, *FRUS* 1950, V, p. 1382.

55. Embassy New Delhi telegram 491 to the State Department, August 28, 1950, *FRUS* 1950, V, p. 1427.

56. Embassy New Delhi telegram 799 to the State Department, September 29, 1950, *FRUS* 1950, V, p. 1433. Abdullah argued for independence with at least one other Western ambassador during this time. See Walter Crocker, *Nehru: A Contemporary's Estimate* (London: George Allen and Unwin), p. 95. Crocker was Australian high commissioner to India at that time.

57. In early 1951, the commonwealth comprised only a handful of members— Britain, the original settler dominions of Canada, Australia, New Zealand, and the Union of South Africa, and the three newly independent South Asian states—India, Pakistan, and Ceylon (Sri Lanka).

58. Department of State telegram 1395 to New Delhi, March 2, 1951, *FRUS 1951*, VI, part 2, p. 1740. The draft included one further plebiscite option: an all-state vote with regions to be subsequently divided between India and Pakistan on the basis of local majorities. It called for the stationing of UN troops in the state during the plebiscite period and for reference to arbitration on issues on which the two sides could not agree.

59. Henderson expressed his misgivings in connection with Admiral Nimitz's continuing inability to assume his responsibilities as plebiscite administrator. The ambassador was convinced that India no longer wished a retired American military officer in that role and would not cooperate with the admiral. Moreover, Henderson warned, if Nimitz ever did take up his duties, he would become the target of venomous allegations in the Indian press that he was promoting U.S. interests in Kashmir. Henderson urged that Nimitz be replaced by an outstanding commonwealth personage or someone from a small country who would not be vulnerable to similar defamation. (Embassy New Delhi telegram 1142 to the State Department, February 3, 1951, *FRUS 1951*, VI, part 2, p. 1716.)

60. Washington believed that Pakistan would not accept Bunche because of his association at the United Nations with the Palestine dispute and the creation of the state of Israel. Bunche's friendship with Nehru also hurt him with the Pakistanis. They believed that the Afro-American Bunche admired Nehru because Nehru championed the colored races. In their view, this would limit his objectivity.

61. Department of State memorandum, "India-Pakistan Relations—Kashmir, for Review at the NSC," August 21, 1951, *FRUS 1951*, VI, part 2, p. 1817.

62. Memorandum, Department of State, "Kashmir Dispute: Future Action," August 27, 1951, *FRUS 1951*, VI, part 2, p. 1822.

63. Elections for the twenty-five seats allocated to Pakistan-controlled areas were, of course, not held.

64. For a useful study of Abdullah's motives in convening the constituent assembly, see Lamb, *Kashmir, A Disputed Legacy*, pp. 192–93.

65. Embassy New Delhi telegram 1660 to the State Department, November 7, 1951, *FRUS 1951*, VI, part 2, p. 1903.

66. Embassy New Delhi telegram 1770 to the State Department, November 16, 1951, *FRUS 1951*, VI, part 2, p. 1904. Like many of the "polls" Bowles conducted and reported during his two assignments to India, the results of this one were almost certainly based on a wishful interpretation of the replies he received from those he questioned.

67. For further details of Bowles's views on the Kashmir issue, see my biography, *Chester Bowles: New Dealer in the Cold War* (Harvard University Press, 1993), pp. 101–4.

68. Department of State telegram 2226 to New Delhi, April 15, 1952, *FRUS 1952–54*, XI, p. 1232.

69. Department of State telegram 2431 to New Delhi, May 3, 1952, *FRUS 1952–54*, XI, p. 1241.

70. Embassy New Delhi telegram 2718 to the State Department, January 30, 1952, *FRUS 1952–54*, XI, p. 1184.

71. For the text of Graham's Fifth Report, see UN document S/2967, New York.

Chapter Two

1. Memorandum from Henry Byroade and John Hickerson to the Secretary of State, March 14, 1953, *FRUS 1952–1954*, XI, p. 1314.

2. Dulles-Eisenhower memorandum, March 24, 1953, and Eisenhower-Dulles memorandum, March 25, 1953, *FRUS 1952–54*, XI, p. 1316

3. Embassy New Delhi telegram 3873 to the State Department, April 17, 1953, *FRUS 1952–54*, XI, p. 1316.

4. Hoffman-Dulles letter, April 28, 1953, *FRUS 1952–54*, XI, p. 1319.

5. Alan R. Raucher, *Paul G. Hoffman, Architect of Foreign Aid* (University Press of Kentucky, 1985), p. 121.

6. Memorandum of Bogra-Dulles conversation, May 23, 1953, *FRUS 1952–1954*, IX, p. 121; memorandum of Zafrulla Khan-Dulles conversation, May 23, 1953, *FRUS 1952–1954*, IX, p. 127; memorandum of Ayub Khan-Dulles conversation, May 23, 1953, *FRUS 1952–1954*, IX, p. 131.

7. Consulate General Istanbul telegram 802 to the State Department (no. 10 from the secretary), May 26, 1953, *FRUS 1952–1954*, IX, p. 147.

8. Ibid.

9. Memorandum of discussion at the 147th Meeting of the National Security Council, June 1, 1953, *FRUS 1952–1954*, IX, p. 379.

10. Walter Johnson, ed., *The Papers of Adlai E. Stevenson*, vol. 5 (Boston: Little Brown, 1974), p. 225; John Bartlow Martin, *Adlai Stevenson and the World* (Garden City, N.Y.: Doubleday, 1977), p. 54. Asked by a Pakistani journalist for his views on a Kashmir settlement at a press conference he held in New Delhi shortly after his visit to the state, Stevenson said, "I would be very bold indeed if I thought I had found a solution to the Kashmir question, and I haven't. But I think step number one would be consultations and conferences between the Chiefs of [Government] of India and Pakistan directly, Prime Minister Nehru and Prime Minister [Bogra]. I think discussions would be in a spirit of good will. . . . [The problem] presents nothing that is insoluble and . . . it could be resolved" (Johnson, *Papers of Adlai E. Stevenson*, vol. 5, p. 225). Stevenson's statement came only a few weeks before the Nehru-Bogra meetings, which Washington also welcomed.

11. "Will India Turn Communist?" *Look*, July 14, 1954, pp. 42–44.

12. Embassy New Delhi telegram 79 to the State Department, July 13, 1953, *FRUS 1952–1954*, XI, p. 1323.

13. Department of State telegram 48 to New Delhi, July 15, 1953, *FRUS 1952–1954*, XI, p. 1324; Embassy New Delhi telegram 128 to the State Department, July 17, 1953, SDCF 690D.91. The Indian Ministry of External Affairs also discouraged Allen's vacationing in Kashmir despite his assurances that he did not intend to

see Abdullah or other political personalities. The reason it gave was unusually lame: the Communists, the ambassador was told, were planning a demonstration on his arrival.

14. Two American embassy officers and their families were vacationing in Kashmir at the time Abdullah was arrested. According to one of them, J. Wesley Adams, the officers were accused of having been conspirators in these events (Adams, Oral History, Truman Presidential Library, pp. 82–85).

15. Embassy New Delhi telegram 278 to the State Department, August 10, 1953, SDCF 690D.91.

16. Embassy New Delhi telegrams 275 and 283 to the State Department, August 10, 1953, SDCF 690D.91.

17. Embassy New Delhi telegram 392 to the State Department August 26, 1953, SDCF 690D.91. Embassy New Delhi telegram 315 to the State Department, August 13, 1953, *FRUS 1952–1954,* XI, p. 1330.

18. For an incisive account of the widespread Indian acceptance of the allegations of a U.S. hand in Kashmir, see W. G. Dildine's article in the *Washington Post,* August 23, 1953. Dildine found that Indian leaders across the political spectrum, from Communists, to moderates, to right-wingers, were convinced of American involvement. He quoted the popular socialist leader, Dr. Ram Manohar Lohia: "America is playing a game of international intrigue in Kashmir and I would say, as the entire Indian people would say, 'America, hands off Kashmir!'"

19. *NYT* editorial, August 18, 1953.

20. S. Gopal, *Jawaharlal Nehru, A Biography,* vol. 2 (Harvard University Press, 1979), p. 182.

21. Embassy Karachi telegram 172 to the State Department, August 16, 1953, *FRUS 1952–1954,* XI, p. 1331.

22. Sir N. R. Pillai, the secretary general of the Indian Ministry of External Affairs, raised the Nepal issue informally with Ambassador Allen in March 1954. Pillai told Allen that while "he personally put little credence in reports that Americans were intriguing against Indian interests in Nepal, . . . the conviction was growing among people of both India and Nepal that it was true." The ambassador scoffed at such reports. "Certainly," he assured Pillai, "we had no desire to disrupt Indo-Nepalese relations and throw Nepal into the hands of Communist China." (Embassy New Delhi telegram 1450 to the State Department, March 20, 1954, *FRUS 1952–1954,* XI, p. 1350.) There is no available evidence to substantiate the reports, which typify allegations of U.S. intervention in the smaller South Asian countries the Indians repeatedly made during the cold war.

23. The term *fireside chat* seems to have come from Bogra himself. He may have picked it up during his assignment in the United States as Pakistan ambassador. For

anyone who has wilted in the heat of a Pakistani September, the usage seems quite bizarre.

24. Acting secretary of state David Bruce–Nimitz memorandum of conversation, May 28, 1952, *FRUS 1952–1954*, XI, p. 1251. Nimitz's characterization of Nehru seems remarkably restrained for an old navy salt.

25. Secretary Dulles–Rear Admiral Bernard L. Austin, USN, memorandum of conversation, September 1, 1953, *FRUS 1952–1954*, XI, p. 1333.

26. Ibid., p. 1334.

27. Embassy Karachi Telegram 196 to the State Department, September 3, 1953, *FRUS 1952–1954*, XI, p. 1334. Hildreth's alarm echoed the position taken a couple of years earlier by Avra Warren, his predecessor at Embassy Karachi. Reacting to reports that Washington might find a candidate other than Nimitz as plebiscite administrator, Warren warned that this would "have a shocking effect on public opinion already acutely inflamed in Pakistan." (Embassy Karachi telegram 725 to the State Department, February 9, 1951, SDCF 845.00.) Reacting to this message at Embassy New Delhi, Ambassador Loy Henderson argued tartly that "Nimitz or any other prominent American citizen not known to be opposed to present U.S. foreign policy would be greatly handicapped [in dealing with the Indians]." (Embassy New Delhi telegram 2063 to the State Department, February 13, 1951, SDCF 845.00.)

28. Embassy Karachi strongly backed the projected arrangement and fatuously forecast that "while India would not be pleased over U.S. military aid to Pakistan, the result on the Kashmir question might in the end be beneficial." It called for a hardening of U.S. positions on Kashmir that would benefit Pakistan. (Embassy Karachi telegram 172 to the State Department, August 26, 1953, *FRUS 1952–1954*, XI, p. 1331.) Not surprisingly, Embassy New Delhi sharply disagreed with this assessment. In a hard-hitting cable, Ambassador Allen pointedly asked whether America was becoming more involved with the Kashmir question than its national interests justified. "It would be a very serious matter," he wrote, "for the United States to get tied up militarily or become morally committed to assist physically either side in territorial disputes so far from U.S. shores." In Allen's view, the United States should help where it could, through the UN wherever possible, but should avoid bilateral commitments. (Embassy New Delhi telegram 399 to the State Department, August 27, 1953, *FRUS 1952–1954*, XI, p. 1331.)

29. For excellent studies of the development of U.S.-Pakistan security relations in 1953–1955, see Robert J. McMahon, *The Cold War on the Periphery* (Columbia University Press, 1994), pp. 154–88, and Dennis Kux, *The United States and Pakistan, 1947–2000, Disenchanted Allies* (Woodrow Wilson Center Press and Johns Hopkins University Press, 2001), pp. 54–73. Selig Harrison's series in *The New*

Republic, written closer to the event, in 1959, also provides useful insights into how and why the relationship was brought about; see "The Cost of a Mistake," August 1959; "Undoing a Mistake," September 1959.

30. For an example of Embassy New Delhi's dire forecasts, see its telegram 654 to the State Department, October 19, 1953, *FRUS 1952–1954,* IX, p. 423. In this message, Chargé d'Affaires Sheldon T. Mills reported that senior officers at the embassy believed that India's response to direct military aid to Pakistan will be "bitter and vigorous." It would "color and perhaps change the course of the U.S.-India relationship for a long time to come." The embassy strongly urged Washington to adopt a method of indirect aid to accomplish American objectives in Pakistan. A senior State Department official rejected that approach: "If we decide to help Pakistan, we shall just have to ride out the storm." (Letter from John Jernigan, deputy assistant secretary for Near Eastern, South Asian, and African affairs, to Loy Henderson, U.S. ambassador to Iran, November 19, 1953, *FRUS 1952–1954,* IX, p. 432.) Canadian High Commissioner to India Escott Reid has an interesting insider's account of the embassy's ultimately unsuccessful campaign. According to Reid, Ambassador Allen had little hope that his arguments would tip the balance in Washington. See Reid, *Envoy to Nehru* (Oxford University Press, 1981), pp. 99–116.

31. Some of the most trenchant of Nehru's warnings about the implications of the agreement are in the letters he wrote to Indian state leaders in late 1953 and early 1954. See in particular those of November 15, 1953, December 31, 1953, and April 26, 1954, in Jawaharlal Nehru, *Letters to Chief Ministers* (New Delhi: Government of India, 1987), pp. 440–42, 472–478, 529.

32. Commenting on these expressed concerns, Embassy Karachi said it was "convinced that U.S. arms assistance will not lead to a GOP [Government of Pakistan] attempt to reach a military decision in Kashmir but it is obvious that as a result of the arms assistance promise, the Pakistanis feel they are in a better bargaining position." (Embassy Karachi telegram 708 to the State Department, March 9, 1954, *FRUS 1952–1954,* XI, p. 1340.)

33. Nehru, *Letters to Chief Ministers,* letter of March 15, 1954, pp. 504–5.

34. "Nationality of Aides Called No U.N. Issue." *NYT,* March 11, 1954. Department of State telegram 1058 to New Delhi, March 10, 1954, *FRUS 1952–1954,* XI, p. 1343. Legal precedents support Hammarskjöld's position.

35. Telegram to the Indian Mission at the United Nations, March 6, 1954, quoted in Gopal, *Jawaharlal Nehru,* vol. 2, p. 189.

36. Memorandum of conversation, Allen–Pakistan Ambassador Syed Amjad Ali, September 9, 1955, *FRUS 1955–1957,* VIII, p. 59. By then Allen was assistant secretary of state for Near Eastern, South Asian, and African affairs.

37. Reid, *Envoy to Nehru,* p. 123.

38. Department of State memorandum of conversation, July 29, 1955, SDCF 690D.91.

39. Dennis Kux, *India and the United States: Estranged Democracies, 1941–1991* (Washington: National Defense University Press, 1993), p. 118.

40. "The Russians in Kashmir." *NYT,* December 11, 1955. The newspaper featured the story on its front page.

41. The Soviets had generally abstained on Western-sponsored resolutions on Kashmir. This did not deter them from sharply castigating the United States and Britain. In 1952, for example, Soviet deputy foreign minister Jacob Malik charged at the United Nations that American and British efforts to settle the Kashmir dispute were part of an imperialist plot to seize control of the state and turn it into a military base.

42. Department of State telegram 1292 to Karachi, December 17, 1955, *FRUS 1955–1957,* VIII, p. 61. The U.S. official was Assistant Secretary of State George Allen, who after completing his New Delhi assignment had replaced Henry Byroade in that position. The ambassador of Pakistan was again Mohammed Ali Bogra. Bogra had only recently returned to Washington following his ouster as prime minister in another demonstration of the power Pakistan's military-bureaucratic hierarchy wielded over the country's weak politicians.

43. Embassy Karachi telegram 1175 to the State Department, December 20, 1955, SDCF 690D.91.

44. Embassy New Delhi dispatch 783 to the State Department, January 19, 1956, SDCF 690D.91.

45. *Department of State Bulletin,* March 19, 1956, p. 448. In addition to the United States and Pakistan, the member nations of the Southeast Asia Treaty Organization were Australia, France, New Zealand, the Philippines, Thailand, and the United Kingdom. All were represented at the meeting by their foreign ministers.

46. Dulles telegram 19 to the State Department (from New Delhi), March 10, 1956, *FRUS 1955–1957,* VIII, p. 66.

47. For example, see Embassy New Delhi telegram 271 to the State Department, August 1, 1956, *FRUS 1955–1957,* VIII, 94.

Chapter Three

1. For an account of U.S.-Indian relations during the second Eisenhower administration, see my book, *Ellsworth Bunker: Global Troubleshooter, Vietnam Hawk* (University of North Carolina Press, 2003), pp. 51–74, from which this passage is drawn.

2. S. Gopal, *Jawaharlal Nehru, A Biography,* vol. 3 (Harvard University Press, 1984), p. 40. Memorandum of telephone conversation, December 19, 1956, Eisenhower Library, Dulles Papers, White House telephone conversations.

3. "Statement of Policy on U.S. Policy [sic] toward South Asia," *FRUS 1955–1957,* VIII, pp. 29–43.

4. As Ambassador Henry Cabot Lodge pointed out, the Security Council's rejection of the Kashmir Constituent Assembly's vote to accede to India was basically a reaffirmation of a statement it issued in March 1951, when the Kashmir government, then led by Sheikh Abdullah, was considering convoking the assembly. (See *Department of State Bulletin,* February 11, 1957, pp. 231–32, for Lodge's statement on this issue and the text of the resolution.) The Indian government disregarded the resolution. Three days after the Security Council adopted it, New Delhi formalized the accession of Kashmir on India's national day, January 26, 1957, when the constituent assembly was replaced by a state legislature similar to those elsewhere in India.

5. The resolution's other cosponsors were the United Kingdom, Australia, Colombia, and (pre-Castro) Cuba.

6. Embassy New Delhi reported that the Security Council's overwhelming vote for the resolution "shocked and disappointed the Indian press and leaders but did not diminish the spate of self-righteous stories and editorials condemning Pakistan, the five powers sponsoring the resolution, the Security Council, and everyone except themselves for what has happened." (Embassy New Delhi telegram 2093 to the State Department, January 29, 1957, SDCF 690D.91.)

7. The resolution was cosponsored by the United States, the United Kingdom, and Australia. For the text of both resolutions and the statements U.S. representatives made in the debate about them, see *Department of State Bulletin,* March 18, 1957, pp. 457–63.

8. Embassy Karachi telegram 2326 to the State Department, February 28, 1957, SDCF 691D.91.

9. For a detailed account of how Nehru and his government assessed and dealt with the issue during this period, see Gopal, *Jawaharlal Nehru,* vol. 3, pp. 40–52.

10. Embassy New Delhi telegram 2726 to the State Department, April 3, 1957, *FRUS 1955–1957,* VIII, p. 128. For a summary of Bunker's assessment of the Kashmir issue and India-Pakistan relations, see Schaffer, *Ellsworth Bunker,* pp. 64–66.

11. The final results gave the National Conference sixty-eight of the seventy-five seats. (The twenty-five seats reserved for the Pakistan-administered parts of the state remained unfilled.)

12. The other sponsors were Australia, Britain, Colombia, and the Philippines. India, which was not a member of the Security Council, considered even the revised

resolution unacceptable. But in line with earlier precedents, it said it would extend "a hospitable welcome" to the UN representative. *Department of State Bulletin,* December 23, 1957, pp. 1011–17, provides important statements made by U.S. representatives at the United Nations on the evolving American position on the issue.

13. Embassy New Delhi telegram 691 to the State Department, September 12, 1957, SDCF 690D.91. Bunker, who surely knew Krishna Menon was right, diplomatically chose not to respond to the defense minister's jibe.

14. Robert J. McMahon, *The Cold War on the Periphery* (Columbia University Press, 1994), p. 241–42, has an insightful study of the initiative.

15. Dulles-Eisenhower memorandum, April 17, 1958, *FRUS 1958–1960,* XV, p. 81.

16. Following his return from consultations in India and Pakistan in March, Graham told U.S. representatives that he planned to recommend the stationing of UN forces in the Pakistan-administered parts of Kashmir and a meeting between the Indian and Pakistani prime ministers. He also favored another Security Council session to consider the issue. The United States recognized that the UN forces proposal was not viable—according to Graham, the Indians had rejected it when he raised the idea with them. Washington also adamantly opposed a UN Security Council debate, which it believed would only exacerbate tensions, fail to bring the issue closer to solution, diminish the prestige of the council, and weaken the UNCIP resolutions. Embassy Karachi and Embassy New Delhi agreed with this conclusion. Both feared that another debate would delay moving forward on the package proposal and even destroy it. In the end, American representatives talked Graham out of his proposals other than the idea of a prime ministerial summit.

17. Eisenhower-Dulles memo, April 21, 1958, *FRUS 1958–1960,* XV, p. 82.

18. Eisenhower did not spell out the issues in his letter, but they were included in the "talking paper" sent to the ambassadors for their sessions with Nehru and Mirza. The list of issues was expanded to include financial problems stemming from the partition, including the resettlement of refugees. These additional matters were considered ancillary to the "big three." (*FRUS 1958–1960,* XV, p. 78.)

19. Eisenhower-Nehru/Eisenhower-Mirza letters, May 2, 1958, *FRUS 1958–1960,* XV, p. 100.

20. Embassy New Delhi telegram 1225 to the State Department, November 6, 1957, SDCF 690D.91.

21. Arthur Z. Gardiner of the Office of South Asian Affairs appears to have been the only senior naysayer in the State Department. Gardiner had recently returned from an assignment at Embassy Karachi and was known for his pro-Pakistan views. He held that the proposal would cause problems for the United States with the Pakistanis, run counter to the principle of Kashmiri self-determination, and denigrate

the position of the United Nations. (Gardiner memorandum to William Rountree, November 15, 1957, *FRUS 1955–1957*, VIII, p. 152.)

22. The provisions included regard for religious concentrations *whenever possible*; contiguity of geographic area; existing district and administrative boundaries; terrain and natural communications and trade routes; existing or potential irrigation and hydroelectric projects; national security, *with particular reference to the northern frontiers*; and control over river segments or headwaters in relation to any settlement of the Indus waters dispute. (Emphases added.) Many of these criteria were vague and ambiguous. Did regard for religious concentrations "whenever possible" offer an out that would provide a basis for India's retaining the Valley? Did particular reference to the northern frontiers mean that India should have access through the Valley to the areas in Ladakh it disputed with Communist China? Did the natural communications and trade routes refer to the pre-1947 situation, when the Valley's connection with the rest of undivided India was through areas that became part of Pakistan, or did the phrase also take into account new construction, including the building of a tunnel and the upgrading of roads that connected the Valley with present-day India through Jammu? See Rountree-Dulles memorandum, April 10, 1958, *FRUS 1958–1960*, XV, p. 75.

23. Nehru-Eisenhower letter, June 7, 1958, *FRUS 1958–1960*, XV, p. 117.

24. Gopal, *Jawaharlal Nehru*, vol. 3, p. 85.

25. Embassy New Delhi telegram 3137 to the State Department, June 8, 1958, *FRUS 1958–1960*, XV, p. 119.

26. Department of State telegram 2868 to New Delhi, June 11, 1958, *FRUS 1958–1960*, XV, p. 124.

27. After an uneasy three-week duumvirate, Ayub forced out Mirza on October 27 and became president.

28. Embassy Karachi telegram 169 to New Delhi, October 21, 1958, *FRUS 1958–1960*, XV, p. 142. Embassy Karachi telegram 1096 to the State Department, November 1, 1958, *FRUS 1958–1960*, XV, p. 143.

29. Allen Dulles's memorandum of the 404th meeting of the National Security Council, April 30, 1959, *FRUS 1958–1960*, XV, p. 166.

30. *Department of State Bulletin*, October 10, 1960, p. 577.

31. This position was reflected in the briefings U.S. officials provided to the media. See the *NYT* front-page account, December 9, 1959, for a good example of the way American papers played the story. It was headlined "Eisenhower Cool to Pakistan's Bid on Indian Dispute." Subheads read: "President is reluctant to take initiative for talks on Kashmir with Nehru. 'Good offices' sought. Karachi aides disappointed but stress close ties."

32. Memorandum of Eisenhower-Ayub conversation, Karachi, December 8, 1959, *FRUS 1958–1960*, XV, p. 781. Kashmir was not specifically mentioned in the joint communiqué the two sides issued at the end of Eisenhower's visit. The text said only that "the American people especially hope that Pakistan and the other nations in South Asia will succeed in their efforts to improve relations among themselves." This was unusually bland even for a communiqué.

33. Gopal, *Jawaharlal Nehru*, vol. 3, p. 104.

34. Embassy Karachi telegram 1483 to the State Department, December 23, 1959, *FRUS 1958–1960*, XV, p. 197. For a recent detailed discussion of the foiled no-war treaty and the bilateral exchanges in which it was unsuccessfully revived in the 1980s, see A. G. Noorani's article in the *Daily Times* (Lahore), July 21, 2008. Noorani, an Indian journalist, scholar, and lawyer, argues that "as talks on Kashmir progress the no-war Treaty must be revived with greater realism and sincerity than before. It should either cap a Kashmir settlement or be signed when talks on Kashmir achieve a breakthrough." Earlier in 1959, Ayub had offered Nehru a proposal for joint India-Pakistan defense. This offer fitted well with Washington's long-standing interest that the two South Asian countries work together to deter Communist aggression. Nehru rejected it out of hand.

35. Embassy Karachi telegram 1483 to the State Department, December 23, 1959, *FRUS 1958–1960*, XV, p. 197.

36. Embassy New Delhi telegram 2428 to the State Department, January 22, 1960, *FRUS 1958–1960*, XV, p. 202.

Chapter Four

1. See letter from Rountree to T. Eliot Weil, February 8, 1961, *FRUS 1961–1963*, XIX, p. 6.

2. Embassy Karachi dispatch 936 to the State Department, June 2, 1961, SDCF 690D.91.

3. Memorandum of Johnson-Ayub conversation, Karachi, May 20, 1961, *FRUS 1961–1963*, XIX, p. 47.

4. Embassy Karachi telegram 2087 to the State Department, June 2, 1961, *FRUS 1961–1963*, XIX, p. 52.

5. Embassy Office Murree airgram G-16 to the State Department, June 17, 1961, SDCF 690D.91.

6. Embassy New Delhi telegram 2946 to the State Department, June 9, 1961, SDCF 690D.91. Embassy New Delhi telegram 3122 to the State Department, June 28, 1961, *FRUS 1961–1963*, XIX, p. 59.

7. Phillips Talbot, message to the author, July 2007. Talbot was assistant secretary for Near East and South Asian affairs in the Kennedy administration.

8. SNIE 32-61, "Prospects for Pakistan," July 5, 1961, *FRUS 1961–1963*, XIX, p. 60.

9. See Muhammad Ayub Khan's political autobiography, *Friends Not Masters* (Oxford University Press, 1967), p. 137.

10. Memorandum of conversation, "Kennedy-Ayub talks," July 11, 1961, *FRUS 1961–1963*, XIX, p. 66. Kennedy later told Assistant Secretary Talbot and Ambassador Rountree, who had participated in the meeting, that at the proper time the administration should appraise the possible consequences of renewed UN consideration of the Kashmir question and counsel the Pakistanis strongly if prospects were negative.

11. Arthur M. Schlesinger Jr., *A Thousand Days* (Boston: Houghton Mifflin Company, 1965), p. 526.

12. Memorandum of conversation, November 7, 1963, *FRUS 1961–1963*, XIX, p. 128.

13. Embassy New Delhi airgram 258 to the State Department, December 29, 1961, SDCF 690D.91.

14. Embassy Karachi telegram 1096 to the State Department, December 28, 1961, and Embassy Karachi telegram 1106 to the State Department, December 30, 1961, SDCF 690D.91.

15. Paper prepared by the Bureau of Near Eastern and South Asian Affairs, "U.S. Relations with South Asia: Major Issues and Recommended Courses of Action," undated (probably early January, 1962), *FRUS 1961–1963*, XIX, p. 181.

16. U.S. Mission Geneva telegram 654 to the State Department, December 31, 1961, SDCF 690D.91. Galbraith was vacationing in Switzerland at the time.

17. Department of State telegram 2810 to USUN, April 25, 1962, SDCF 690D.91.

18. Embassy New Delhi telegram 4165 to the State Department, June 24, 1962, SDCF 690D.91.

19. Embassy New Delhi telegram 4183 to the State Department, June 25, 1962, *FRUS 1961–1963*, XIX, p. 292.

20. Consulate General Calcutta telegram 1 to the State Department, July 1, 1962, *FRUS 1961–1963*, XIX, p. 293. Department of State telegram 6 to New Delhi, July 2, 1963, *FRUS 1961–1963*, XIX, p. 296. McGeorge Bundy–Galbraith special channel message, July 3, 1963, *FRUS 1961–1963*, XIX, p. 297.

21. Author's conversation with Anthony C. E. Quainton, July 2007. Quainton was a political officer at Embassy Karachi during McConaughy's tenure there. Phillips Talbot message to author, July 2007.

22. Embassy Karachi telegram 154 to the State Department, July 13, 1962, *FRUS 1961–1963*, XIX, p. 303.

23. Consulate General Calcutta telegram 1 to the State Department.

24. Department of State memo to the President, June 15, 1962, *FRUS 1961–1963,* XIX, p. 273.

25. It was this negotiation that Galbraith had cited in his complaint that support for Pakistan at the United Nations had not advanced U.S. interests.

26. McGhee-Talbot memorandum, May 14, 1962. Talbot-McGhee memorandum, May 26, 1962. Both documents are in SDCF 690D.91. Talbot wrote his memo before the Security Council debate on Kashmir had ended. But it seems very unlikely that he would have argued any differently once it was over.

27. Department of State telegram 660 to Karachi, October 21, 1962, *FRUS 1961–1963,* vol. XIX, p. 339. Department of State telegram 664 to Karachi, October 22, 1962, *FRUS 1961–1963,* XIX, p. 339.

28. Memorandum of Kennedy-Ayub Conversation, September 24, 1962, National Security Files, Country Series, Pakistan, Kennedy Presidential Library.

29. Kennedy-Ayub letter, October 28, 1962, transmitted in Department of State telegram 681 to Karachi, October 28, 1962, *FRUS 1961–1963,* XIX, p. 359. In *Ambassador's Journal, A Personal Account of the Kennedy Years* (Boston: Houghton-Mifflin, 1969), Galbraith describes in some detail his successful effort to win Nehru's permission to allow the Americans to pass word to Ayub that he would warmly accept such assurances and would respond to them.

30. McConaughy handed to Ayub an aide-mémoire stating that "the Government of the United States of America reaffirms its previous assurances to the Government of Pakistan that it will come to Pakistan's assistance in the event of aggression from India." (Embassy Karachi airgram 883 to the State Department, February 23, 1963, *FRUS 1961–1963,* XIX, p. 372.)

31. McConaughy's conversations with Ayub are reported in Embassy Karachi telegram 764 to the State Department, October 27, 1962, and Embassy Karachi telegram 820 to the State Department, November 5, 1962, *FRUS 1961–1963,* XIX, pp. 355, 369. The text of Ayub's message to Kennedy is in Department of State telegram 754 to Karachi, November 13, 1962, *FRUS 1961–1963,* XIX, p. 377. Ayub sent the message on November 5, 1961. He also reproduced its full text in *Friends Not Masters,* p. 141.

32. Komer-Kennedy memo, November 12, 1962, *FRUS 1961–1963,* XIX, p. 375. For Komer's dim view of the value of the U.S.-Pakistan alliance, see his January 1962 memo to McGeorge Bundy, "A New Look at Pakistani Tie," *FRUS 1961–1963,* XIX, p. 179.

33. Embassy Karachi telegram 804 to the State Department, November 2, 1962, SDCF 690D.91.

34. Department of State telegram 2329 to New Delhi, November 25, 1962, *FRUS 1961–1963*, XIX, p. 405. Kennedy sent this message to Ambassador McConaughy and special envoy W. Averell Harriman. It provided them with talking points for their imminent discussions with President Ayub.

35. David T. Schneider letter to the author, July 2007.

36. Department of State telegram 782 to Karachi, November 18, 1962, *FRUS 1961–1963*, XIX, p. 391.

37. Department of State telegram 2172 to New Delhi, November 20, 1962, *FRUS 1961–1963*, XIX, p. 400.

38. Memorandum of conversation, President Kennedy-Indian Ambassador B. K. Nehru, December 17, 1962, *FRUS 1961–1963*, XIX, p. 439.

39. Department of State telegram 2329 to New Delhi, November 25, 1962, *FRUS 1961–1963*, XIX, p. 405.

40. Ibid.

41. Embassy New Delhi telegram 2178 to the State Department, November 30, 1962, *FRUS 1961–1963*, XIX, p. 414.

42. Memorandum of Ayub-Sandys-Harriman conversation, Rawalpindi, November 28, 1962, *FRUS 1961–1963*, XIX, p. 409. Memorandum of Ayub-Harriman conversation, Rawalpindi, November 29, 1962, *FRUS 1961–1963*, XIX, p. 413.

43. Memorandum of meeting of the NSC Executive Committee, December 3, 1962, *FRUS 1961–1963*, XIX, p. 418. Department of State circular telegram 1066, December 8, 1962, *FRUS 1961–1963*, XIX, p. 426. Department of State telegram 2550 to New Delhi, December 3, 1962 (from Harriman), SDCF 690D.91.

44. Department of State telegram 2599 to New Delhi, December 8, 1962, *FRUS 1961–1963*, XIX, p. 423.

45. Embassy Office Murree telegram 16 to the State Department, December 28, 1962, SDCF 690D.91.

46. For a firsthand account of the reaction of the Indian delegation to the announcement, see Y. D. Gundevia, *Outside the Archives* (Hyderabad: Sangam Books, 1984), pp. 260–63. As commonwealth secretary in the Ministry of External Affairs, Gundevia was a major player in developing Indian policy toward Pakistan. Galbraith and others regarded him as a hard-liner on Pakistan and Kashmir and tried when possible to go around him. Gundevia's memoir provides interesting insights on the negotiations and other Indian diplomatic moves but should be read with this in mind.

McConaughy reported his conversation with Swaran Singh in Embassy Office Murree telegram 13 to the State Department, December 27, 1962. His report on his meeting with Ayub is in Embassy Karachi telegram 1205 to the State Department,

January 4, 1963. According to McConaughy, Swaran Singh told him that the Sino-Pakistan agreement was bound to have a lasting effect on India's attitude and position. The ambassador also said that he had persuaded Ayub to explain the timing and limited purpose of the agreement personally to Swaran Singh in conciliatory terms. Ayub's assertion to McConaughy that the agreement had a limited purpose is probably a reference to its provision that it would be replaced by a formal treaty after India and Pakistan had resolved the Kashmir issue. When McConaughy chided him about the agreement, Ayub came up with several arguments. The most disingenuous of these was his claim that the agreement formalized a favorable boundary that China could not later violate without committing clear and unconcealable aggression. As such, he argued, it fitted in well with U.S. containment policy. Ayub told James that he had learned of the agreement, which was signed in Beijing, only *after* he had met Swaran Singh (Embassy Karachi telegram 1267 to the State Department, January 4, 1963.) All three messages are in SDCF 690D.91.

47. Interestingly, the embassies in New Delhi and Karachi came to quite different conclusions about the delegations their host governments were sending to the talks. Embassy New Delhi reported that "almost all members of the Government of India delegation . . . were old hands at India-Pakistan relations and none of them, if left to their own devices, was likely to bring any significantly new approach to the problem." (Embassy New Delhi telegram 2364 to the State Department, December 13, 1962.) Embassy Karachi was much more enthusiastic about the Pakistan delegation: "With the exception of one [foreign office official], Ayub could hardly have assembled a group more conducive to adopting a reasonable approach to the negotiations, under his personal control and guidance." In what soon came to be seen as a monumental misjudgment, the embassy also found that "Bhutto's relative freedom from Indophobia constitutes an important plus factor." (Embassy Karachi telegram 1076 to the State Department, December 14, 1962.) Both messages are in SDCF 690D.91.

48. The best single account of the negotiations is in Sir Morrice James, *Pakistan Chronicle* (Oxford University Press, 1993). Like his American colleague, Walter McConaughy, James played an important role on the margins of the talks. So did his counterpart in New Delhi, Sir Paul Gore-Booth. Gore-Booth has also written his memoirs, *With Great Truth and Respect* (London: Constable, 1974). This book offers useful insights into the negotiations, but its coverage of them is less detailed than is James's.

49. Embassy New Delhi telegram 2834 to the State Department, January 19, 1963, *FRUS 1961–1963*, XIX, p. 477.

50. Embassy New Delhi telegram 2853 to the State Department, January 21, 1963, SDCF 690D.91.

51. The proposed division was spelled out in Department of State telegram 1093 to Karachi, January 21, 1963: (1) Indian authorities to retain control over the eastern and southern parts of the Kashmir Valley and enjoy unimpeded transit through it to Ladakh; (2) In order to protect its interests in Gilgit and Hunza, Pakistan must have improved access to these areas. Accordingly, the international border would enter the Valley just south of the Jhelum River and run to the outlet of Wular Lake so that the entire Muzaffarabad–Sopor road and a two-mile strip of territory to its southeast would be within Pakistan's control, thence along the main course of the Mash Matti River, thence northward to a trijunction northeast of Burzil Pass where the Astor district line and the Skardu and Kargil tehsil lines intersect. The territory to the north and west of this line would be assigned to Pakistan, the balance of the Valley remaining with India. (In a subsequent message, Department of State telegram 3004 to New Delhi, January 28, 1965, the department mentioned that it had told the British that Pakistan would get Bara.) (3) Outside the Valley, Punch, Mirpur, and Muzaffarabad districts would come under Pakistan's control. (4) The international border would divide Riasi District along the Chenab River northward to the point where the river turns east, then northward to the Riasi district line, then westward along the district line between Punch and Anantnag, between Punch and Baramulla, and between Muzaffarabad and Baramulla. District lines would be followed to a point just south of where the Jhelum River and the Baramulla-Muzaffarabad road cross exiting the Valley; (5) Northeast of the Burzil Pass the international border would follow the tehsil line separating Skardu from Kargil and Ladakh tehsils up to the Chinese border. (Both cited messages are in SDCF 690D.91.) In a subsequent message to Assistant Secretary Talbot, National Security Council senior staffer W. Howard Wriggins suggested possible adjustments to the department's proposal to bring it closer to the Pakistan government's requirements. These changes included giving Pakistan territory that would provide it with control of more of the drainage basin of the Chenab River. McConaughy made a similar proposal. The Chenab issue was an important one for the Pakistanis, who stressed it at the third round of negotiations and elsewhere. (Wriggins-Talbot memo, January 26, 1963; Embassy Karachi telegram 1385 to the State Department, January 28, 1963, both in SDCF 690D.91.)

52. Komer-Kennedy memo, January 26, 1963, *FRUS 1961–1963*, XIX, p. 485.

53. Embassy New Delhi telegram 2900 to the State Department, January 25, 1963 and Embassy New Delhi telegram 3091 to the State Department, February 6, 1963, SDCF 690D.91.

54 Embassy Karachi telegram 1385 to the State Department, January 28, 1963, SDCF 690D.91.

55. Department of State telegram 2932 to New Delhi, January 21, 1963, Embassy New Delhi telegram 2998 to the State Department, January 31, 1963, SDCF 690D.91.

56. Embassy London telegram 2969 to New Delhi, February 5, 1963, Embassy New Delhi telegram 3202 to the State Department, February 16, 1963, SDCF POL 32-1 India/Pakistan.

57. Embassy New Delhi telegram 3168 to the State Department, February 13, 1963, SDCF POL 32-1 India/Pakistan.

58. Talbot memorandum for the NSC Executive Committee, February 7, 1963, *FRUS 1961–1963,* XIX, p. 494. Department of State telegram 3181 to New Delhi, February 16, 1963, *FRUS 1961–1963,* XIX, p. 498.

59. Informal notes on discussion with President Kennedy on Kashmir negotiations, February 21, 1963, *FRUS 1961–1963,* XIX, p. 508.

60. In his message to Nehru, Kennedy argued that "if only the [Kashmir] issue could be settled, it would open new perspectives in terms of India's role on the world stage. . . ." American diplomats continue to this day to make this point to the Indians in discussing the need for progress in the India-Pakistan peace process, which focuses importantly on Kashmir. (Department of State telegram 3098 to New Delhi, February 6, 1963, *FRUS 1961–1963,* XIX, p. 490.) Also see chapter 8.

61. Embassy New Delhi telegram 3804 to the State Department, April 4, 1962, SDCF POL 32-1 India/Pakistan.

62. Plans for the internationalization of the Valley were also drawn up as a fallback. Galbraith consistently opposed this approach and was convinced that India would never accept it. Following the failure of the Calcutta round, he told Washington: "We can't ask the Indians to fight in Ladakh to defend a Valley which is under the UN or a consortium consisting of Ghana, Ceylon, and the Congo. . . ." (Embassy New Delhi telegram 3501 to the State Department, March 10, 1963, SDCF POL 32-1 India/Pakistan.)

63. Consulate General Dacca telegram 329 to the State Department, March 11, 1963, SDCF POL 32-1 India/Pakistan.

64. Department of State telegram 1282 to Karachi, February 22, 1963, and Embassy Karachi telegram 1609 to the State Department, February 24, 1963, SDCF POL 32-1 India/Pakistan. Memorandum of Secretary Rusk's conversation with Pakistan Ambassador Aziz Ahmed, February 23, 1963, *FRUS 1961–1963,* XIX, p. 510. Rusk was unusually tough with Ahmed, who lamely tried to blame the Chinese for insisting, or so he said, that Pakistan be represented at the foreign minister level.

65. Rusk-Kennedy Memo, "Kashmir: Tactics for Fifth Round, March 31, 1963, Attachment: "Elements of a Settlement," *FRUS 1961–1963,* XIX, p. 534.

66. Rostow-Kennedy memorandum, April 8, 1963, *FRUS 1961–1963,* XIX, p. 538. See also W. W. Rostow, *The Diffusion of Power* (New York: Macmillan, 1972), pp. 203–6 and 651–53.

67. Embassy Karachi telegram 2048 to the State Department, April 20, 1963, SDCF POL 32-1 India/Pakistan.

68. Nehru-Kennedy letter, quoted in S. Gopal, *Jawaharlal Nehru, A Biography,* vol. 3 (Harvard University Press, 1984), p. 259.

69. Ibid.

70. Embassy New Delhi telegram 4101 to the State Department, April 22, 1963, SDCF POL 32-1 India/Pakistan.

71. Galbraith, *Ambassador's Journal,* p. 564.

72. Notes on Karachi-New Delhi Visit, Washington, May 5, 1963, *FRUS 1961–1963,* XIX, p. 575.

73. Memorandum for the Record, president's meeting on India, April 25, 1963, *FRUS 1961–1963,* XIX, p. 561.

74. Timothy W. Crawford, "Kennedy and Kashmir, 1962–63: The Perils of Pivotal Peacemaking in South Asia," *India Review* 1, no. 3 (July 2002): 8.

75. Embassy New Delhi telegram 3693 to the State Department, March 25, 1963, *FRUS 1961–1963,* XIX, p. 526.

76. Rusk-Kennedy memorandum, "Kashmir: Tactics for Fifth Round," March 31, 1963, *FRUS 1961–1963,* XIX, p. 530.

77. Embassy New Delhi telegram to State Department, May 16, 1963, and Komer memo to President Kennedy, May 17, 1963, Kennedy Presidential Library.

Chapter Five

1. Department of State memorandum to the NSC, January 27, 1964, SDCF POL 32-1 India/Pakistan.

2. Embassy Karachi telegram 1343 to the State Department, January 18, 1964, SDCF POL 32-1 India/Pakistan.

3. State-NSC memorandum, January 27, 1964, "Pakistan's Referral of Kashmir to Security Council," *FRUS 1964–1968,* XXV, p. 18.

4. Embassy New Delhi telegram 2177 to the State Department, January 18, 1964, SDCF POL 32-1 India/Pakistan.

5. Critchfield received valuable assistance in making contacts in the Valley from Farooq Kathwari, then a student at Kashmir University and a leader in the peaceful demonstrations that had followed the theft of the holy relic. Despite his family's misgivings, Kathwari was similarly helpful to me when I visited the Valley in early March 1964. The authorities were not happy with his activities, and Kathwari had to leave India. In 1965 he made his way to the United States and embarked on a remarkably successful business career. He is now chairman, president, and CEO of Ethan

Allen Interiors, a Fortune 500 company that is one of the country's largest manufacturers and retailers of quality furniture. Kathwari's continuing interest in the plight of the Kashmiris is reflected in his leadership of the Kashmir Study Group, which he founded in 1996 (see ch. 6).

6. Bowles also had some trouble convincing the State Department that an official embassy visit was a good idea. The department had agreed that it would be desirable to have a firsthand report, but told him that he should hold off implementing the idea, presumably because of the sensitivity of the Kashmir situation. (Department of State telegram 1637 to New Delhi, February 14, 1964, SDCF POL 32-1 India/Pakistan.)

7. I detailed my findings in Embassy New Delhi airgram to the State Department A-934, March 24, 1964, SDCF POL 32-1 India/Pakistan.

8. Embassy London telegram 4705 to the State Department, March 25, 1964, *FRUS 1964–1968,* XXV, p. 67. Talbot discussed this issue further in a July 2007 message to the author.

9. Komer-McGeorge Bundy memorandum, March 26, 1964, *FRUS 1964–1968,* XXV, p. 71. As special assistant to the president for national security, Bundy was Komer's boss at the National Security Council. His reply, in which he supported Talbot's position, is in a footnote at *FRUS 1964–1968,* XXV, p. 73

10. In his July 2007 message to the author, Talbot wrote: "I have never known where the 'Talbot Plan' idea originated, except that after 1962 India clearly braced to deal with whatever policy compensation the United States might claim for its help with the China border war. My visit to New Delhi in March 1964 . . . was seen by some as the expected occasion for the United States to claim its price. The 'Yankee Talbot Go Home—Kashmir Not for Sale' poster that hangs in my den as a memento of my government service is a reminder of the mood at that time. Its call to 'Join in the Thousands—Down with the Talbot Plan' stirred a peaceful crowd of about forty people, I heard later."

11. Embassy New Delhi telegram 2573 to the State Department, March 2, 1964, SDCF POL 32-1 India/Pakistan. The *Hindustan Times* report was quoted in the embassy's telegram 2567 to the State Department, March 2, 1964, SDCF POL 32-1 India/Pakistan.

12. Embassy Karachi telegram 1465 to the State Department, February 3, 1964, SDCF POL 32-1 India/Pakistan.

13. Embassy New Delhi telegram 2423 to the State Department, February 17, 1964, SDCF POL 32-1 India/Pakistan.

14. Embassy Karachi telegram 1935 to the State Department, April 11, 1964, *FRUS 1964–1968,* XXV, p. 80.

15. Embassy New Delhi telegram 3266 to the State Department, May 4, 1964, SDCF POL 32-1 India/Pakistan.

16. Talbot message to the author, July 2007.

17. Embassy New Delhi telegram 3818 to the State Department, June 20, 1964, SDCF POL 32-1 India/Pakistan.

18. Memoranda of conversation, "Military Assistance to India," July 7, 1964, *FRUS 1964–1968*, XXV, p. 132. "President's Conversation with Ambassador McConaughy," July 15, 1964, *FRUS 1964–1968*, XXV, p. 136.

19. Department of State telegram1250 to New Delhi, December 18, 1964, SDCF POL 32-1 India/Pakistan.

20. Embassy Karachi telegram 1730 to the State Department, March 16, 1965, SDCF POL 32-1 India/Pakistan.

21. Harold H. Saunders, "Narrative and Guide to the Documents," 6, NSF, NSC Histories, South Asia, Johnson Presidential Library.

22. Embassy New Delhi telegram 3095 to the State Department, April 30, 1965, SDCF POL 32-1 India/Pakistan.

23. Talbot-Rusk memorandum, April 30, 1965, SDCF POL 32-1 India/Pakistan.

24. This message is referred to in Department of State telegram 2305 to New Delhi, May 3, 1965, SDCF POL 32-1 India/Pakistan.

25. Department of State telegram 2509 to New Delhi, 1267 to Karachi, June 1, 1965, SDCF POL 32-1 India/Pakistan.

26. Just before Abdullah's rearrest, Parker T. Hart, the American ambassador to Saudi Arabia, met the sheikh, who was passing through the kingdom on his way back to India. Hart reported that Abdullah had no prescription for a Kashmir solution other than self-determination. (Embassy New Delhi had come to the same conclusion earlier.) Abdullah had urged that the United States not let India sleep on the Kashmir problem, which would not go away. He wanted Washington to bring Kashmir to India's repeated attention and not permit India to be so reassured by U.S. aid that it would continue to defy American and world opinion regarding the UN resolutions. (Embassy Jidda airgram A-335 to the State Department, May 18, 1965, SDCF, POL 32-1 India/Pakistan.)

27. Embassy New Delhi telegram 3574 to the State Department, June 7, 1965, SDCF POL 32-1 India/Pakistan.

28. Embassy Karachi telegram 2363 to the State Department, June 9, 1965, SDCF POL 32-1 India/Pakistan.

29. Talbot memo to Secretary Rusk, June 20, 1965, *FRUS 1964–1968*, XXV, p. 275.

30. Embassy Karachi telegram 209 to the State Department, August 11, 1965, SDCF POL 32-1 India/Pakistan.

31. Embassy Karachi telegram 254 to the State Department, August 18, 1965, SDCF POL 32-1 India/Pakistan.

32. Department of State telegram 177 to New Delhi, *FRUS 1964–1968,* XXV, p. 328.

33. Komer-Johnson memorandum, August 9, 1965, *FRUS 1964–1968,* vol. XXV, p. 329.

34. Department of State telegram 248 to New Delhi, August 19, 1965, SDCF POL 32-1 India/Pakistan.

35. Specifically, how to deal with the rescheduling for September 23 of the Aid-to-Pakistan Consortium pledging session that had been postponed in June at U.S. behest. The Pakistanis had reacted sharply to the postponement. In the U.S. view, their reaction was "inconsistent with the mutual respect expected among allies, and the continued massive flow of U.S. aid. Its predictable effect was to resurface all the basic concerns about U.S.-Pakistan relations which were growing in the minds of the people of America." (Department of State telegram 284 to Karachi, September 5, 1965, *FRUS 1964–1968,* XXV, p. 357. Rusk had told McConaughy to use this talking point at his upcoming meeting with Ayub and to say that he was speaking under instructions.)

36. Embassy New Delhi telegram 411 to the State Department, August 28, 1965, SDCF POL 32-1 India/Pakistan.

37. Department of State telegram 253 to USUN, August 31, 1965, SDCF POL 32-1 India/Pakistan.

38. Embassy New Delhi telegram 411 to the State Department, August 28, 1965, SDCF POL 32-1 India/Pakistan.

39. Komer-Johnson memo, August 31, 1965, *FRUS 1964–1968,* XXV, p. 342.

40. Memorandum for the record, "Meeting with the President on Kashmir, September 2, 1965," *FRUS 1964–1968,* XXV, p. 345.

41. Department of State telegram 266 to Karachi, September 2, 1965, *FRUS 1964–1968,* XXV, p. 347.

42. Embassy New Delhi telegram 458 to the State Department, September 2, 1965, SDCF POL 32-1, India/Pakistan; Department of State telegram to New Delhi 330, September 2, 1965, Box 24, NSF, Johnson Presidential Library; Embassy New Delhi telegram 478 to the State Department, September 4, 1965, *FRUS 1964–1968,* XXV, p. 350. For a fuller account of Bowles's activities during this period, see my biography, *Chester Bowles: New Dealer in the Cold War* (Harvard University Press, 1993), pp. 268–69.

43. Embassy Karachi telegrams 343 (September 2, 1965) and 360 (September 4, 1965), both to the State Department, SDCF POL 32-1 India/Pakistan.

44. Department of State telegram 343 to New Delhi, September 3, 1965, *FRUS 1964–1968,* XXV, p. 348.

45. Embassy Office Rawalpindi telegram 38 to the State Department, September 6, 1965, *FRUS 1964–1968*, XXV, p. 360.

46. Department of State telegram 290 to Karachi, September 6, 1965, *FRUS 1964–1968*, XXV, p. 365; Embassy Karachi telegram 428 to the State Department, September 9, 1965, *FRUS 1964–1968*, XXV, p. 379.

47. Rusk-Johnson memo, September 9, 1965, *FRUS 1964–1968*, XXV, p. 376.

48. Embassy Office Rawalpindi telegram 91 to the State Department, September 20, 1965, *FRUS 1964–1968*, XXV, p. 415.

49. Ayub-Johnson telephone conversation, September 23, 1965, *FRUS 1964–1968*, XXV, p. 427.

50. Referred to in Komer-Johnson memorandum, October 1, 1965, *FRUS 1964–1968*, XXV, p. 437; Embassy New Delhi telegram 829 to the State Department, September 29, 1965, *FRUS 1964–1968*, XXV, p. 441.

51. Embassy office Rawalpindi telegram 121 to the State Department, September 29, 1965, *FRUS 1964–1968*, XXV, p. 441.

52. Bundy-Komer memorandum to Johnson, October 6, 1965, *FRUS 1964–1968*, XXV, p. 444.

53. Embassy New Delhi telegram 734 to the State Department, September 21, 1965, *FRUS 1964–1968*, XXV, p. 422.

54. Bundy-Komer telegram to Johnson, December 1, 1965, *FRUS 1964–1968*, XXV, p. 483.

55. Memorandum of conversation, "Visit of President Ayub Khan; Official Call by Acting Secretary Ball on . . . Ayub," December 14, 1965, *FRUS 1964–1968*, XXV, p. 506.

56. Memorandum of Johnson-Ayub conversation, December 15, 1965, ibid., p. 509. For a good description of the atmospherics of the Ayub visit, see Dennis Kux, *The United States and Pakistan, 1947–2000, Disenchanted Allies* (Washington: Woodrow Wilson Center Press, 2001), pp. 165–68.

57. Dean Rusk Oral History Statement, Interview III, Tape 1:27, Johnson Presidential Library. January 2, 1970.

58. Embassy New Delhi telegram 12 to the State Department from Secretary Rusk, January 13, 1966, *FRUS 1964–1968*, XXV, p. 533.

59. Johnson-Kosygin letter, January 24, 1966, Johnson Presidential Library.

60. Johnson-Humphrey telephone conversation, February 4, 1966, *FRUS 1964–1968*, XXV, p. 561. Johnson later told Ayub that he "greatly admired" the accomplishments at Tashkent and said he shared Ayub's hope that the agreement would enable India and Pakistan to turn over a new leaf so that there could be real progress toward removing differences between the two countries. (Johnson-Ayub letter, February 10, 1966, Johnson Presidential Library.)

61. Department of State telegram 3171 to Paris, January 11, 1966, SDCF POL 32-1 India/Pakistan.

Chapter Six

1. Minutes of Secretary of Defense Laird's Armed Forces Policy Council Meeting, December 6, 1971, *FRUS 1969–1971*, XI, p. 652. Minutes of Washington Special Actions Group Meeting, December 6, 1971, *FRUS 1969–1971*, XI, p. 652.

2. According to the report, Gandhi's other objectives were the liberation of Bangladesh and the destruction of Pakistani armored and air force capabilities. CIA Intelligence Information Cable, December 7, 1971, *FRUS 1969–1971*, XI, p. 686. Minutes of Washington Special Action Group Meeting, December 8, 1971, *FRUS 1969–1971*, XI, p. 690. See also *NYT*, January 15, 1972, which carries the report of the meeting that was leaked to columnist Jack Anderson. The leaked report said that Kissinger suggested that "the key issue if the Indians turn on West Pakistan is Azad Kashmir. If the Indians smash the Pak air force and the armored forces, we would have a deliberate Indian attempt to force the disintegration of Pakistan." Seeking to calm the national security adviser, Assistant Secretary of State Joseph Sisco noted that "it must . . . be kept in mind that [all of] Kashmir is really disputed territory." This was of course the long-standing U.S. position.

3. Department of State telegram 222636 to New Delhi, December 10, 1971, *FRUS 1969–1971*, XI, p. 734.

4. USUN telegram 4965 to the State Department, December 12, 1971, *FRUS 1969–1971*, XI, p. 795.

5. Lee Lescaze, "Indo-Pakistan Accord a Giant Step," *Washington Post*, July 4, 1972.

6. Official U.S. satisfaction was paralleled in the American press. The *Washington Post* (July 4, 1972) reported that the agreement "surpassed all expectations" and showed the way for resolution of conflicts elsewhere. The *New York Times* (July 7, 1972) also hailed the agreement and the realism that Gandhi and Bhutto showed in reaching it, but sensibly warned that like Tashkent, Simla fell far short of bringing about a durable peace.

7. Interview with William Clark, April 2007.

8. Communications from Walter Andersen, May and September 2007.

9. Interview with R. Grant Smith, May 2007.

10. Interview with Teresita C. Schaffer, March 2007.

11. Dennis Kux, *The United States and Pakistan, 1947–2000, Disenchanted Allies* (Washington: Woodrow Wilson Center Press, 2001), p. 305.

12. Interview with Robert Oakley, October 2007.

13. P. R. Chari, Pervaiz Iqbal Cheema, and Stephen Philip Cohen, *Perception, Politics, and Security in South Asia: The Compound Crisis of 1990* (London: Routledge Curzon, 2003), p. 68. Also see these authors' *Four Crises and a Peace Process* (Brookings, 2007), p. 88.

14. Robert Pear, "State Dept. Moves to Expel Top Kashmir Separatist," *NYT,* April 18, 1990.

15. Gates was accompanied by Richard Haass, the senior National Security Council member responsible for South Asia, and John Kelly, assistant secretary of state for the Near East and South Asia.

16. The Gates mission statement mentioned as an objective "begin[ning] the sort of political dialogue which could not only reduce tension but could lead to a peaceful and permanent resolution of the Kashmir problem, as called for under the Simla Agreement. . . ." But this had been standard Washington rhetoric for eighteen years and in no way suggested U.S. willingness to become involved in helping devise a settlement.

17. Ambassador Robert Oakley, who sat in on the talks, recalls that during the meetings with the two leaders—Prime Minister Benazir Bhutto, the third member of the shaky governing triumvirate was out of the country—Gates told them that Washington was aware that Pakistan's nuclear program had been reactivated, thus ending the self-imposed restraint that Islamabad had applied a year earlier to avoid U.S. sanctions. Gates added that unless the new activity was quickly suspended, the Bush administration would be obliged to impose the sweeping sanctions called for by the Pressler Amendment. This statute required annual presidential certification that Pakistan neither possessed nor was developing a "nuclear explosive device" for military and economic aid to continue. The Pakistanis, in Oakley's account, turned a deaf ear. As noted, the administration imposed the strictures the legislation called for four months later. (Interview with Oakley, October 2007.)

18. Chari, Cheema, and Cohen, *Perception, Policy, and Security in South Asia,* p. 111.

19. Ibid.

20. U.S. Department of State, "India Human Rights Practices, 1993," January 31, 1994 (http://dosfan.lib.uic.edu/ERC/democracy/1993_hrp_report/93hrp_report_sasia/India.html).

21. Interview with William Clark, April 2007. Interview with R. Grant Smith, May 2007.

22. Testimony of John H. Kelly, to the Subcommittee on Asian and Pacific Affairs of the House Foreign Affairs Committee, March 6 and November 2, 1990.

23. Interview with John Malott, March 2007. Malott was interim director and principal deputy assistant secretary of the newly organized South Asia bureau from June 1992 to July 1993.

24. Some referred to them as "Burton's Freak Show."

25. Like many other senators and representatives (and administration officials) who were vigorous critics of India in the 1990s and earlier, Burton has since become an India fan. On a 2007 visit he hailed the improvement in U.S.-Indian relations that he had zealously tried to prevent and welcomed India's economic progress. According to one observer, Burton's conversion may have been helped along by his discovery that a factory in his district had a lucrative contract to sell equipment to the Indians. (Stephen P. Cohen, communication to the author, October 2007.)

26. Interviews with John Monjo, April 2007, and John Malott, March 2007.

27. Douglas Jehl, "Pakistan Is Facing Terrorist Listing," *NYT,* April 25, 1993.

28. Communication from Alan W. Eastham, April 2007.

29. John F. Burns, "No Answers for Wife of U.S. Hostage in Kashmir," *NYT,* July 6, 1997.

30. Eastham communication. See also Victoria Schofield, *Kashmir in Conflict* (London: I. B. Tauris, 2000), pp. 187–88, 196–97, for a good account of the kidnappings and their aftermath

31. Interview with R. Grant Smith, May 2007. Smith held senior positions in the State Department and Embassy New Delhi during that time.

32. Interview with Teresita C. Schaffer, April 2007.

33. Testimony of John H. Kelly, Subcommittee on Asian and Pacific Affairs of the House Foreign Affairs Committee, March 6, 1990.

34. Testimony of John Malott, Hearings and Recommendations for U.S. Foreign Assistance to Asia and the Pacific before the Subcommittee on Asian and Pacific Affairs of the House Foreign Affairs Committee, April 28, 1993. Rep. Dana Rohrabacher, a California Republican, was dissatisfied with Malott's answers. He told Malott that his archival searches ought not to have stopped in 1948 but gone back to 1776, when the Declaration of Independence laid out guiding principles on issues such as Kashmir.

35. Ibid.

36. Walter Andersen, who then and later was the leading South Asia specialist in the State Department's Bureau of Intelligence and Research, points out that others in the department who dealt with the region made a similar assessment. (Andersen communication, February 2008.)

37. The silly allegation that Robin Raphel was pro-Pakistan seems to have been based in part on the fact that she had served at Embassy Islamabad in the 1970s with her then-husband, Arnold Raphel. Arnold Raphel later became ambassador to Pakistan and died in the mysterious 1988 plane crash that killed President Zia ul-Haq, a fellow passenger. Some of Robin Raphel's critics claimed that this strengthened the attachment to Pakistan she had developed when she worked there in the late 1970s.

In fact, the Raphels had been divorced well before the crash and Arnold Raphel had remarried.

38. Interview with Robin Raphel, April 2007.

39. Adhay Vaidya, "Kashmir Disputed Territory: US," *Times of India*, October 30, 1993.

40. Communication from Walter Andersen, September 2007.

41. Raju Santhanam, "Why India's Reaction on J &K Is All Sound and Fury," *Statesman* (Calcutta), October 30, 1993.

42. The examples are drawn from stories in the *Statesman, Times of India*, and *Hindustan Times*, October 30–November 7, 1993. For example, see N. C. Menon, "Anti-India Tilt in US Policy on Kashmir," *Hindustan Times*, November 1, 1993.

43. J. N. Dixit, *India-Pakistan in War & Peace* (New Delhi: Books Today, 2002), p. 314. Dixit also alleged that "the unfortunate aspect [of Raphel's remarks] was that the United States not only backed Pakistan's viewpoint but also picked up this issue to pressur[e] India to fall in line with Washington's agenda on nuclear non-proliferation and missile development" (p. 311). Dixit was very critical and condescending about Raphel's low rank in comments he made to me in 1994. He sniffed that he had been obliged to tell his unhappy Ministry of External Affairs colleagues to accept her appointment since "that is the way Americans handle such things."

44. Inter-Press Service, "Kashmir: India Calls Clinton's Pakistan Views 'Unfortunate,'" February 17, 1994.

45. Aziz Haniffa, "Raphel Warns on Two Asian Conflicts," *India Abroad*, February 18, 1994.

46. Clinton remarks, April 11, 1995. The president was answering a reporter's query about his statement that "I told the Prime Minister that, if asked, we will do what we can to help these two important nations work together to resolve the dispute in Kashmir and other issues that separate them." Joint Press Conference with P. M. Bhutto (http://archives.clintonpresidentialcenter.org/?u=041195-joint-press-conference-with-pm-bhutto.htm).

47. House of Representatives International Relations Committee, Subcommittee on Asia and the Pacific, October 22, 1997 (http://commdocs.house.gov/committees/intlrel/hfa47327.000/hfa47327_0f.htm).

48. Embassy Islamabad–based officers also routinely visited Azad Kashmir. But since there was no insurgency in the region nor any significant popular objection to the region's link with Pakistan, these visits were much less important. (The American officials were not allowed to hunt for insurgent camps, of course.)

49. Schofield, *Kashmir in Conflict*, p. 163.

50. Assistant Secretary of State Robin Raphel, in testimony before the House of Representatives International Relations Committee, Subcommittee on Asia and the

Pacific, March 12, 1997 (http://commdocs.house.gov/committees/intlrel/hfa43264.
000/hfa43264_0f.htm).

51. Full disclosure: I am a charter member of the KSG.

52. Long led by Dr. Fai, its energetic executive director, the council actively seeks
the support of U.S. officials, senators and representatives, the media, and influential
private Americans for Kashmiri self-determination. It sponsors seminars, meetings,
and studies built around the self-determination cause and a demand for an improvement in the Indian government's human rights performance in the parts of Kashmir New Delhi controls. The high point in its annual calendar of events is a
much-publicized meeting and roundtable in a congressional office building on Capitol Hill that draws members of Congress, Kashmiri political leaders (all of an anti-
Indian flavor), American and South Asian academic specialists, Kashmiri-Americans,
ethnic journalists, and Pakistan Embassy officers (www.iakf.org/main/).

At the seventh annual session, in July 2007, a half-dozen legislators spoke briefly
in support of the Kashmiri cause. Dr. Fai maintains ties with some of the Hurriyet
leaders and often sponsors their public appearances when they come to the United
States. The council is widely believed to receive financial backing from the Pakistan
Embassy. Fai also has links with European-based Kashmiri organizations.

53. The Indo-American Kashmir Forum was established in 1991, soon after the
Pandit community was expelled from the Valley. Its main purpose is to win sympathetic American attention to the plight of the Kashmiri Pandits as "victims of Islamic
fundamentalists and terrorists," an accurate description. It also supports the reha-
bilitation of the community throughout the world through financial grants and by
enlisting backing from national and international relief organizations. The end goal
of its advocacy is "(1) to promote the safety and security of Kashmiri Pandits living
in the Valley and to create conditions acceptable for the return of displaced Pandits
outside the Valley . . . with dignity and (2) to create a society in which Kashmiri Pandits are integral members with a proportionate representation and voice in the affairs
of the state" (http://www.iakf.org/main/).

Dr. Sazawal, its energetic overseas coordinator and past president, has become a
well-known figure to U.S. government officials and influential private Americans
interested in the Kashmir issue. In an August 2007 interview, he told me that the
forum enjoyed some support in Congress, but its ability to expand this is inhibited
by the lack of interest on the part of the Indian Embassy in Washington in promoting the Pandits' cause among pro-Indian senators and representatives. He dismissed
as unrealistic the call of some Kashmir Pandits for a state of their own inside the
Valley. According to Dr. Sazawal, 350,000 Pandits left the Valley and only 5,000
remain there. He estimates that there are 1,300 to 1,500 Pandit families in the United
States, mostly in New York, New Jersey, northern California, Houston, Chicago, and

Washington, D.C. They easily outnumber the Kashmiri Muslims resident in this country, he says (www.kashmirforum.org).

54. Kashmir Study Group, *Kashmir: A Way Forward,* February 2000. Larchmont, N.Y. (www.kashmirstudygroup.net/).

55. Kashmir Study Group, *Kashmir: A Way Forward,* February 2005. Larchmont, N.Y. (www.kashmirstudygroup.net/).

56. Clad later became a senior official in the Department of Defense. He made his proposal as a private citizen.

57. The Kashmir Study Group's first (2000) report includes an addendum in which Hannum spells out his findings (www.kashmirstudygroup.net/).

58. Teresita C. Schaffer, *Kashmir: The Economics of Peace Building* (Washington: Center for Strategic and International Studies, 2005) (www.csis.org/media/csis/pubs/kashmirexecsummary.pdf).

59. These proposals are summarized in a Stimson Center report, "Kashmir Forum Proposals," issued in 2005. The report also includes proposals offered by many non-American scholars and observers, mostly South Asian. Summaries of all the proposals appear on the Stimson Center website (www.stimson.org/southasia/?SN+SA20050202678). Professor Wirsing's proposal is drawn from his book *Kashmir in the Shadow of War: Regional Rivalries in a Nuclear Age* (London: M. E. Sharpe, 2003).

60. See Dalia Dassa Kaye, *Talking to the Enemy: Track Two Diplomacy in the Middle East and South* Asia (Santa Monica: Rand Corporation, in press), ch. 3, for a valuable summary of the work of these and other organizations involved in Kashmir-related track two diplomacy.

61. "Members Create Kashmir Forum," website of Representative Joe Pitts, Republican of Pennsylvania, June 6, 2002 (www.house.gov/pitts/initiatives/kashmir/020606kfr-announcement.htm).

Chapter Seven

1. K. R. Narayanan, the left-leaning Indian president, took issue with this assessment when Clinton visited New Delhi in March 2000. "It has been suggested," Narayanan declared in his formal toast at the banquet honoring his American guest, "that the Indian-subcontinent is the most dangerous place in the world today and Kashmir is a nuclear flash-point. These alarmist descriptions will only encourage those [read Pakistan] who want to break the peace and indulge in terrorism and violence." Narayanan's unscripted outburst, which surprised some of the Indian diplomats present, did not change Clinton's views. (Speech by President K. R. Narayanan, March 21, 2000.)

2. Strobe Talbott, *Engaging India* (Brookings, 2004), p. 57.

3. Talbott provides a fascinating account of his efforts in Pakistan; *Engaging India*, pp. 56–72.

4. Bruce Riedel, background paper prepared for the Institute for the Study of Diplomacy at Georgetown University, Washington, D.C., May 2007.

5. These included bringing to a rapid conclusion the long negotiation to end the production of fissile material; avoiding putting nuclear warheads on their missiles and bombers; and preventing the export of nuclear equipment, materials, and technology that could help nonnuclear weapons states and nonstate actors acquire nuclear weapons or ballistic missiles.

6. Talbott's account of the talks is in *Engaging India*. Jaswant Singh became minister of external affairs in the course of the discussions.

7. Interview with William B. Milam, May 2007.

8. Assistant Secretary of State Inderfurth quoted these presidential comments in a hearing of the Senate Foreign Relations Subcommittee on the Near East and South Asia, May 25, 1999. Ironically, Inderfurth's testimony came only a couple of days before the Indians discovered that the Pakistanis had crossed the Line of Control in the Kargil area some time earlier.

9. In *Four Crises and a Peace Process* (Brookings, 2007), P. R. Chari, Pervaiz Iqbal Cheema, and Stephen P. Cohen discuss the sharply different views they found among their Pakistani and Indian interlocutors regarding the origins of the Kargil conflict. Pakistanis maintained that the Kargil intrusion "fell within the genre of accepted 'nibbling' operations" that had been going on along the Line of Control for years. It was also designed to meet specific Indian military threats. An apparent second Pakistani military objective was to tie India's armed forces down so they could not mount an attack across the international border. In the Indian view, Pakistan's paramilitary forces along with Islamic militants had blatantly violated the Line of Control in a long-planned attack much greater than a nibbling operation (pp. 124–30).

10. Celia W. Dugger, "No Halt to Kashmir Strikes, Even for Talks, India Leader Says," *NYT*, May 30, 1999.

11. Both Riaz Khokhar and Naresh Chandra were outstanding diplomats whom Washington could count on to get the U.S. message straight in their reports to their home governments. Khokhar, a career foreign service officer, had been Pakistani high commissioner (ambassador) to India and Bangladesh before his U.S. assignment. He went on to become ambassador to China and retired as foreign secretary, the top position Pakistani Foreign Service officers can hold. Naresh Chandra had a civil service background. Before coming to Washington he had held multiple positions at the apex of the Indian bureaucracy and was widely regarded as one of the most influential government officials of his generation.

12. Phone interview with Thomas Pickering, July 2007.

13. Bruce Riedel, *American Diplomacy and the 1999 Kargil Summit at Blair House* (Philadelphia: Center for the Advanced Study of India, University of Pennsylvania, 2002), p. 5.

14. Interview with Milam.

15. Talbott, *Engaging India,* p. 157.

16. Pervez Musharraf, *In the Line of Fire* (New York: Free Press, 2006), pp. 87–98. Musharraf wrote that the Kargil operation was "only the latest in a series of moves and countermoves at a tactical level by India and Pakistan along the Line of Control in the inaccessible, snowbound Northern Areas [of Kashmir]." He held that it was "the Kashmiri freedom fighting" mujahedin who had occupied the Kargil heights. He suggested that the Pakistan Army's moves, which he said were coordinated with the mujahedin, were designed only to fill the gaps in Pakistan's defensive position on the Line of Control in anticipation of an attack by superior Indian forces. Astonishingly, Musharraf failed to mention the Lahore Summit meeting anywhere in his book.

17. In his memoir, Zinni claims that at his final meeting with Sharif, the prime minister agreed to order a withdrawal of Pakistani forces and requested the general to set up a meeting for him with Clinton. See Tom Clancy with General Tony Zinni [Ret.] and Tony Koltz, *Battle Ready* (New York: G. P. Putnam's Sons, 2004), p. 347. Other American officials who played a role in the Kargil crisis disagree with this interpretation. In their view, which I share, Sharif agreed to withdraw only when he met Clinton in Washington on July 4.

18. Riedel, *American Diplomacy,* p. 7.

19. Ibid., p. 15. Interview with Inderfurth, April 2007.

20. Interview with Walter Andersen, April 2007. Andersen also recalled that aside from taking notes, he also presented to Shahbaz Sharif a history of the Kashmir issue as the United States saw it. Prepared to answer questions from Shahbaz, he was disappointed when there were none, "perhaps because Shahbaz's major message was . . . to warn the United States about 'unconstitutional' threats to his brother's rule." According to Andersen, Shahbaz's body language and vehemence suggested that he really believed that a coup was a serious possibility. (Communication to author from Andersen, September 2007.)

21. Reuters, September 20, 1999. The official was widely believed to have been Assistant Secretary Inderfurth.

22. Walter Andersen has argued that the term "sanctity" was a kind of code word that suggested that the Line of Control would eventually become the international boundary in Kashmir. (Communication from Andersen, March 2008).

23. Howard B. Schaffer and Teresita C. Schaffer, "Kashmir: Fifty Years of Running in Place," in *Grasping the Nettle,* edited by Chester A. Crocker, Fen Osler Hampson,

and Pamela R. Aall (Washington: United States Institute of Peace Press, 2005), pp. 295–318. Clinton made his remarks on March 25, 2000.

24. Clinton news conference, Washington, February 16, 2000, *2000–2001 Public Papers of the President of the United States* (Washington: Government Printing Office).

25. Clinton's speech to the Indian Parliament, March 22, 2000; Clinton's TV address to the people of Pakistan, March 25, 2000, *2000–2001 Public Papers.*

26. Clinton's interview with Peter Jennings of ABC's World News Tonight in New Delhi, March 21, 2000, *2000–2001 Public Papers.*

27. This was the work of Under Secretary Thomas Pickering, who persuaded Musharraf to agree to the initiative and then badgered senior officials to work out an agreement. (Interview with Pickering, July 2007.)

28. Clinton's Statement on "Action by India and Pakistan to Reduce Tensions in Kashmir," December 20, 2000, *2000–2001 Public Papers of the President.*

Chapter Eight

1. One of the causes of Indian government pique was Musharraf's surprising agility in dealing with the local media. Ironically, the military president proved much better at spinning events at the summit than did the politician prime minister, who seemed ponderous in comparison.

2. Arun R. Swamy, "India in 2001," *Asian Survey* (January/February 2002), pp. 165–77.

3. In his crucial TV broadcast to the nation on September 19, Musharraf accused New Delhi of attempting to take full advantage of the crisis arising from the attacks in the United States and said that preserving the unity and integrity of Pakistan was a primary consideration behind his decision. According to the account in the reliable Indian newspaper *The Hindu,* he said that the Indians "have offered all military facilities to America. They want America on their side. The objective is to get Pakistan declared as a terrorist state and harm our strategic interest and the Kashmir cause."

4. Interestingly, Blackwill never visited Pakistan during his tenure in New Delhi and, in a throwback to earlier decades, did not enjoy good relations with his opposite number at Embassy Islamabad.

5. The Pakistan-based group Jaish-e-Mohammed initially claimed responsibility but later disavowed any role.

6. Lt. Gen. V. K. Sood (retired) and Pravin Sawhney, *Operation Parakram—The War Unfinished* (New Delhi: Sage Publications, 2003), p. 9.

7. Patrick E. Tyler and Celia W. Dugger, "Powell's Message: America's Courting of Pakistan Will Not Come at India's Expense." *NYT,* October 18, 2001.

8. More recently, the Indians alleged that Lashkar-e-Taiba was also responsible for the much deadlier attack on Mumbai in November 2008.

9. Polly Nayak and Michael Krepon, *U.S. Crisis Management in South Asia's Twin Peak Crisis* (Washington: Henry L. Stimson Center, 2006), p. 22. This study offers a collection of fascinating insider accounts based on interviews with U.S. government participants who dealt with the crisis in Washington, New Delhi, and Islamabad.

10. P. R. Chari, Pervaiz Iqbal Cheema, and Stephen Philip Cohen, *Four Crises and a Peace Process* (Brookings, 2007), p.165.

11. Interview with Wendy Chamberlin, May 2007.

12. Interview with a U.S. official, June 2007.

13. Todd S. Purdom, "Powell Lauds Pakistan's Efforts against Extremists," *NYT,* January 17, 2002.

14. Thom Shanker and Elizabeth Bumiller, "Citing Tension, U.S. Advises Americans in India to Leave," *NYT,* June 1, 2002; Celia W. Dugger, "Little Feeling of Emergency in American Exit from Delhi," *NYT,* June 2, 2002; Nayak and Krepon, *U.S. Crisis Management,* p. 34.

15. Interview with a former U.S. official, September 2007.

16. In their study, Nayak and Krepon found that Powell and Armitage were the dominant figures in devising and implementing U.S. policy in the crisis. They quote several State Department officials: "Secretary Powell excelled at 'working the phones. . . . Armitage was the 'go-to' guy and a 'gifted trouble shooter.'" Nayak and Krepon, *U.S. Crisis Management,* p. 26.

17. Celia W. Dugger with Thom Shanker, "Indian Sees Hope as Pakistan Halts Kashmiri Militants," *NYT,* June 9, 2002.

18. Conversation with Ambassador Nancy Powell, May 2007. See also Chari, Cheema, and Cohen, *Four Crises,* p. 160: "By [the time of Armitage's visit in early June 2002] . . . the [Indian] political leadership had recognized that further provocations would be risky and made ready for the actual drawdown, in October. . . ."

19. Nayak and Krepon, *U.S. Crisis Management,* p. 27.

20. In the dynastic tradition of South Asian political democracy, the National Conference was led by Omar Abdullah, the grandson of Sheikh Abdullah and son of Farooq Abdullah.

21. See Navnita Chadha Behera, *Demystifying Kashmir* (Brookings, 2006), p. 61.

22. Powell press conference, New Delhi, July 28, 2002 (http://2001-2009.state.gov/secretary/former/powell/remarks/2002/12228.htm).

23 Powell press briefing, Islamabad, July 28, 2002 (http://2001-2009.state.gov/secretary/former/powell/remarks/2002/12229.htm).

24. Department spokesman (Richard Boucher), press statement, October 10, 2002 (http://2001-2009.state.gov/r/pa/prs/ps/2002/14278.htm).

25. Powell press conference, New Delhi, July 28, 2002 (http://2001-2009.state.gov/secretary/former/powell/remarks/2002/12228.htm).

26. State Department daily press briefing, May 6, 2003 (http://2001-2009.state.gov/r/pa/prs/dpb/2003/20274.htm).

27. *NYT,* May 3, 2003.

28. Amit Baruah, "Pakistan Needs to Take Firm,Credible Steps," *The Hindu,* May 7, 2003; State Department daily press briefing, May 6, 2003 (http://2001-2009.state.gov/r/pa/prs/dpb/2003/20274.htm).

29. Amy Waldman, "Gambling on Peace: India's Leader Tries Again." *NYT,* May 5, 2003.

30. David Rohde, "American Official Praises India's Moves to Defuse Tensions with Pakistan." *NYT,* May 11, 2003.

31. Despite Armitage's disavowal, Prime Minister Jamali felt obliged to reassure his countrymen that the deputy secretary was not pressuring the Pakistanis to accept the Line of Control as a permanent border.

32. Carlotta Gall, "U.S. Official Is 'Optimistic' on India-Pakistan Dispute," *NYT,* May 9, 2003.

33. Qudssia Akhlaque, "Offer Includes Siachen Truce, Says Kasuri," *Dawn* (Karachi), November 24, 2003.

34. Amit Baruah and Sandeep Dikshit, "India, Pakistan Cease-Fire Comes into Being." *The Hindu,* November 25, 2003.

35. State Department daily press briefing, November 26, 2003 (http://2001-2009.state.gov/r/pa/prs/dpb/2003/26009.htm). The cease-fire applied to the Line of Control, the Siachen Glacier, and the so-called "working boundary" that divides Indian-administered Kashmir from Pakistan proper.

36. Reuters, "Vajpayee Willing to Hold Talks with Musharraf. Indian P.M. Arrives in Islamabad," *Dawn,* January 7, 2004.

37. One prominent Pakistani politician, Senator Mushahid Hussain, an ally of Musharraf, told the *New York Times* that the reduction of hostility toward India also found support among the religious right. For this political group, he claimed, "Anti-Indianism has been replaced by anti-Americanism." The comment could not have gone over well with American policymakers. Amy Waldman, "Sense of Mortality Gave Push to India-Pakistan Talks," *NYT,* January 8, 2004.

38. Interviews with Nancy Powell and other State Department officials, June-July 2007.

39. Secretary Powell's "Interview with the *USA Today* Editorial Board," October 18, 2004 (http://2001-2009/state.gov/secretary/former/powell/remarks/37184.htm).

40. Neena Vyas, "Jaswant Flays U.S. Foreign Policy," *The Hindu,* October 22, 2004.

41. Associated Press of Pakistan, "Kashmir Issue Will Be Solved, Hopes U.S," *Dawn,* January 10, 2004.

42. Secretary Powell's press conference, January 8, 2004 (http://2001-2009.geneva. usmission.gov/press2004/0109powell.html).

43. India had insisted that passengers carry passports, which Pakistan argued would constitute recognition of the Line of Control as an international border. The Indians eventually backed down. But the bus service proved to have greater symbolic than practical significance. Travel was restricted to Kashmiris who had relatives on the other side of the Line and documentation took months to obtain. In 2008 few buses made the run and those that did carried only a handful of passengers. Most Kashmiris reportedly find it easier to cross the international border at Wagah in the Punjab, a much longer and more expensive route.

44. Somini Sen Gupta, David Rohde, Salman Masood, and Hari Kumar, "Quake Strains 58-Year-Old Fault Line," *NYT,* October 24, 2005.

45. Musharraf's seven regions included two now held by Pakistan (Azad Kashmir and the Northern Areas) and five held by India. To come up with these five, Musharraf divided the predominantly Hindu Jammu province, breaking out its Muslim-majority districts into a separate "region." He did the same with Buddhist-majority Ladakh division, separating from it Kargil district, where Shiite Muslims predominate. He left the Valley intact.

46. The Indians rejected out of hand Musharraf's public call for reductions of Indian forces in specific areas, identified as Baramulla and Kupwara in the Kashmir Valley. Musharraf reportedly tried to sell the idea to President Bush. Prime Minister Singh reported that he had told Bush that Pakistan was not doing enough and "clearly enunciated how violence and terror cast a shadow on our ability to carry this [peace] process forward." (Harish Khare, "We Won't Let Terrorism Hinder Peace Process," *The Hindu,* September 16, 2005.)

47. Amit Baruah, "Manmohan Wrong to Link Normalization with Kashmir," *The Hindu,* March 25, 2006.

48. See, for example, the State Department spokesman's comment of October 27, 2004: "We encourage all interested parties to take a careful look at any proposal which could advance peace in the region, which engage their own publics." The departing American ambassador to Pakistan, Nancy Powell, said the same day that "the president's recent proposal is trying to encourage debate, which . . . needs to be encouraged as it may help the two sides reach a decision" (*Asia Pulse,* October 28, 2004). Deputy Secretary Armitage, visiting Islamabad a few weeks after Musharraf initially broached his idea, was similarly noncommittal on the substance of the proposals when he told a Pakistan TV interviewer that Musharraf had "caused a great

deal of thinking both here and in India." (B. Murlidhar Reddy, "Armitage Lauds Musharraf Proposals on Kashmir," *The Hindu*, November 10, 2004.)

49. Amit Mukherjee, "Lesson from Another Insurgency," *NYT*, March 4, 2006.

50. White House website, September 22, 2006 (http://georgewbush-white-house.archives.gov/news/releases/2006/09/20060922.html).

51. There seems no serious basis to the speculation that Bush continued to defer to the Indians on an American role in a Kashmir settlement because he did not want to queer efforts to negotiate a civil nuclear agreement with New Delhi. The president had adopted this position, which he inherited from a succession of White House predecessors, long before he initiated this "U.S.-India nuclear deal" in 2005.

52. A. G. Noorani, "There Is Much to Gain Mutually," *Frontline*, August 12–25, 2006.

53. Pervez Musharraf, *In the Line of Fire* (New York: Free Press, 2006), p. 305. Musharraf listed four "elements" of what he described as a "possible 'outside the box' solution." These were identification of geographic regions; demilitarization including "curb[ing] of all militant aspects of the struggle for freedom"; introduction of self-governance or self-rule in the identified region or regions: "Let the Kashmiris have the satisfaction of running their own affairs without having an international character and remaining short of independence" and "Most important, have a joint management mechanism with a membership consisting of Pakistanis, Indians, and Kashmiris overseeing self-governance and dealing with residual subjects common to all identified regions and those subjects that are beyond the scope of self-governance." Musharraf did not mention the status of the Line of Control in his proposal, which he described as "purely personal and [needing] refinement."

54. The spokeswoman for the Pakistan Ministry of Foreign Affairs claimed the following day that Musharraf's remarks did not reflect a change in Pakistan's position on Kashmir. The president, she said, has only reiterated the well-known view that "in step with India, Pakistan is willing to be flexible in pursuit of an acceptable negotiated settlement." "Musharraf's Comments Invoke Mixed Response in Occupied Kashmir," *Dawn*, December 6, 2006,

55. Somini Sen Gupta, "Pakistani Says Concessions Could Produce Kashmir Pact," *NYT*, December 6, 2006.

56. Former Pakistan Foreign Secretary Tanvir Ahmad Khan, "Showdown in Peace Process," *Dawn*, September 10, 2007. Praveen Swamy, "An Explosion on the Road to Peace," *The Hindu*, February 27, 2008.

57. Luv Puri, "Make Line of Control 'Line of Peace': Manmohan." *The Hindu*, July 15, 2007.

58. http://2001-2009.state.gov/r/pppa/prs/dpb/2006/77453. Conversation with a senior State Department official, April 2007.

59. Javed Naqvi, "Asif Talks of Strong Kashmir Policy," *Dawn*, March 1, 2008.

60. Iktikhar A. Khas, "President Will Be Subservient to Parliament: Asif," *Dawn*, September 10, 2008.

61. "Our Reporter," "Revisit Presidential Powers—Zardari's Offer to Parliament," *Dawn*, September 21, 2008.

62. Anwar Iqbal and Masood Haider, "We Are in a State of War–Asif." *Dawn*, September 25, 2008.

63. Like the longer mass upheavals in 1963–64 and 1989–90, the crisis was triggered by a specific event. This time it was the state administration's ill-conceived decision to make 100 acres of public land available to a Hindu religious organization to build facilities for pilgrims to a popular shrine. The land transfer provided ammunition to Kashmir's anti-Indian politicians, who made wild claims that it was part of a conspiracy to reduce the state's Muslim majority to minority status. Amid growing unrest, the government rescinded the transfer. Nationalist leaders in Jammu started violent demonstrations against the revocation. Scores were killed in firing by police and military in both parts of the state and in Hindu-Muslim clashes in Jammu.

Chapter Nine

1. http://swampland.blogs.time.com/2008/10/23/the_full_obama_interview/.

Index

Abdullah, Farooq, 124, 146, 253n20

Abdullah, Sheikh Mohammed: 1950 elections, 32–33; continued influence through dynastic tradition, 198, 253n20; death, 124; independence vs. accession to India position, 10, 19–20, 23, 30–31, 40–41; mentioned, 56; Nehru friendship, 102; overthrow and detention (1953), 33, 42, 102; rearrest and detention (1965–68), 107, 108; release from detention (1947), 11; release from detention (1964), 99–100, 102–03; release from detention (1968), 119; return to influence (1964), 102–04; state chief minister appointment, 123; Stevenson visit, 40, 41

Abdullah, Omar, 198, 253n20

Acheson, Dean, 24, 27–28, 29, 31, 33

Ackerman, Gary, 139–40

Adams, J. Wesley, 225n14

Adams, Sherman, 59

Afghanistan: Al Qaeda and U.S. on terrorism in, 169–70, 173, 178; Durand Line border settlement with Pakistan, 84; Soviet withdrawal, 124, 125, 128, 130

Agra summit, 170, 185

Albright, Madeleine, 22, 144, 159

Al-Faran kidnappings, 136–38

Allen, George V., 41, 42, 48, 50

All-India Muslim League, 10, 11

Alling, Paul, 15

All Parties Hurriyet Conference, 146, 179, 186, 198

Al Qaeda, 17, 171, 178, 196

Andersen, Walter, 126, 164

Armitage, Richard, 172, 177–78, 181–82, 185, 253n16, 255n48

Arunachal Pradesh, 75

Attlee, Clement, and government, 12, 15, 27

Austin, Warren R., 14–15, 16, 18, 19, 30

Ayub Khan, Muhammad, 1947–60: call for U.S. action, 39; Eisenhower meeting, 62–63; Indus Waters Treaty signed, 1960, 62; military coup, 1958, 61; Nehru proposal for peaceful negotiations, 63, 66